ARCHAEOLOGY AND ITS DISCONTENTS

Archaeology and its Discontents examines the state of archaeology today and its development throughout the twentieth century, making a powerful case for new approaches.

Surveying the themes of twentieth-century archaeological theory, Barrett looks at their successes, limitations, and failures. Seeing more failures and limitations than successes, he argues that archaeology has over-focused on explaining the human construction of material variability and should instead be more concerned with understanding how human diversity has been constructed. Archaeology matters, he argues, precisely because of the insights it can offer into the development of human diversity. The analysis and argument are illustrated throughout by reference to the development of the European Neolithic.

Arguing both for new approaches and for the importance of archaeology as a discipline, *Archaeology and its Discontents* is for archaeologists at all levels, from student to professor and trainee to experienced practitioner.

John C. Barrett is Emeritus Professor of Archaeology at the University of Sheffield, having previously taught at the Universities of Leeds and Glasgow. He is the author of *Fragments from Antiquity* (1994) and co-author, with Michael Boyd, of *From Stonehenge to Mycenae* (2019). His research has focused upon British and European prehistory and archaeological theory.

Themes in Archaeology

https://www.routledge.com/Themes-in-Archaeology-Series/book-series/SE0460

ARCHAEOLOGY AND ITS DISCONTENTS

Why Archaeology Matters

John C. Barrett

Routledge
Taylor & Francis Group

LONDON AND NEW YORK

First published 2021
by Routledge
2 Park Square, Milton Park, Abingdon, Oxon OX14 4RN

and by Routledge
52 Vanderbilt Avenue, New York, NY 10017

Routledge is an imprint of the Taylor & Francis Group, an informa business

© 2021 John C. Barrett

British Library Cataloguing-in-Publication Data
A catalogue record for this book is available from the British Library

Library of Congress Cataloging-in-Publication Data
A catalog record has been requested for this book

ISBN: 978-0-367-56020-1 (hbk)
ISBN: 978-0-367-55645-7 (pbk)
ISBN: 978-1-003-09611-5 (ebk)

Typeset in Bembo
by Apex CoVantage, LLC

For the ground keeps on giving the illusory image of a greater depth, and when we seek to reach this, we keep on finding ourselves on the old level.

Our disease is one of wanting to explain.

Wittgenstein – *Remarks on the Foundations of Mathematics*, VI §31

'How am I able to obey a rule?' – if this is not a question about causes, then it is about the justification for my following the rule in the way I do.

If I have exhausted the justifications I have reached bedrock, and my spade is turned. Then I am inclined to say: 'This is simply what I do.'

Wittgenstein – *Philosophical Investigations*, § 217

CONTENTS

FIGURES

ACKNOWLEDGEMENTS

I must thank all my colleagues and friends who have discussed their views with me, optimistic or otherwise, as to the possibilities and potential of archaeological practice. I owe a particular debt of gratitude in this regard to my students, and in particular to those Masters students at The University of Sheffield, who have argued for and against the central theme of this book. Kathryn Barrett, Michael Boyd, Alexandra Ion, and Artur Ribeiro read and commented upon an earlier draft of this text and Brian Boyd and Ihong Ko read sections of this text, I apologise to all of them if I have failed to adequately adopt their recommendations and the errors remain my own. I must also thank Penny Bickle, Amy Bogaard, Despina Catapoti, Irene Garcia, Daniela Hofmann, Glynis Jones, Lesley McFadyen, Theresa Nelson, and Michael Wallace, all of whom have answered questions from me that have arisen while writing this text. My thanks go to Matthew Gibbons, Katie Wakelin, and Marc Stratton at Routledge, Jenny Doole for the index and Laura Kopp for copy-editing my text. I also acknowledge the unstinting helpfulness of the library staff at the University of Sheffield. I remain grateful to Gill Andrews, Andrew Gibson, and John Lewis who allowed, and indeed encouraged, me to explore some of the practical implications of these ideas in the context of a large-scale commercial project at Heathrow Airport, and my thanks and gratitude extend to all those who co-operated with me while they worked on that project. I owe my use of the term *humanness* to Niels Johannsen.

INTRODUCTION

The central argument of this book is that archaeology must enable us to understand how different forms of human life have emerged historically through their desire to understand, and to engage with, the worlds that they have encountered. I have termed these forms of human life different kinds of 'humanness' (Barrett 2014a) in an effort to emphasise their diversity, and I have identified the mechanisms that brought them into existence as 'biocultural' processes.

If understanding the historical conditions under which human diversity has been created is indeed the main purpose of archaeology, then we obviously need to specify how that purpose might be achieved. This will require us to be clear as to the kinds of evidence that are available to archaeology, and the means by which such an investigation can be facilitated. It has often been assumed that the kinds of evidence with which archaeology deals is evidence that represents a particular kind of process, providing us with a record resulting from the actions of that earlier humanity. This assumption is put to one side here; indeed, I will argue that it is an assumption that has contributed to the failure of archaeology to realise its wider potential. I will argue that the fundamental issue that archaeology confronts concerns the relationship between the various material conditions that once existed and the ways that the various forms of humanness emerged by their learning how to live within those material conditions.

If we characterise archaeology as an investigation of how forms of humanness created themselves by bringing the material conditions of their world into view, then the way that the concept of *culture* has been used by archaeology needs to be reviewed. As Benjamin Roberts and Marc Vander Linden have emphasised, the term has been widely used as the means to group similar levels of variation amongst the material assemblages: an 'empirically based framework within which to place new data from excavations and surveys' (Roberts & Vander Linden 2011b, 5). However, by treating archaeological evidence as if it represented the actions of an extinct human presence in this way, the question is raised as to what these cultural assemblages might represent in terms of human behaviour? This has traditionally been answered by asserting that patterns of cultural materials simply represent the ways people once did things according to certain cultural norms and traditions. Of course, this then introduces the further question of how these human motivations might have originated, and it has been in attempting to deal with this further question that archaeology's failures in reasoning have been exposed.

Most practising archaeologists (who today are widely involved in various aspects of Cultural Resource Management) are concerned with the recovery and analysis of ancient materials. These materials gain their significance for archaeology because they are believed to have been structured by processes that once operated in the human past. Indeed, their importance is that it was to a now extinct human existence that these materials are assumed to have once made reference. It is as if that earlier human presence had somehow caused, and had thus been recorded by, the form of the material residues. The American archaeologist Michael Schiffer (1976) once distinguished between the human or culturally motivated 'c-transformations' of the material, and the record of 'natural' processes of erosion and transformation (so-called 'n-transforms'). The discovery of artefacts has therefore resulted in describing them as the representations of the processes of their creation, use, discard, and their subsequent erosion. In addition, some aspects of soil and vegetational history and of soil erosion have been taken to represent a history of human cultivation and land-use. The motivations of human behaviour have then been divided between cultural motivations, which are the learnt procedures of how to do things, and the consequences of those actions in terms of their function, or the requirements that they appear to have satisfied.

Recording the stratigraphic context of sequences of material residues such as these is a basic requirement of field procedures. This was emphasised by Wheeler (1956), and the excavation, recording, and analytical procedures concerning soil stratigraphy have been variously refined in the UK by, for example, Philip Barker (1982), Edward Harris (1989), Steve Roskams (2001), and Martin Carver (2009). It has been by the means of stratigraphic analysis that the patterns across broadly contemporary residues have been identified, and these have been treated as indicating the ways human behaviour was once organised and executed. Sequences in this material have thus been treated as indicating periods of stability or change in the organisation of that behaviour, with the ultimate aim of establishing the forces that might have structured, and might thus explain, the history of that behaviour. This has placed the forces motivating human behaviour at the heart of any archaeological attempt to explain the patterns of material. The challenge 'to explain' is considerable, and as Colin Renfrew and Paul Bahn (2004, 469) have commented, '[t]o answer the question "why" is the most difficult task in archaeology'.

In trying to address the task of explanation, archaeology has moved away from earlier attempts that explained human behaviour by reference to its supposed cultural motivations, and has moved instead towards explanations in terms of what that behaviour had achieved, and these achievements are believed to have been structured by the demands of environmental or social adaptation, or by the playing out of conceptual schemes of moral and political order. As a result, archaeology has seemed to have been more concerned with the humanity behind the artefacts, and with the forces that had structured that humanity's behaviour, than it has with the material context of that humanity's existence. This apparent bias has prompted the view that 'things . . . are too often treated as secondary expressions of society, social structures and cultural values' (Olsen et al. 2012, vii), and as a reaction against this archaeology of structural explanations (that are often expressed in highly theoretical terms), archaeology has recently been characterised, by some at least, as 'the discipline of things' (cf. Olsen 2010).

This move towards archaeology as the discipline of things, prompted by the desire to turn away from viewing the world 'from a perspective presupposing humans in a privileged position with respect to nature' (Webmoor 2007, 568), has also recognised that all things display an agency (Olsen 2012, 20) because they changed historical conditions by their very existence. While this accepts that the historical conditions that are glimpsed by archaeology arose from an assemblage of all existing things, human and non-human, living and non-living (Latour 1993 & 2005; Witmore 2007; Olsen et al. 2012; DeLanda 2016; Jervis 2019), precisely how that mixing had occurred, that is, how it was structured, does not seem to have been discussed. As a result, the attempt to centre archaeological analysis upon the existence of things alone (Olsen et al. 2012, 136–156; Pétursdóttir 2017), rather than upon the making of the phenomena of humanness that had arisen amongst those things (cf. Marshall & Alberti 2014; Barad 2007; Braidotti 2019a), appears to have been little more than the removal of life's otherwise messy existence.

All forms of archaeological recording and analysis have depended upon three things: the perspective of the investigator (including their various expectations and prejudices as to the nature of existence); the methodology that should be employed in analysis; and a belief as to the historical reality that is being observed. When taken together these things contribute towards an agreed scheme of working, or what Thomas Kuhn (1970) once referred to as a *paradigm*. The archaeological community has tended to work within a single paradigm, enabling that community to share a perspective upon the status of archaeological data, and to agree upon the kinds of things that need investigating (past processes), and how they should be investigated (through a theoretically informed analysis of archaeological materials). This has also enabled archaeology to work 'cross-culturally' on the assumption that the cultural differences witnessed between the peoples, represented by different assemblages of material, were no more than the merely apparent differences in the execution of behaviours that were determined by the structure of a limited number of underlying processes. The paradigm that dominated twentieth-century archaeology can therefore be characterised as a *representational paradigm* simply because archaeological residues have been taken to represent the target condition of human behaviour, and, behind that, the processes that had structured that behaviour.

The failure of this representational paradigm has been expressed in the complaint that claims that the material evidence is never enough to provide for an understanding of the historical process. Instead that material merely indicates the existence of the forces of history that are the real object of archaeological concern because it was these forces that supposedly directed or compelled certain historical conditions to come into being (Webmoor & Witmore 2008, 53). If we accept this complaint then it means that we can no longer explain the changing patterns of archaeological materials by theorising the existence of this or that determinate force that supposedly operated behind the backs of the contemporary human populations. By way of an alternative, I will argue that the task of archaeology is to gain some understanding of how human diversity brought itself into existence by means of the growing and developing familiarity of people with the material conditions amongst which they had lived and developed, and to which archaeological research can now attest.

The diverse forms of life that have brought themselves into existence, did so without being formed by some pre-existing process: they were not created, instead they created themselves within certain given material conditions. Forms of life therefore act intentionally, in the technical meaning of that term; namely that a form of life emerges by means of its own development, orientating itself towards the things that are of relevance for it.

This argument is developed in this book in the following way. Chapter 1 distinguishes between the processes of explanation and those involved in understanding. Given that claims were once made that archaeology should *explain* the changes that it had described in sequences of material residues, and the desire to express those explanations in terms of the generally applicable causes for cultural change, we must allow that the formulation of all such explanations will be informed by our own perceptions of how the world seems to work. The alternative that I seek is an archaeology that attempts to *understand* how others were able to bring themselves into being by their occupation of the different kinds of material conditions that are attested for by archaeological residues. The long-recognised historical and geographical diversity of material culture might therefore be understood as contributing to the material conditions within which different kinds of humanness could emerge.

Chapter 2 reviews the way that archaeological materials became accepted as the testimonies for the existence of a now absent, but nonetheless singular humanity. When these materials were recognised as being recovered from various geological contexts, they were used to argue for the antiquity of that humanity. The principle that a human presence is attested for by the recovery of material residues in an earth-bound or geological context, and that these deposits can be interpreted in light of the principle of uniformitarianism, continues to inform current archaeological practice. During the latter part of the twentieth century an increased emphasis was placed upon attempts to explain the ways that human lives have been ordered by various indigenous forces, and these explanations replaced earlier models of diffusion and cultural influences.

Chapters 3, 4, and 5 consider the various ways that archaeology has, since the 1950s, been used to explain the order observed amongst archaeological residues, not as sequences comprising individual cultural traits but in terms of the systematic organisation of the past, firstly with reference to the system's adaptation to available ecological resources, secondly with reference to the logic of its social organisation, and thirdly with reference to the way that human systems were likely to have been structured by the cognitive perceptions of their members. Because these chapters concern the changes that occurred in the ways that the past was thought about during the latter half of the twentieth century, many readers might regard a review of these changes as redundant, given the various critiques that have been directed towards them more recently. Consequently, those readers might conclude that there is no point in dealing with these earlier ways of thinking. The need to revisit these traditions is however warranted by the problems that we have inherited in contemporary archaeology. These problems lie not with archaeology's commitment to the study of human behaviour, but with the ways in which that behaviour, which had resulted in a particular form of material residue, was treated as if it was determined by forces of an uncertain origin. The same working assumption, that archaeological data represent the consequences of one or other of these relatively abstract processes, is shared by all three traditions of analysis. All three have also expressed their failure to recognise what is unique concerning the archaeological understanding of human diversity. Consequently, all three have demonstrated a reliance in their interpretations upon analogies drawn from the neighbouring disciplines of History, Anthropology, and more widely across the Social Sciences. These analogies are assumed to illustrate, or to model, the processes that are believed to have resulted in cultural change. The problem with all such models is that if these analogies do represent the ultimate achievement of archaeological interpretation, then it is unclear why we bother to collect archaeological data, if we are to assume that other disciplines are better able to supply the explanations for human diversity.

Chapter 6 establishes that the basis for understanding human diversity lies in the biology of life, not in terms of biological determinism, as might be implied by the recent emphasis upon genetic analysis, but by treating the histories of human diversity as if they were the products of biological growth, development, and adaptation. Each of these processes of development has resulted from the phenomenological interpretations that have been played out within the biological and cultural context of an evolving ecology. It is the material traces of these ecologies that are partially preserved as archaeological data.

The histories of populations are constructed by the biocultural developments of the individuals who were members of those populations. Such an understanding requires that we accept that humanity, as a form of life, has grown and developed biologically. This process of coming into being is one shared with all other living things, and the growth of a form of life is achieved by means of its interpretation of the material ecologies within which its life is able to develop. Forms of humanness can only ever have brought themselves into existence, therefore, by means of their recognition of those things that had a significance for them. Archaeology studies the various conditions of human possibility which survive today, at least in part, as a material residue. The point of this kind of archaeology is not to explain the reasons for the changing patterns of these residues, as if such changes represented changes in behaviour, but to understand how the diversity of humanness has been created by living amongst these changing material conditions. Whilst neither cultural nor biological resources have been determinant in this process, biological and cultural materials were nonetheless resources necessary for the processes of interpretation that brought a population into existence. This is the theme explored in Chapter 7.

By rejecting the dominant archaeological model in which material residues are explained as if they were the products of past human behaviour, we need to re-evaluate the critique of Cultural Archaeology that had been formulated in the latter half of the twentieth century. This critique had claimed that the explanations offered for the large-scale patterns of apparent cultural uniformity were inadequate. The extensive regions of common cultural patterns in the material have subsequently been ignored by archaeological schemes of explanation, although they have continued in use as the conventions of archaeological description (cf. Roberts & Vander Linden 2011). While we might continue to reject claims that these patterns represent patterns of normative behaviour, it remains entirely possible that they map environments that sustained patterns of common human development. Chapter 8 explores this argument from the perspective of the early Neolithic in Europe.

The traditional sequence of analytical procedures in archaeology that runs from the methods of recovery to the theoretical modelling of the past as a process, has enforced a distinction in the practice of archaeology, between the description of things on the one hand, often undertaken by field technicians, and their academic interpretation and explanation on the other. This has resulted in the eclectic adoption of various theoretical fashions in the hope that they will not only facilitate the processes of interpretation, but also enhance the reputation of the interpreter (Bintliff 2011). Recent attempts to reject the claim that the collection, and the study, of things is only 'important insofar as they provide access to the human beings assumed to lie behind them' (Olsen et al. 2012, 7) have resulted in asserting the centrality of things to archaeological experience. Given that archaeologists 'labor hard to collect their data, their information' (Olsen et al. 2012, 58), we might hope that the reasons for that labouring would extend beyond a desire simply to care for antiquities. What is it that archaeology might hope to achieve as the results of these labours? The craft of excavation (Shanks & McGuire 1996) has its rewards in the confidence that is gained from participating in that process, in team working, and in the romanticism of discovering things that have been long forgotten. But what is it that makes this work the scene of 'active individual engagements with *the past*' (Olsen et al. 2012, 62 emphasis added) rather than merely being an engagement with things? When Colin Renfrew wrote so evocatively of 'the sense of mystery and solitude when I was the first to enter, perhaps for thousands of years, one of the side chambers at Quanterness' (Renfrew 2003, 40), what did he think that he was encountering?

This is not a book about archaeological theory, instead it is a book that enquires into the purpose of archaeology. The purpose that is suggested here is that archaeology should establish a relationship between our contemporary lives and the historical lives of others in such a way that it enables us to understand some of the ways that those other lives were constructed. This should support our realisation that humanity has been determined neither as the creation of God nor as the creation of genetics. Throughout history, different kinds of human-ness have brought themselves into existence with reference to the material con-ditions amongst which they lived, and whose fragmented residues survive today (Kronfeldner 2018, 8). They have done this out of the desire to understand the nature and the origins of the worlds amongst which they lived. An archaeology of what remains of those material conditions matters because it can, and indeed it should, confront some of the political and ethical challenges that we face today in terms of our current diversities. Fundamental to these modern challenges is our ability to understand, and indeed to tolerate, those others whose lives are different from our own. This will require us to recognise that what is unfamiliar to us in those other lives, along with the familiar normality of our own lives, are not given but are constructed out of the resources that each of us has to hand. This is what, in my view, archaeology should teach us, and it is towards an understanding of this point that this book is dedicated.

1

EXPLANATION AND UNDERSTANDING

What might an archaeologist expect to know and how might they expect to know it?

In 2014 a group of fifteen academics, all but one of whom were resident in north America, identified what they claimed to be the most important scientific challenges that archaeology might be expected to address in a subsequent twenty-five-year period (Kintigh et al. 2014). The exercise was certainly optimistic. It assumed that researchers should be able to synthesise the very large data sets that archaeology had collected (Kintigh 2006), and that these data sets would provide 'knowledge of the long-term trajectories of past societies' (Kintigh et al. 2014, 6). It is with this knowledge that archaeology could, or so it was claimed, address current problems of a global and a contemporary significance. This claim was supported by the assertion that archaeological interpretations had already contributed to debates about 'human responses to climate change, the eradication of poverty and the effects of urbanism and globalization on humanity' (Kintigh et al. 2014, 6). The proposal outlined by Kintigh and his colleagues resulted in the 2018 founding of a Coalition for Archaeological Synthesis (archsynth.org).

The search for the various 'archaeological challenges' had originally involved enquiries directed to the major 'North American and European professional (archaeological) organisations' and a work-shop that was run for key participants, all of which resulted in twenty-five 'grand challenges' being identified. Instead of focusing upon individual historical events, these challenges focused upon analysing the *general* ways that human and cultural systems were organised and coupled together with their environments. The entire programme seems to echo an earlier observation that 'the conviction is widely held that the discovery of cultural laws is an ultimate goal of anthropology, to be attained when fact-collecting and detailed analyses of particular cultures and sequences are sufficiently advanced' (Steward 1949, 2).

The challenges that were identified by Kintigh and others can be grouped under five broad themes. These describe particular kinds of human historical trajectories that might be characterised as: (1) emergence, communities, and complexity; (2) resilience, persistence, transformation, and collapse; (3) movement, mobility, and migration; (4) cognition, behaviour, and identity; (5) human–environment interactions. All these challenges express the belief that archaeologists can, and should, co-operate to investigate the regularities that can be identified as operating through, and might thus explain, the various historical trajectories of humanity.

The Kintigh proposal maintains the belief that a clear distinction exists between archaeological data that are given and might describe something of what happened in the past, and their interpretation, for which we are responsible and which might seek to explain why those things happened. This reflects the current working practice in which the methodologies of fieldwork and analysis appear to be untroubled by changes that occur in theories that might impact upon historical interpretation (cf. Lucas 2012). Data are thus the archived results of excavation, survey, and collecting, where the archive contains the descriptions and samples of material residues that relate to the human past. Interpretation, on the other hand, establishes the significance of these data for our understanding of the past. The relationship between data and interpretation, between observation and understanding, is perhaps more complex than has sometimes been allowed, given that the data are collected, described, and catalogued with the expressed purpose that those data will then submit to interpretation. It would seem likely, therefore, that the means by which the data are to be interpreted must reflect something of the ways in which they have been collected and catalogued.

Archaeology has been defined as the discipline that enables us to examine the past by means of its surviving residues (cf. Chapman & Wylie 2016). We will review the kinds of historical knowledge that archaeologists have sought to establish, and how they have gone about establishing it, before considering the basis for an archaeological alternative. It was by assuming that they knew how the analysis of archaeological data should be undertaken that Kintigh and his colleagues established the priorities that, in their view, justified a financial investment by the National Science Foundation of the United States of America in the archaeologically directed development of information technologies. Whilst these technologies are intended to synthesise archaeological data and thus produce a form of historical knowledge, the entire process is obviously grounded upon knowing the kind of 'historical knowledge' that we want, and how the kinds of data that have been collected can furnish us with that knowledge.

The archaeological convention is that the surviving residues provide us with a material record of human history (Lucas 2012), and how they do this is one thing that this book is designed to investigate. Indeed, the ways in which archaeologically recovered residues might be interpreted have recently become matters of contention (cf. Moro Abadía 2017), and the processes of interpretation have often been expressed in terms that are both theoretical and abstract (Johnson 2010). One obvious point that must be emphasised is that these are our interpretations of a past that we do not inhabit. We might be tempted to treat such pasts as if they had once existed 'apart from the present' (Olsen et al. 2012, 6), and of course the lives that interest us were once lived in worlds that existed before our time, but the historical accounts of those other lives remain our accounts, we do not discover *the* past. This bequeaths to us a considerable responsibility, for the assumptions that we are prepared to make about those other lives will inform the assumptions that we will also be prepared to employ in our attempts to understand all other people, including our contemporaries.

By treating the material as if, in its degraded form, it represented or was in some way derived from human activity, it has seemed reasonable to distinguish between the ways that people once chose to do things, and the functions that their activities fulfilled. Thus, whilst all people need to eat, for example (providing food with its function), what they have chosen to eat and how they have chosen to eat it are matters of cultural convention and material availability. This distinction has proven to be remarkably important in the history of archaeological thinking because it has facilitated a distinction between the stylistic (cultural) traditions that were specific to particular historical and geographical contexts, and the more general themes of function and organisation that appear to have been shared across different cultures (Dunnell 1978).

The revitalisation of archaeological practices that occurred in the latter half of the twentieth century employed this distinction between the cultural style of an activity and the kind of function that activity had fulfilled. This revitalisation is often taken to have originated with the publication of Binford's 1962 'Archaeology as Anthropology', with its reference to the earlier assertion by Willey and Phillips that 'American archaeology is anthropology or it is nothing' (1958, 2). In his paper, Binford argued that archaeological data 'represent the structure of the total cultural system' and that 'change in the total cultural system must be viewed in an adaptive context both social and environmental' (Binford 1962, 217). The emphasis upon the context of a cultural system's adaptation underscored the need to establish how human activity had functioned, rather than a concern with the stylistic ways in which those activities had been executed. Previously, archaeology's emphasis had been upon tracing the history and the geographical distribution of different patterns of cultural styles, and this had meant, according to Binford, that whilst archaeology had made a major contribution in elucidating 'the total range of physical and cultural similarities and differences characteristic of the entire spatial-temporal range of man's [*sic*] existence', it had nonetheless 'made essentially no contribution in the realm of explanation' (Binford 1962, 217). It was in the realm of *explaining* material-cultural change, expressed in terms other than the supposed spread of cultural influences, that Binford and others came to believe the particular contribution of archaeology lay. Twenty years after Binford's paper was published Colin Renfrew commented that:

> [a] recurring theme in the thinking and writing of most contemporary archaeologists – indeed perhaps the single dominant theme – is the need for

archaeology to go beyond the mere reconstruction and description of the past and to seek insight enabling us to *explain* how that past came about. An essential characteristic of what is today called 'processual archaeology' is the intention to seek explanations for the archaeological record of the past in terms of valid general statements . . . . (Renfrew 1982, 5 emphasis original)

Kintigh and his colleagues have now repeated the demand that archaeology should be able to *explain* why the human past, as represented by archaeological materials, followed the direction that it did. Given that it has been more than fifty years since the first of these calls for a New Archaeology were made, we might begin to wonder why so little appears to have been achieved.

The impact upon the ways different observational data are prioritised as a result of the shift from reading the material record as the product of a variety of *cultural* influences, individual motivations, and past conventions of how to make and how to do things, to treating that record instead as if it attested to the economic and social *functions* which various activities had arisen to satisfy, can be illustrated by the way that Colin Renfrew re-orientated the study of the stone-built monuments that had been erected by the first agricultural communities of western Europe (Renfrew 1976).

The megaliths of western Europe

The earliest surviving stone-built (megalithic) monuments of Europe, the so-called chambered tombs of the Neolithic, are distributed along the Atlantic seaboard of Europe, from southern Sweden to Iberia, and were erected by some of the first European agriculturalists. Regarded as the representations of a single phenomenon of tomb building (Laporte & Scarre 2016), no independent radiocarbon chronology for these structures was established until the early 1960s. With that chronology now in place we know that the earlier estimated dating of this building tradition was both too short in its duration, and too recent in its origin (Daniel 1963 [1962], 143–146). Until the 1960s, these monuments of the Neolithic agriculturalists of western Europe were treated culturally, as representing the regional developments of a building tradition that expressed people's ideas as to how their dead should be treated. These ideas were assumed to have been influenced both by the common origin of a single category of monument, and by the regionally developing techniques of tomb construction (Daniel 1963). The tradition of tomb building was therefore believed to represent the spread of a cult of communal burial, the origins of which were assumed to have lain in the eastern Mediterranean (Childe 1940, 46–80; Childe 1958, 124–134). Consequently, archaeological analysis was directed towards establishing the history, and the spread, of the megalithic cultural tradition by focusing upon the details of what were believed to have been sequences of regional architectural developments (cf. Daniel 1950b & 1960; Powell et al. 1969). This was the approach that Colin Renfrew sought to overturn by establishing a more generally adaptive and functional reason for why early European agriculturalists might have built these tombs in this part of Europe. While these monuments were still accepted to be the tombs that represented a cultural tradition concerning the ways that the dead should be buried, the dominant question that Renfrew posed was: what additional adaptive requirement might these monuments have satisfied?

Renfrew's interpretation of the data exploited the implications derived from the first radiocarbon dates. These indicated that the tombs predated, by a considerable margin, their previously claimed Mediterranean precursors, and the new chronology implied that some of the earliest of these monuments were found in western France (Renfrew 1976 & 1973b, 120–146; cf. Schulz Paulsson 2019). By providing the grounds for rejecting accounts of cultural diffusion, whilst also hoping to explain the emergence of megalithic tombs as a class of monuments, a category that Renfrew accepted was the product of 'a taxonomic decision of our own', he maintained that the tombs arose as the manifestation of:

> a particular set of conditions [that] existed in the Atlantic region at this time, conditions that were not seen elsewhere in Europe, and that these favoured the construction of stone monuments by the small-scale societies of the time. Such a general formulation . . . would explain for us the essentially independent genesis of stone monuments, no doubt of widely different forms in several areas. (Renfrew 1976, 199)

Renfrew argued that the category of 'megalithic tomb' was unified not by its derivation from a common origin and the subsequent diffusion of an evolving cultural idea, but rather by the functional role of tomb building in securing the ongoing claims of segmentary units of agriculturalists to territories of land (Figures 1.1 & 1.2). It was this role that had resulted from the conditions that pertained in several different regions along the Atlantic facade of Europe during the early Neolithic, and it was these conditions that therefore determined the ways that people had behaved. Renfrew's argument was:

> to see in these monuments an expression of territorial behaviour in small-scale segmentary societies . . . [and] to suggest that such forms of territorial behaviour may be particularly frequent in small-scale segmentary societies of this kind in circumstances of population stress. (Renfrew 1976, 200)

The existence of 'population stress' was an entirely hypothetical explanation, given that no empirical data was offered to support its existence. Instead Renfrew argued that this 'stress' had arisen as the result of an advancing wave of colonising agriculturalists, arriving from central Europe, who were forced to adapt to the absence of any further opportunities for westward dispersal by the existence of the Atlantic seaboard (cf. Giot 1963, 3). The resulting population pressure was assumed to have been exacerbated because these migrants had arrived in coastal and riverine environments that might still have been heavily settled by hunter-gatherers

FIGURE 1.1 Renfrew's map indicating the proposed regions for the independent development of chambered tombs (Renfrew 1973c, Fig. 25).

(Renfrew 1976, 213). Thus, whilst cultural archaeology had treated the detailed architectural comparisons of individual monuments as signifying the execution of certain cultural ideas that had been transmitted from one place to another, Renfrew's interpretation abandoned the treatment of architectural form as expressing cultural influences and turned instead to treat the pattern of tomb distributions as signifying the emergence of a form of territorial land-holding.

Both the earlier cultural analysis, and the alternative offered by Renfrew, employ general assumptions, in the first case about people's own deployment of cultural rules, and in the second about the possible development of small-scale segmentary societies responding to the presumed pressures of population growth. Both kinds of analysis therefore accepted that the material residues, classified archaeologically, signified the kinds of process that had resulted in the formation of those residues, and each also employed those aspects of the data (tomb form *versus* locational analysis) that best fitted with the explanation they sought to construct. In this way the earlier studies, which claimed to trace cultural histories, referenced the

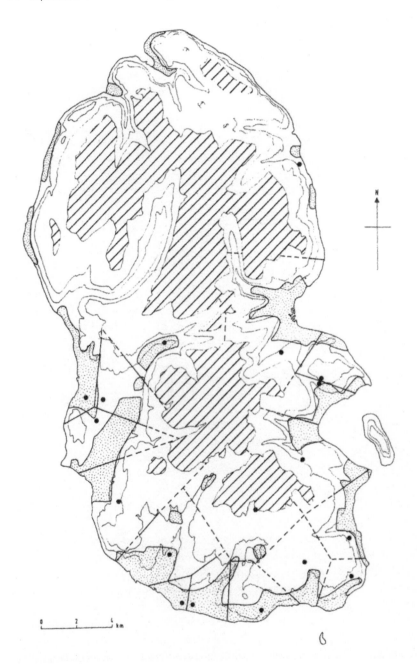

FIGURE 1.2 Renfrew's map of tomb locations on the Isle of Arran, Argyll, with hypothetical territories outlined, and with modern arable land indicated by stippling (Renfrew 1976, Fig. 6).

architectural detail of particular monuments arising from what were claimed to have been culturally transmitted and locally executed rules of behaviour. The form of the monuments was not the kind of data that was addressed by Renfrew whose concern lay instead with the geographical distribution of the monuments as indicative of the early agricultural adaptation to the landscape by means of territorially based activities (Figure 1.2).

From explanation to understanding

In 1942 Carl Hempel published what was to become a widely referenced paper on the function of general laws in historical analyses (Hempel 1942). Hempel's argument here and in its later development (cf. Hempel & Oppenheim 1948), was that the occurrence of an event that required to be explained (the *explanandum*) could be explained by an *explanans,* which expressed a combination of the initial and the boundary conditions that had operated within the context of one or more general laws. A historical event, according to the Hempel model, is therefore explained when the antecedent conditions are subsumed within what William Dray characterised as a 'covering law' (Dray 1957). From this perspective, historical generalities were not to be described simply as organised assemblages of activities and material conditions. Instead the historical conditions that had generated the assemblages of residue had been governed by the laws of historical process which resulted in predictable, or at least statistically probable, outcomes (Salmon 1993).

The Hempel model found enthusiastic support among many archaeologists in the 1970s who saw it as providing a basis for the scientific analysis of the historical conditions to which they were able to attest archaeologically. These archaeologists regarded the ultimate aim of archaeology as establishing the covering laws that had governed the historical processes, to which archaeological residues attested, and within which human activities had once operated (Fritz & Plog 1970; Watson et al. 1971). This enthusiasm was not shared by all, however (Levin 1973; Morgan 1973). Indeed, Colin Renfrew argued that to subsume the particulars of any one historical circumstance within a model providing for a more general explanation, did not necessitate that the general model should be elevated to the status of a law of history (Renfrew 1973a). The argument that Renfrew used to explain the emergence of European megalithic tombs did not utilise any laws of historical development that would have been recognised by Hempel, but it did employ a generalisation about specific historical conditions. It did not, for example, offer a general law for why collective burial might be expected under certain boundary conditions, nor did it offer a general law that determined that burial sites should be used as territorial markers under certain historical conditions (cf. Saxe 1970). Instead Renfrew expected similar conditions to be explained by high-level generalisations that were specific to the period (the European Neolithic) and that referred to processes, such as those resulting from a growing population confronting the limited possibilities of economic expansion. These conditions had supposedly accommodated the variables whose cultural execution in tomb design was particular to each case

(Renfrew 1973a; cf. Braithwaite 1964, 319ff.). This argument leaves us to question how the sufficiency of explanations such as those offered by Renfrew is to be judged, given the lack of empirical data that were available to support the processes that were proposed. The obvious answer might be that the explanations seemed to work, given what was known, and that nothing more should be demanded of them. If this is so, then the problem simply becomes whether the target towards which the explanation is directed, namely the apparent emergence of territorial behaviour, is itself a valid description of the historical reality.

A generalising procedure for the archaeological identification of past processes therefore requires reducing the specific, cultural, detail of the material (a detail that is often painstakingly recorded by archaeologists) to represent the more general processes that had supposedly resulted in the creation of that material. Archaeological residues are therefore now treated as being significant because they inform on the ways that human activities were organised to satisfy certain functional requirements. It was upon this basis that the New Archaeology argued that the changing conditions represented by the sequences of material residues could be explained.

An early critique of Hempel's model was provided by William Dray (1957). He accepted that historians work with generalisations that tend to group together historical conditions under certain common themes, as if each specific historical case were the representation of more generally applicable processes. An example that Dray offered was the ways that the general process that the historian might classify as a 'revolution' was manifested in a number of specific events. Dray then argued that the historian's task was to investigate the characteristics that guided a historically specific example of such a condition. It was the historically specific variables that undermined the idea that historical events might ever be explained simply as the playing out of more general laws, and the historian's task was to identify the historically specific variables in a particular case, rather than confirm some overarching law of process. The history of the French Revolution, for example, is, in Dray's terms, to be understood by reference to the conditions and the strategies that were at work among the different sections of the population in eighteenth-century France: it was these strategies that gave rise to that particular revolution, rather than the events of 1789–1799 being explained by the operation of a supposedly timeless law governing all revolutionary conditions.

In Dray's argument the historian's task has always been to clarify what distinguished the particular historical trajectory within a more general kind of process (cf. Dray 1959). This is presumably how the records of events might initially have been perceived in archaeology, as attesting to the specifics of a cultural strategy, such as a cultural group belonging to the western European Neolithic, rather than as having satisfied a more general, functional requirement. The expectation of a cultural archaeology was therefore that its statements were always likely to refer to various cultural changes in material conditions, and these changes would tell us something about the influences that brought those changes about. In his study of megalithic tombs, Renfrew perceived what happened in history not in this way, but as an organisational change which he characterised in terms of a geographical pattern. Thus, for Renfrew, what happened in western Europe after 5000 BCE was the colonisation of the land by agriculturalists who had developed their mortuary rituals, and the associated monuments, to signal their claim on certain areas of land. The need to adjust to population pressures by means of establishing a territorial organisation for the allocation of land became the explanation as to why the monuments were apparently regularly spaced in those agricultural regions that Renfrew offered as examples of the process (Figure 1.2). However, this did not explain why it was *tombs* that were developed as territorial markers (cf. Chapman 1981), nor did it explain the architectural form of the tombs themselves. Indeed, it appears that the material itself (the megalithic tombs of western Europe) was not what was being explained in Renfrew's model at all, rather it was the more general process that was hypothesised as being represented by those tombs. Renfrew does not therefore explain the development of megaliths; instead he offers some reasons for believing that *what happened* in western Europe with the arrival of agriculturalists was the emergence of a territorial form of settlement organisation. He offers an empirical reason for accepting that such an organisation arose (given by the distribution of monuments), and he argues for a reason as to *why* that organisation might have occurred (the hypothetical pressure on resources). We will return to consider the various ways in which we might understand the building of these monuments in Chapters 5 and 8.

Even allowing for the conflicts over the ways we might characterise what happened in history, explanations as to *why* it happened obviously confront the 'problem of limitation'. If the explanation for an emergent condition is treated as if it were a causal reason – that is, as necessarily occurring in some antecedent condition – then the problem is that we lack any guide for selecting the conditions that might have been causally significant. Any number of factors will exist from the vast array of antecedents (Botterill 2010, 289). These antecedent conditions will include all those conditions that have left no archaeological trace at all. Botterill considers the target towards which an explanation is directed, and he distinguishes between those explanations that address the interrogative 'why?' questions and those that address 'how?' questions. He characterises the latter as 'process explanations' (Botterill 2010, 295), and argues that these could prompt narrative accounts that search for agencies that were end-directed or teleological in their form.

Causal and teleological explanations have traditionally been held to be in contrast one with the other (von Wright 1971, 83). Causal explanations point towards the past to identify the prior conditions that might explain 'why' something happened, such as the pressure on resources triggering a concern for the control over a territory. These explanations tend to be mechanistic in their form and deterministic in their operation (thus reflecting the earlier archaeological interest in laws under which historical explanations might be subsumed). Teleological explanations on the other hand point to a future state to explain the direction towards which processes were directed. They explain why certain things might have occurred by detailing 'how' such end-directed processes might have operated to achieve their goal, such as a project to build, maintain, and use a megalithic tomb. Von Wright noted that the explanandum of a teleological explanation is 'in typical cases, an item of behavior – or it is the product or result of behavior' and where 'behavior which has a genuine teleological explanation might be called *action-like*' (von Wright 1971, 86 emphasis original). This directs our attention towards the purpose of an agent, which we will take to be the direction of an agent towards certain conditions of possibility. This reading of purpose therefore results in an archaeological concern with understanding how certain historical processes might have been possible. Therefore, an *understanding* of how historical conditions might have been possible stands in contrast to *explaining* why such conditions may have occurred.

> Understanding is also connected with *intentionality* in a way explanation is not. One understands the aims and purposes of an agent, the meaning of a sign or symbol of a social institution or religious rite. The intentionalistic or . . . semantic dimension of understanding has come to play a prominent role in more recent methodological discussion. (von Wright 1971, 6 emphasis original)

Teleological explanations in archaeology have tended to be called upon when the function of the innovation to be explained is identified. In this way a new arrangement of things might be explained as if those innovations were designed to do what they are now assumed to have done. The obvious problem with such arguments is that the function of things is often not realised until those things exist. Megalithic tombs might indeed have been a way of establishing the territorial claims of early agricultural communities, although it would be difficult to understand how such a role was conceived before these tombs existed. They might, after all, have been built with the intention of simply housing the dead and, once built, only then might they have functioned as territorial markers. However, all this might seem to be little more than supposition. The obvious lack of either a living informant or a literary testimony that would enable archaeological investigators to understand the motivation of an agent's actions, has long been held either to make such a task impossible, or to render it little better than informed speculation (cf. Binford 1987).

The claim that archaeology can identify the general processes that instigated the patterns of archaeologically recovered materials which are believed to represent the ways that human behaviours were organised economically and socially, has accompanied attempts to 'justify the broad cross-cultural and diachronic scope of our work' (Drennan et al. 2012, 1). However, Drennan and others have complained that '[i]n the past two decades, the pendulum seems to have swung away from comparative research in archaeology. Many archaeologists focus on detailed contextual descriptions of individual cases, and only a few have dedicated themselves to explicit comparative work' (Drennan et al. 2012, 1).

The archaeological task as set out by Kintigh and his colleagues, and with which we began this chapter, would seem to return us to the quest for comparative historical studies upon which general explanations of causation may be founded, and this reads like one of the programmatic statements associated with the literature of the New Archaeology which appeared in the 1960s and 1970s. That literature was optimistic about the possibility that archaeology could establish the general characteristics of any historical change, and the continuing commitment to this approach is expressed by the challenges that Kintigh and his colleagues have listed as addressing one of three kinds of question. The first of these is that of cause (as in: 'how did certain material conditions emerge, or what prompted such conditions to arise?'). The second is the question of function (as in: 'what was the role of certain patterns of organised behaviour?'). Functional questions often reduce to questions of cause simply because, as I have argued above, the function of a kind of behaviour is offered as explaining the cause for its existence (as in: 'what were the consequences of such and such a condition?' as if this explained its cause – which it doesn't). The third kind of question concerns the available analytical procedures (as in: 'how might archaeology best understand these material patterns and the forms of the organised behaviour that are indicated by those patterns?'). This entire approach thus characterises the past as if it comprised systems of material conditions (made up of material culture and the material conditions of the wider environment), and patterns of human behaviour. These systems are represented today by their material residues and can be described in terms of different kinds of human and material organisation (expressed in such terms as settlement, economic or social organisations, and environmental conditions).

If we could indeed define the kinds of systemic organisations that have occurred in the past, then the historical challenge would seem to be one of either explaining or understanding why these kinds of organisation might have arisen. Colin Renfrew and Paul Bahn have commented that '[t]o answer the question "why?" is the most difficult task in archaeology' (Renfrew & Bahn 2004, 469). We might wonder if the question 'how?' would prove to be equally difficult.

Conclusion

The optimism expressed by Kintigh et al. in assuming that archaeology can contribute to the historical characterisation of the human condition, has also been expressed by others, whilst some have expressed their concern that archaeology is failing to live up to that optimism. Writing in the 1973 Redman-edited *Research and Theory in Current Archaeology*, John Fritz stated his belief that the volume reflected 'a long-standing dissatisfaction with archaeology felt by many', a dissatisfaction that was expressed in the commonly held view that 'archaeology is primarily or "merely" a technique' (Fritz 1973, 59). The problem, Fritz suggested, was that despite the data that archaeology made available for the study of the historical processes that had generated long-term change amongst human populations, the potential of those data remained insufficiently exploited. Indeed, he and Fred Plog had previously suggested that 'unless archaeologists find ways to make their research increasingly relevant to the modern world, the modern world will find itself increasingly capable of getting along without archaeologists' (Fritz & Plog

1970, 412). Five years after Fritz wrote, Redman and others continued to refer to 'the feeling of many archaeologists that the discipline isn't doing enough, that it isn't saying enough about our subject matter, and that archaeologists aren't being listened to by the rest of anthropology' (Redman et al. 1978, 2): it is a complaint that continues to be made today (e.g. Smith 2012; Gonzáles-Ruibal 2018).

My concern in writing this book has been to reject the problem that is most often expressed for archaeology, namely that it confronts data that are either limited or ambiguous in what they might represent, and that these data are therefore impoverished, when compared to the data that are available to other domains of social science and historical research (Hawkes 1954; Smith 1955). The problem, as I see it, is that the kinds of understandings and explanations that archaeology has been attempting to offer depend upon the kind of historical object that is taken to be represented by archaeological data. Despite all the theoretical differences that have been expressed in the ways that those data have been interpreted, they have all shared the same assumption, that the data are the static representations of past dynamics. My argument is that the current object of archaeological enquiry is mis-cast: it is not a matter of how we might explain the conditions of the past, and this means that the current interpretation of archaeological data, as representing those conditions, is also mis-directed.

Archaeological methodologies construct a perspective upon once existing historical conditions. These methodologies are constructed from a particular perspective that is not value-free. Archaeologists do not, as Sir Leonard Woolley once implied, simply 'dig up the past' (Woolley 1960 [1930]), and to suggest otherwise by claiming that archaeology reconstructs a now absent reality based upon the representations that are provided by the material, is to slip into what Bhaskar called 'the epistemic fallacy' which assumes that 'statements about being can always be transposed into statements about our knowledge of being' (Bhaskar 1997, 16). The archaeological problem, as I hope to characterise it, is to establish how we might credibly characterise the once existing conditions of human life, and upon that basis understand those particular forms of life from an archaeological perspective. But the more important question is, perhaps: why do we bother? What is the significance of an archaeological understanding to our contemporary world? My reply to that question starts from the assertion that archaeology is not the study of things that represent some aspect of a past reality, nor is it initially the study of the human actions that had caused those things to occur. Instead archaeology is the study of how forms of life had once become possible by their development within the contexts of the particular material conditions that archaeology enables us to glimpse. My intention is that this will lead to an understanding of how the diversity witnessed by life as a whole, and by human life in particular, has been constructed, and for this kind of archaeology to be possible it will be necessary to re-think some of the ways that we characterise the conditions of history.

2

THE ARCHAEOLOGICAL RECORD

Introduction

In June 1797, the Society of Antiquaries of London received a short communication from John Frere, a Norfolk landowner (Frere 1800). The gentlemen members of the Society had been meeting since the beginning of the eighteenth century 'for their mutual improvement in the Study of Antiquity and in the History of Former Times', although sadly those gentlemen present at that June meeting seemed unable to grasp the significance of what Frere told them (Evans 1956, 104 & 202–203). Frere's communication concerned the discovery of some 'flint weapons' (Figure 2.1), a discovery that he described by using what archaeologists have come to accept as the basic methodological assumptions employed by field archaeology. By so doing Frere was able to explore the profound significance of the discoveries that he communicated to the Fellowship of the Society.

The flint implements had been recovered from a quarry-pit dug for clay extraction at Hoxne in eastern England, and Frere described the implements as being 'fabricated and used by a people who had not the use of metals'. Having been found at a depth of some four metres in clays, and below a layer of sand and shell, he also reasoned that this sequence would 'tempt us to refer them to a very remote period indeed, even beyond that of the present world' and buried by deposits that 'may be conjectured to have been once at the bottom, or at least the shore, of a sea' and below strata containing 'some extraordinary bones . . . of some unknown animal' (Frere 1800, 204).

The logic involved in Frere's reasoning is important. He accepted that the stone implements were humanly produced, an acceptance based, we must assume, partly upon analogies drawn with the collections that Europeans had accumulated during their destructive encounters with the non-European communities who were employing stone-based technologies (Daniel 1964, 38–41), and partly upon the regularity of the form of the implements, implying the execution of an intentional design in their production, and which Frere presumably equated with human activity. The timeless characteristics of the human presence were therefore recognisable amongst this material, and we must also assume that it was the shape of the implements that prompted Frere to suggest that they were intended to function as weapons. Frere's reasoning therefore employed a commitment to humanity as being a single and behaviourally distinctive form of life, and where the functionality of the artefacts produced could be ascertained from their form. Having thus accepted that the objects had been formed by human manufacture, the implications of their recovery, stratified within fluvial deposits and below the bones of presumably extinct animal species, were clear: those humans had lived a very long time ago.

The reasoning that Frere employed to understand the significance of these findings must have drawn upon ideas that were in circulation at that time, and these provided the basis for three important claims that continue to be made by archaeology. First, that the presence and the activities of humans are recognisable historically by the distinctive form of their material products, the function of which might still be ascertained from their shape. Neither depend upon the current presence of humans themselves and their verbal testimony. In Frere's case, recognition of the now absent humanity came from the form of the flint implements. The assumption was that all humans, at all times, have made things intentionally, and that those intentions remain understandable to us simply because the form of things attests to the purpose for which they were designed. If this reasoning holds, then it would mean that we should be able to understand why other people either made, or did, certain things, despite the absence of those people from the field of our enquiry, and despite the considerable distances in time and in cultural beliefs that separate us from them. It is a claim based upon the assertion that a single form of humanity has existed throughout its history. The second claim was that the things people made, and the ways, and the technologies, that they used to make them can be observed to have changed over time. Thus, whilst people have remained the same kinds of people their behaviours have nonetheless changed. In Frere's view, for example, there was a time in which people 'had not the use of metals'. The third claim was that the sequences of deposits in which these objects were found provided two kinds of additional information. One was that the relative sequences in which different materials were deposited, with one above the other, ran from the earliest to the latest. The other is that the kind of environment that resulted in the formation of those deposits, such as the shore of a sea that Frere had proposed in the case of some of the Hoxne deposits, could be reconstructed based upon a uniformity with present-day processes. Although Frere's speculation of a time 'beyond that of the present world' is ambiguous (it might imply his commitment to the existence of an antediluvian age), he nonetheless accepted that the geological *processes* of formation must have remained constant over time (Daniel 1950a). This so-called 'principle of uniformitarianism' was established by the late eighteenth century and was formalised with the publication of Lyell's *Principles of Geology* between 1830 and 1833.

FIGURE 2.1   One of the handaxes reported upon by Frere from Hoxne, Suffolk (Frere 1800).

These three volumes, which laid the basis for accepting the geological antiquity of the earth, had a considerable impact upon the thinking of Charles Darwin.

The uniformitarian principle that 'the key to the past lies in the present' evokes the existence of timeless and mechanistic processes that have always linked certain kinds of productive processes to a particular kind of product. The suggestion that the physical processes of production are recorded by their products has been of fundamental importance to the development of archaeological, as well as geological, reasoning. It has allowed archaeologists to assume that the form of archaeological materials is the product of a mechanism of transformation that had occurred in the past in the same way as it would occur today, and that the nature of such a process is recorded in the form taken by the material. Uniformitarian reasoning also allowed geological deposits to be read as recording the earth's tectonic processes, and the processes of rock and soil erosion and deposition. It has been upon a similar basis that humanly produced artefacts have been read as recording the mechanistic processes involved in their making by the transformation of raw materials, and where those processes of production were directed by factors that are believed to have been possessed by, or to have acted on, humanity as a whole.

Frere's reasoning was therefore based upon the claim that historical conditions and present conditions share a number of common processes that render the former understandable by analogy with our own experiences of the latter. Thus, the conditions by which sand and shells are deposited along a sea-shore comprised processes that are assumed to have remained uniform over time. In addition, the symmetry of the flint implements and the flake scars, which attest to the mechanical ways in which this symmetry was created, are taken to imply a purposeful designer, and Frere accepted that such a designer was a human rather than an animal or a mythical being. This assumption would not be widely contested today, and it implies that human behaviour is recognisable in virtue of the ways that its products attest to their purposeful design, and purposeful design is treated as a quality associated with human action. Thus, whilst we might doubt Frere's assertion that the implements were designed to act as weapons of war, we are nonetheless likely to accept that they were intended for some purpose, such as butchery of a carcass. But if we equate human intentions with purposeful design, and thus with the regularity of the form of the things created, then what are we to make of other regularities that are manufactured by other species? This was a question that Marx raised when he noted that:

> [a] spider conducts operations that resemble those of a weaver, and a bee puts to shame many an architect in the construction of her cells. But what distinguishes the worst architect from the best of bees is this, that the architect raises his structure in imagination before he erects it in reality. (Marx 1867, 127)

Marx offered the powerful, and widely accepted, assertion that humanity is distinguishable from the rest of the natural world by virtue of its possession of a particular kind of cognitive ability, one that facilitates a process of forward planning in the initiation of an action. If this generalisation were indeed to be accepted then the handaxes from Hoxne would presumably have been 'raised in imagination' before being flaked into reality.

The claim that long-term human history can be traced in terms of a technical development in the making of objects, running from the use of stone to that of metals, was formalised in the nineteenth century by the eventual adoption of the sequence of the three ages of Stone, Bronze, and Iron (Rowley-Conwy 2007). And in 1859, the same year that saw the publication, in its first edition, of *On the*

Origin of Species by Means of Natural Selection (Darwin 2009 [1859]), John Evans and Joseph Prestwich read a paper to the Royal Society in London in which they accepted the implications that Boucher de Perthes's recovery of stone tools from deep within the gravels of the Somme had for the presence, and thus for the considerable antiquity, of human beings. John Frere was therefore part of the long intellectual revolution that occurred between the late eighteenth and mid-nineteenth centuries which resulted in seeing the world, and humanity's place within it, not as the products of momentary and relatively recent creations, but as the products of long-term processes of geological, behavioural, and biological development. Humanity's place in nature was largely established through archaeological procedures.

The possibility of archaeology

Archaeology's claim to provide an account that extends across what Frere had come to recognise as the lengthy history of humanity, is only sustainable if it can be demonstrated that the history of the various forms of human behaviour, and the various ways in which that behaviour had been organised, can be understood by reference to the residue of the surviving things that were involved in that behaviour. Understanding in the context of a historical enquiry presumably means more than simply describing what had happened at that time, and yet we might wonder what more could ever be achieved. The traditional practice of archaeology has accepted that the form and the patterning of the residues that we recover are mainly the results of human activity, and that this material can provide for an intelligible understanding of the processes by which the form of, and the associations deposited with, those material things were created. This reasoning develops the principle that all of humanity has registered a particular kind of material presence that is archaeologically distinguishable from other non-human processes of material transformation. This principle was clearly expressed in such book titles as *Man* [sic] *the Toolmaker* (Oakley 1967), and it follows that it should be possible to chart the ways in which human activity, as the producer of things, has varied throughout its history. Humans, in other words, do things in ways that we can recognise but in ways that have varied historically and geographically. The simplest expression of this idea in archaeology has been to argue that human behaviour is distinctive because its material products have always been designed to express both a functional requirement and a particular kind of cultural or stylistic order. This is rather like saying that, to communicate, 'all humans have language', whilst also recognising that, in communicating, humanity has spoken in many different languages and in many different dialects.

The obvious challenge for archaeology in extending our understanding of human behaviour beyond the description of its existence, is the considerable distance that separates our own cultural understandings of the world from that of those who inhabited the historical conditions that we are hoping to characterise. To pursue the analogy with language, it would be as if we knew that people in the past were communicating by speaking, and that we could hear fragments of what they were saying, but where those fragments were nothing more than a meaningless babble to our own ears. Not only that, but what was being said expressed a different perception of the world from that which was held by us, but it was a perception that we nonetheless seek to understand. Archaeology has therefore needed to establish the basis upon which a cross-cultural understanding of others might be possible, based upon the relics that have survived from those earlier times, and this is a considerable challenge. Whilst the distances between languages can be transcended by means of translation, and where the question might be whether the same kind of procedure might be offered to transcend the differences in the production of material culture, it is important to note that linguistic translation is not concerned with transliteration, but with rendering what is understood as being evoked in one linguistic tradition comprehensible to those operating in another. This should warn us against assuming that the 'meaning' of individual things could ever provide us with an absolute by which the user of any one cultural assemblage could understand that of another. Things of the same shape, and indeed of the same function, could vary considerably in terms of the cultural significance they held for different users.

Clearly, archaeological claims to understand others will always be based upon some very significant claims about humanity in general. These generalisations have been widely employed to define what it is to be human, and to distinguish humanity from the rest of nature, not only in the terms already mentioned (*Man the Tool-Maker*), but also in such terms as *The Believing Primate* (Schloss & Murray 2009), and *The Symbolic Species* (Deacon 1997). The ability to represent things that were immediately experienced as if they were 'merely apparent' and represented the workings of a more profound, possibly sacred, order appears to mark one characteristic of human behaviour. It is also possible, however, that the emergence of some symbolic behaviour does not correlate with clearly demarcated stages in hominin species evolution – for example, when primates that seemingly lack the anatomically modern features of *Homo sapiens*, such as those whose skeletal remains have been classed as *Homo naledi* from the Rising Star cave in South Africa, appear to have been involved in the selective deposition of their dead deep within that cave system (Shreeve 2015; see also https://www.homonaledi.org/ and https://www.newscientist.com/article/2128834-homo-naledi-is-only-250000-years-old-heres-why-that-matters/). Finds such as these raise the possibility that symbolic and ritualised responses to death had occurred amongst individuals who were physically unlike modern humans. Indeed such 'mourning' behaviour might be extended to include species other than our own (cf. Pettitt 2011; Pettitt & Anderson 2020; Barrett 2013; Anderson et al. 2018; Piel & Stewart 2016), and there are times when the distinction that we draw between human behaviour, as culturally mediated, and animal behaviour, as the product of biologically determined instinct, can seem far less clear-cut than we might once have assumed (de Waal 2016).

Perhaps we should allow that whilst an archaeological methodology will continue to be based upon the general characteristics that are assumed to render all human presences materially recognisable, the specific forms of particular material cultural conditions will also describe something of that humanity's internal diversity. This would require an archaeological methodology that defines the basis for understanding others, and it is the widespread doubt concerning the usefulness of archaeological knowledge in establishing anything more than the most general confirmation for an earlier human presence, that accounts for archaeology's marginality in the study of human diversity. As Gonzáles-Ruibal (2013) has commented, reference to archaeology beyond the discipline itself is normally in terms of a metaphor, not one for the seeking of origins and histories, but simply for the act of *seeking*, as in 'excavating', the underlying structures that might determine the appearance of things (e.g. Foucault 1972). However, if archaeology is treated as a metaphor for peeling away the surface appearances of things, then the practice of archaeology itself seems to be almost obsessively concerned with that surface flotsam of materials. Archaeologists certainly excavate, but this process of going beneath the surface of the ground is merely designed to recover the material debris left by a now absent humanity. Occasionally that debris includes 'wonderful things', such as those glimpsed by Carter when he broke the seal of Tutankhamun's tomb, but more often than not it appears to be the fragmentary detritus of quite unlovely materials (cf. Olsen 2013). How this detritus could ever provide us with a secure understanding of the structures and motivations that have governed the diverse histories of human life continues to pose a significant challenge. Archaeologists have themselves continued to question the extent to which they might ever get 'behind' the artefact or the deposit, and to see at last the lives of others that were once lived.

The archaeological record

The practice of archaeology has placed an emphasis upon the processes of survey, excavation, and with it the recovery of ancient objects: this is what archaeologists are supposed to do, after all. The initial result of the work of excavation is a descriptive archive of the things encountered, of the analyses undertaken, and an archived collection of the recovered materials (Lucas 2012). These are the cumulative bodies of data for which Kintigh and his colleagues hope to provide a synthesis. The object of archaeological analysis therefore encompasses a number of different kinds of things, either those things 'in the field', or the accumulation of things in museums, along with the archived descriptions of things that are encountered by archaeologists and by others. In the eighteenth century, and some sixteen years before Frere offered his observations to the London Antiquaries, the philosopher Immanuel Kant had provided an account of our experience of things that distinguished between the things in themselves, and the human, subjective awareness of those things (Kant 2007 [1781]). Kant's point was that these are not one and the same, and that whilst things in themselves certainly exist, our access to those things is only ever through the medium of our experiences of them.

It would be an understatement to say that much has been written regarding the distinction that Kant drew, and even a cursory consideration of the resources now available for archaeological analysis will recognise that whilst these resources obviously include things in themselves, they are archived, displayed, and described in terms that are chosen by archaeologists and will conform with the disciplinary conventions of a contemporary methodology (Shanks & Tilley 1987a, 68–99). Nonetheless, the argument has been made that because things-as-such have an existence well beyond the human experience of them (Meillassoux 2008), and because this larger non-human-related existence must be recognised as having operated as long as those things have existed, then a critical account of the archaeological resource should reflect upon the brute fact that things exist beyond our perceptions of them. However, the conclusion that archaeology should be seen purely as the 'discipline of things' (Olsen et al. 2012) is itself questionable.

My aim is to develop the argument for an archaeology that seeks to understand how humans have coped with, and developed through, their own relationships with things, rather than merely acknowledging the existence of those things-in-themselves. For this argument to work it will require us to examine the assumption that the material residues represent a record of humanly generated processes involved in their production. Let us therefore begin by asking 'what is it that we want to know and what is it that we hope to understand from our own engagements with these relics?'

It has been easy to assume that archaeological perceptions of the past arise from the material itself, simply because the material records what we can know whilst also defining those things that can never be known. Lewis Binford expressed the relationship between the record and what it records as being the relationship between a contemporary static pattern of things (the residues) and the dynamics involved in their formation (past processes). As Binford saw it, this relationship clearly distinguished between the object that is the focus of present-day archaeological concern and the historical conditions within which that object once functioned. The challenge from this perspective becomes one of linking the contemporary, static patterns of objects to historical dynamics in ways that have a demonstrable validity. If Binford had questioned Frere on this matter, Frere might have asserted that it was self-evident that the 'sand, shells and marine substances' would have been deposited on a sea-shore (the uniformitarian assumption that the same kinds of geological deposits result from the same kinds of formation processes), that the artefacts were humanly designed because that is the way that humans work (a uniformitarian assumption about the nature of human behaviour with implications for how we understand humanity in general), and that these artefacts were weapons because that is what they looked like, an assumption presumably based upon their shape and one that might also have appealed to Thomas Hobbes's assertion that 'primitive' life was 'nasty, brutish, and short' involving a 'war of all against all' (Hobbes 2017 [1651]). The reasoning that Frere might have employed to link the static residues to dynamic processes was therefore grounded upon three assumptions of varying reliability. For Binford the challenge for archaeology was to move away from simply asserting the significance of archaeological things in terms of what they were thought to represent, and to establish how the links between material and its formation dynamics were proven to be demonstrably secure. That security was based upon uniformitarian principles and it arose because the processes resulting in various deposits could be observed ethnographically or could be repeated experimentally (Binford 1983).

It is important to accept that when an archaeologist refers to an archaeological record they are not only establishing the things that are of interest to them but they are also evoking a desire to know something about the past as the condition that once generated, or 'wrote', that record (Patrik 1985). The things that are doing the recording range from single objects, which might be assigned to particular archaeological categories ('Aucheulean' Palaeolithic handaxes), to kinds of deposits (gravels and sands), to the relationships between things (the handaxes stratified in river gravels). Past dynamics are recorded because they transformed the materials in ways that brought those objects, deposits, and the relationships between them, into being.

This current archaeological consensus tends to define the discipline of archaeology by what it studies (material remains) rather than by what it might seek to understand (the conditions of the human past). It assumes that the latter gave rise to the former and that the latter is therefore revealed through our analysis of the former residues. In this way the material defines the object of analysis for, having noticed that antiquities exist in the world around us, archaeologists then ask how those antiquities might have come about. Hence archaeology supposedly discovers something of the historical conditions that determined the production of those antiquities. This is a very different procedure from one that decides, at the outset, what it is that we want to understand before identifying the material, and designing the methodologies, that might enable us to gain that understanding. The current archaeological practice that endows the collection, and the analysis, of ancient materials with analytical priority has a number of practical consequences. Central to these is the need that Binford identified, to establish a secure methodology that will interpret today's static material as the consequence of past dynamics. Binford's research programme therefore became increasingly concerned with explaining the formation of the archaeological record, where such explanations (the historical conditions of the past) are expressed as the causal dynamics resulting in various material residues (Salmon 1982).

The limits of uniformitarianism

Whilst the uniformitarian principle is of importance in the analysis of the mechanistic processes of formation that contributed to the form of their archaeological residues, we might wonder if it is of similar importance for gaining an understanding of the historical conditions of the various kinds of humanity that have also engaged with that material. Because the uniformitarian principle delivers the belief that formation processes occur quite generally and can be read back from the predictability of their residues, this also implies that processes that once operated only locally and in historically specific ways cannot be read off from the record. This has resulted in the assumption that the archaeological record is limited simply because key aspects of earlier, historical conditions are represented in ways that are unpredictable. For example, Margaret Smith once asserted that '[i]t would obviously be impossible to understand the relics of the Trobrianders from the evidence of the material remains alone: they don't even act rationally, on standards we can comprehend, when engaged in growing their subsistence crop' (Smith 1955, 5; cf. Chapman & Wylie 2016, 16).

Upon this basis it appears that the very things in which we might be most interested, namely the specific ways that others once lived and which diverged from our own ways of living, lie beyond the possibility of archaeological understanding (cf. Hawkes 1954), such that our understanding of what it might be to act 'rationally' is quite different from that which was employed by those whom we study.

In negotiating the uncertainties that link specific historical processes to the contemporary data, Adrian Currie has advised that the broad scope of these uncertainties cannot be resolved by any single historical method. In his view the historian/archaeologist should therefore abandon any commitment that they might hold to the ideal of a single method of analysis. I will assume that Currie means us to question the assumption that all archaeological data must be treated as if it recorded the processes of its formation. Instead Currie advises taking a more pragmatic approach, one that develops methods more concerned with what it is that we want to know and that are sensitive to the historical context being analysed (Currie 2018). Thus, for data to become the evidence by which we might gain an understanding of more than the mechanical processes of its formation, we will need to find a way to use that evidence as the evidential traces that are specific to the historical processes that interest us (cf. Wylie 1989).

Lewis Binford recognised that the application of uniformitarian assumptions should enable him to resolve the problem of determining the formation processes that had resulted in the bone debris recovered from a number of French Palaeolithic cave deposits (Binford 1983, 95–108). The predictability offered by the uniformitarian link between the formation process and its resulting faunal deposit meant that the proposed cause-effect relationships could be tested by contemporary observations on environmental conditions that were similar to those that had occurred during the European Palaeolithic. This became the essential step that Binford took towards establishing archaeology as an experimental science, whereby the validity of observations on static residues could be tested by their replication in conditions that were available to contemporary observations.

There is no doubt that such work has had considerable impact on archaeological interpretation, with the greatest impact of this so-called 'middle range' analysis being on our understanding of early hominin behaviour, and on hunter-gatherer archaeology more generally (Binford 1981a; cf. Binford 2001). In the classic example, analysis has allowed patterns of debris resulting from animal behaviour to be distinguished from the patterns that might have resulted from human behaviour.

The South African anthropologist Raymond Dart asserted that he could link a number of animal bone deposits to the activities of very early hunters. By this means Dart claimed to identify the presence of early humans in the archaeological record, not by the presence of fossilised skeletal remains of hominin, but by the apparent presence of residues resulting from behaviour that he regarded as being typically *human* (cf. Binford 1981a, 13). Dart asserted that the relevant deposits were characterised by the discarded debris of early hominin (*australopithecine*) who were meat eaters and therefore hunters, who had butchered their kill and transported selected joints to prepare and consume at a home base, and who had then worked some of the residual animal bone as a source for new tools and weapons (Dart 1949). The humanity of the *australopithecine* was thus attested for by the claimed behaviour of maintaining a home base, sharing food, and by tool manufacture, with all these factors coming at a key point in the evolutionary line that led ultimately to modern humans. This appeared to present hunting and meat sharing, along with tool manufacturing, as if they were key behavioural attributes leading to the evolution of modern humans (cf. Ardrey 1976). Obviously, the link that Dart proposed between *australopithecine* behaviour and animal bone deposits cannot be replicated today, but it is possible to link the formation of contemporary bone deposits with the behaviour of contemporary hunting and scavenging animals. It was upon this basis that C.K. Brain demonstrated that the structure of the fossil bone deposits that Dart had identified as resulting from *australopithecine* behaviour actually matched the structure of bone deposits found today in the dens of hyena. By comparing contemporary scavenger deposits, which included gnawed and split bones, with the fossil record, and by also considering the hunting behaviour of large cats, in particular the bone debris resulting from leopard kills, Brain successfully challenged Dart's behavioural assumptions and relocated the early hominin populations from amongst the hunters to amongst the hunted (Brain 1981).

Binford stressed the need for archaeologists to recognise that complex, taphonomic mechanisms, extending from human, animal, and plant activity to processes of chemical and mechanical erosion, will have contributed significantly to the patterned palimpsest of residues that are the object of archaeological classification. Binford's criticism was that archaeologists had been far too ready, as in the case of Dart, to assert the significance of deposits. This had resulted in archaeological categories of material, such as the assemblages of bones and artefacts, being claimed to derive from so-called 'living floor' deposits that supposedly attested to human behaviour, when in fact these assertions, and the categories that they sustained, were based upon prejudice rather than testable observations. So-called 'living floor' assemblages, for example, have been treated as if they represented the results of short periods of human behaviour, a fossilisation of momentary acts akin to a kind of 'Pompeii premise', rather than, as Binford argued, a palimpsest of complex and ongoing material transformations that had extended across lengthy periods of time (Binford 1981a, 1981b, & 1982; cf. Schiffer 1976 & 1985).

Uniformitarian processes are obviously at work in the world. Hyenas, wherever they might be encountered, will reduce the scavenged carcases of a bovine to a similar pattern of residues. The physical reduction of a flint core by means of soft hammer percussion will generate a similar range of flake debitage whenever and wherever it is executed. We might refer to all such processes as being mechanical. The American philosopher Charles Sanders Peirce offered a typology of signs in which one thing is taken to indicate, or to represent, another when observed by a particular interpretant, and he termed the mechanical relationship between the thing acting as a sign, and what it represented, as an indexical relationship. The classic example of an indexical relationship is that of the weather vane's response to the wind's direction, where the sign of the weather vane's direction is mechanically determined by the direction of the wind. The uniformitarian principle therefore works when the cause has a mechanical consequence, and the indexical reading of archaeological deposits remained Binford's focus for building a methodologically sound process of archaeological interpretation (Binford 1987).

It would be easy enough to present the arguments of Binford as if they provided the basis for an archaeological methodology that calibrated archaeological data indexically and thus ensured that archaeological data were secure in being taken to represent a particular process. However, the uniformitarian principle implies that past dynamics are only securely recognised because they also operate today. If we accept that archaeological data are the product of historical dynamics, and that archaeology should offer not only an account of the formation of those data but also an understanding of how the historical processes had arisen to bring that material into being, then the idea of understanding the cause and effect relationship proposed by Binford presents us with two problems.

First, we obviously have no way of seeing those processes that did not result in a material record, nor those processes where a non-uniformitarian principle links them to a material residue. This is hardly a trivial problem, and, as I have already indicated, it has been taken to limit the relevance of any archaeological analysis of historical processes. If, for example, processes that are of central concern to disciplines neighbouring upon archaeology, such as the ways that kinship systems have tended to operate in anthropological studies, cannot be securely recognised archaeologically, despite the fact that various kinship practices must, presumably, have left material residues, then archaeological analysis is likely to be treated as of marginal relevance to anthropology.

The second problem is that archaeology is surely more than a matter of establishing that currently familiar mechanisms once operated in the past. Frere, for example, believed that what mattered for him was the dramatic implication for human antiquity of his observation that humanity had produced artefacts buried beneath a sequence of geological materials, indicating that such a humanity had existed a very long while ago. Thus, whilst the mechanisms that have transformed the material conditions that comprise an archaeological record are recognisable, archaeological work, if it is to have any value, should surely tell us something that we might not previously have known and allow us to understand the nature of historical conditions that are otherwise unfamiliar to us. If we were to characterise an enquiry into the archaeological record as an attempt to understand why certain recognisable processes happened in the ways that they did, then those processes must include the activities of humans whose activities have long been regarded as historically and culturally specific. Archaeology thus encounters the diversity, complexity, and unpredictable messiness of human history, and if methodological security simply depends upon uniformities linking past processes with their surviving residues, then it remains unclear how we might understand the residues generated by historically specific actions, and by human motivations and intentions that might seem distinctly 'odd' to us today.

Style and function

One attempt to circumvent the problems posed by the desire to understand the subjective intentions, beliefs, and motivations of those populations that are known to us through archaeological analysis, has been by distinguishing two facets of human behaviour. The first relates to those aspects of behaviour that have resulted in the mechanical modifications of materials (that is, the modification to materials that might have happened at any time). The second facet of human behaviour, and its outcomes, are treated as the expressions of particular cultural traditions. Gordon Childe provided one of the clearest expositions of such a distinction by reflecting upon a hypothetical commentary that might have been offered by a middle Palaeolithic flint knapper explaining the manufacture of a flint implement thus:

> [t]o make a D-scraper, collect a flint nodule (1) at full moon, (2) after fasting all day, (3) address him politely with 'words of power' (4) . . . strike him thus with a hammerstone, (5) smeared with the blood of a sacrificed mouse. (Childe 1956, 171)

Childe noted that '[t]echnical and scientific progress has of course just been discovering that (1), (2), (3) and (5) are quite irrelevant to the success of the operation prescribed in (4)' (1956, 172), although the gender-specific nature assigned to the flint nodule might now be questioned.

Childe was drawing a distinction that was similar to the one which Robert Dunnell later claimed represented the 'fundamental dichotomy' in archaeological reasoning (1978). The dichotomy that Dunnell believed operated was one between human actions executed according to certain cultural norms, which found expression in a particular style of working, and the mechanical outcomes that arose as the consequence of that working. The distinction invites us to accept that a difference exists between a way of doing something, such as sacrificing a mouse to make a D-scraper, and the consequences of that 'doing', which was the mechanical production of a functionally useable scraper. This distinction can be read as one that separates the stylistic attributes of an object, which Sackett defined as having a 'highly specific and characteristic manner of doing something' that is 'always peculiar to a specific time and place' (Sackett 1977, 370), from the function of the object or the mechanical achievement of the action. It is a distinction that has dominated archaeological analysis for some time. The mechanical processes are clearly regarded as timeless, and include an understandable relationship between the artefact and its use, such that stone and metal projectile points were, for example, designed to pierce flesh. On the other hand, the style in which such armatures were fashioned is likely to have been learnt as a culturally particular way of undertaking their production, and this was specific to time, place, and made sense to the participant in terms of how they were expected to work (Sackett 1982; cf. O'Brien & Lyman 2003). Culture, from this perspective, becomes the particular way of achieving a commonly understandable result. The analytical distinction between style and function, as proposed by Dunnell, has, however, no valid application if we are attempting to understand the histories of humanly motivated behaviour, for the simple reason that the execution of any action that has functional consequences is only possible by means of a way, or a style, of acting (Boast 1997). To maintain the distinction suggested by Dunnell would be like expecting people to talk, and thus to fulfil the functional need to communicate, whilst expecting them to do so without actually using a particular language. This makes clear the *post hoc* nature of an archaeological reasoning that is unconcerned with the conditions that generated the actions attested for by the material, by focusing instead upon their consequences.

Archaeology has secured a uniformitarian model of human activity by drawing a distinction between a cultural, and therefore a stylistic, way of generating an action, and the functional consequences arising from those actions. From this perception the understandable functional outcomes of an action were achieved by diverse cultural means, and it is the possession of culture that is treated as distinguishing human behaviour from that of the rest of the animal kingdom. Thus, whilst song-birds might well sing in local dialects, few biologists would treat such dialects in the same way that an anthropologist would treat cultural variability (Adkins-Regan et al. 2010), although we might now wonder why this is the case. The reason seems to be that animal behaviour develops partly by copying the behavioural traits of other members of the same species, and has been treated as being in some way biologically determined, whereas human behaviour has long been assumed to express the principle that styles represent certain cultural values which, under various conditions, might have been open to human choice, rejection or negotiation. It is therefore assumed to be unlikely that song-birds reflect upon the significance of the ways that they sing, whereas humans can reflect upon, and indeed rationalise, the proper ways in which they act, although this is not something that they necessarily choose to do very often. To return to the example referred to earlier, the killing and butchering of an animal can certainly provide food for a human community, and humans certainly need to eat, and fulfilling this need might be taken to be the function of hunting. However, how the animal is taken, the relationship between the animal and the hunter (Ingold 2000, 61–76), and the ways that the animal is subsequently butchered, prepared, shared, and consumed are all the practical expressions of maintaining an accepted cultural order.

The distinction here appears to be between the non-negotiable and biologically derived need to eat (or to sing), and the negotiable choices of what we eat, how the food is prepared, and how, when, and with whom we eat (or sing). It is the latter choices that are taken to belong to the development of historically specific, human traditions.

If we accept that 'one of the most striking features of human life is the extraordinary diversity of the ways of living it' (Ingold 1994, 329) then we seem to confront a restriction upon the possible archaeological interpretations and understandings of that extraordinary diversity. Humans may be biologically disposed to think and to act in diverse cultural ways, and this means that the contentious nature of archaeological analysis is brought to the fore when human behaviour becomes the focus for understanding the formation processes of the archaeological record. Binford believed that the only way in which the logic of cultural schemes could be revealed was through the testimony of cultural informants who were asked why they had acted in a certain way. Given that this was not an option available to most archaeologists, Binford was of the view that such concerns should be put to one side by the archaeologist (Binford 1987). The suggestion that verbal testimony is an expression of cultural reasoning therefore chimes with the common assumption that cultural reasoning originates as a mental phenomenon, and that the ideas that are held 'in people's heads' are revealed by verbal expression. It was presumably from this perspective that Binford referred approvingly to the argument of the philosopher and archaeologist R.G. Collingwood who claimed that a distinction exists between the outside and the inside of humanly generated events:

> [b]y the outside of the event I mean everything belonging to it which can be described in terms of bodies and their movements. . . . By the inside of the event I mean that in it which can only be described in terms of thought. (Collingwood 1994, 213)

Whilst 'the historian is never concerned with either of these to the exclusion of the other' (ibid.), Binford argued that archaeological analysis should, to the contrary, identify how the outside events of bodies and movements were represented by material residues and avoid any concern with, and therefore any dependency upon, an unavailable testimony from an extinct humanity that might explain how archaeological deposits might have once expressed the internally derived logic and motivations for that humanity's actions (Binford 1987).

If we were to accept for the moment Collingwood's characterisation of human behaviour as having an inner motivation and an outer application, then Binford's argument that we should only concern ourselves with the latter leaves us with the question of what such a limitation will do for an archaeological understanding of historical conditions. Binford's stance certainly provides us with an understanding of the formation of the archaeological record as a series of physical transformations, but it does not provide us with a historical understanding of human behaviour. We might be able to trace some of the consequences of that behaviour, but have little notion as to the context from which it arose or the mechanisms that sustained it. We might ask, once again, whether this is the remit of archaeology: to merely explain the formation of the archaeological record? Or should archaeology employ the materials that are available to it to gain an understanding of the historical conditions that gave rise to a particular form of humanity and its associated behaviours? If we were to accept the former, then the position that Binford adopted, along with that of many other archaeologists, would appear to be justified, simply because it is on this basis that the formation of the archaeological record is explained as the mechanical outcome of processes, including those of human behaviour. The problem is that no-one outside archaeology seems to be much interested in these results, and who can blame them?

Process and tradition

By treating archaeological data as a record that represented the mechanisms of its formation, many archaeologists have tended to read the data as both a record of short-term events and of long-term processes. Any ongoing process will obviously be known archaeologically by the events that it generated, and the consequent accumulation of particular kinds of residue will trace the path of that process both geographically and chronologically. The traditional archaeological emphasis upon foregrounding human agency as the mechanism that carried forward processes of both environmental and cultural modification has meant that the records of both have been taken to attest to the histories of the continuities, developments, and dislocations occurring in particular traditions of human activity. But to maintain a tradition of practice requires more than the simple repetition of events. For example, whilst a stone flake is predictably formed when a particular force of percussion is directed towards a certain material, the maintenance of a flaking tradition within the history of a human community involves much more than the mechanical repetition of a knapping event. Such behaviour would have had to have been learnt, maintained, developed, and transmitted from the competent practitioner to the novice, and it would have been transmitted and maintained in the context of a range of cultural dispositions and constraints that were of the very kind that Childe listed as being unnecessary to the outcome of the knapping event. But it was these dispositions that would have sustained the knapping tradition. From the perspective of the practitioner, Dunnell's distinction between style and function would be meaningless, given that all tasks were learnt and executed as the particular ways of performing those tasks (cf. Boast 1997).

Different kinds of activity might have been understood, and thus executed, in ways that maintained similarities in their perceived value, or similarities in the duties adopted by or assigned to the same kind of person, and where such activities might have been grouped together in the same place, or have been executed by persons of the same status, to distinguish them from those activities that had expressed different or opposed values.

> Activity areas are spatially restricted areas where a specific task or set of related tasks has been carried on, and they are generally characterized by a scatter of tools, waste products, and/or raw materials; a feature, or set of features, may also be present. (Flannery & Winter 1976, 34)

These differences in activities as lived, and in the archaeological patterning of the resulting deposits, could well have expressed fundamental political and engendered differences (Moore 1982). If archaeology were to neglect the challenge of understanding *how* things were done and consider only the consequences of those activities, then we might wonder about the extent to which archaeology can ever claim to have understood either the behaviour itself or the historical context within which it had arisen.

Hopefully the limited reach of Binford's reasoning is now clear. Whilst mechanical, and therefore uniformitarian, processes will certainly have operated in the mechanisms of past events, and thus in the formation of individual categories of data, such as a spread of flint debitage from a knapping event, the processes that maintained such traditions amongst different communities over time and space, processes that resulted in the formation of repeatable patterns of archaeological data, extended well beyond the repetitive transformation of the material. Each tradition existed by the maintenance, throughout its transmission, of certain behavioural regularities operating within complex and specific social and ecological contexts.

One way to see the problem that archaeological practice faces when limiting itself to the consideration of the mechanical outcomes of human behaviour is to present the explanation for behaviour in terms of proximate and ultimate causes. Proximate causes are the physical mechanisms, including the actual execution of human actions, by which material was transformed: this is the relationship between the process and its record that Binford's theoretical concern with uniformitarian processes was designed to establish. Ultimate causes, on the other hand, concern the conditions that might have guided the ways that traditional patterns of behaviour were maintained. Any attempt to identify these ultimate causes requires more than simply establishing patterns of behaviour; it also requires an understanding of the ways that these behaviours were replicated and guided by motivations, traditions, and historical conditions.

The New Archaeology (Chapter 3) did not proclaim to doubt that some kinds of cultural and conceptual rules contributed to the moulding of human behaviour, but regarded them merely as the 'internal' cultural traditions of motivation that could be analytically 'bracketed off' from the organisation of that behaviour and its adaptive consequences. This returns us to Collingwood's distinction between 'inner' cultural rules and an 'outer' adaptive expediency. The determinants of behaviour were now expressed, not as an 'inner' motivation but as the 'outer' requirement that such behaviour should have adapted to an existing condition, a requirement determined by the availability of natural resources and met by the ways in which behaviour, in its various forms, was organised. Thus, whilst archaeology could not seemingly recover the 'internal' beliefs held by extinct communities because they were not recorded by archaeological data, reassuringly it didn't need to.

Conclusion

The study of the human past is made possible because we are able to recognise that some evidence for that past exists in our contemporary, material world. Archaeology is the process that brings that evidence into view as evidence for an earlier human presence. This is achieved by adopting a series of assumptions that are then applied in fieldwork, and where the assumptions and the fieldwork procedures together describe the current archaeological paradigm. The assumptions are that human actions leave a material trace that is of a particular and recognisable quality, enabling it to be distinguished from the traces resulting from other 'natural' processes. That trace is accepted as deriving from two, recognisable, aspects of human motivation: the intention to do something (function), and the way of doing it (culture). One important way that the trace of a one-time human presence can be interpreted is by reference to the material context in which it is discovered. By employing the assumptions of uniformitarianism and of stratigraphic sequencing it is, for example, possible to interpret something of the physical context of that earlier human behaviour and its relative age.

3

SYSTEMS AND THE DYNAMICS OF HISTORICAL CHANGE

The New Archaeology

Establishing a 'New Archaeology'

For the first half of the twentieth century, archaeology treated the variability of the material residues as if that variability resulted from the different ways that people had once followed – and thus replicated in their behaviour – certain cultural norms. It was by this means that archaeologists assumed that people built various forms of social solidarity (Childe 1956). The archaeological identification of these behavioural norms, achieved by comparing various artefact, monument, and burial styles, was then used to chart the extent to which cultural regularities had spread, been adopted, and had thus influenced the behaviour of now extinct communities. All these claims appeared to depend heavily upon the subjective judgement of the archaeologist (Binford 1972, 4–5). The New Archaeology demanded the establishment of a different kind of methodology. This was to replace the subjective descriptions of differences in the material assemblages with an understanding of material change that could be substantiated by objective procedures of measurement and quantification. This change was predicated upon three claims concerning the future development of an archaeological methodology. First, that the archaeological concern should shift from the cultural motivations behind behavioural traditions to the functional consequences of those traditions. Second, that those consequences were organised in ways that were systemically coherent and had ensured that the total system of behaviours functioned adaptively within a particular environment. Third, that the uniformitarian link between a type of behaviour and its surviving material residue should be validated independently of any proposed theories concerning the ways traditions of behaviour had developed and changed. Underpinning all these claims was the obvious need to render human behaviour archaeologically visible, and the obvious way to do this was by treating the material recovered as the consequences of that behaviour.

Archaeological methodology thus continued the tradition of 'seeing' human behaviour as being represented by certain material residues. Theory's role was to propose the possible reasons for material change. The catch, of course, was that the latter (the reasons for change) also had to be formulated in terms that could be empirically investigated, limiting those reasons to the residues that had resulted from human behaviour within an environment. The environment, in turn, was widely interpreted as being non-cultural, that is as an environment comprising such things as plants, animals, soils, and climate (Binford 1985 & 1987).

It was assumed that the different kinds of human behaviour that generated the different categories of material residue were organised to satisfy a number of generally occurring human needs (Figure 3.1). This is well illustrated by Renfrew and Bahn who consider the ways that materials have been used to enable communities to function, adapt to their environments, provide for subsistence needs, allow for technological development, facilitate trade and exchange, and enable religious, artistic, and symbolic practices to develop (Renfrew & Bahn 2004, 178–428). These different domains of behaviour were assumed to have functioned together coherently, and thus systemically, and the New Archaeology saw its task as explaining why changes in these behaviours, and thus changes in their systemic organisation, had resulted from internal processes of transformation, and not from any externally derived cultural influences. These new explanations were therefore intended to avoid reference to influences supposedly emanating from more 'dynamic' or more 'advanced' cultural communities.

Obviously, the New Archaeologists did not 'dig up the past', they did not find the past 'as it really was'. Instead they adopted methodologies that modelled the residues of behaviour discovered archaeologically to fit their particular ideas as to how the human past must once have operated (cf. Clarke 1972a & 1972b). Thus, diverse archaeological residues were worked into a form of categories, assemblages, distribution patterns, relationships, and systems that brought that particular image of the past into view. The priority was to explain material change by identifying the general processes operating in differently organised systems, whilst those changes had actually been instigated within particular cultural settings. This meant that archaeological residues were treated as resulting from two different facets of human behaviour. One was the way of doing things. This was expressed as a cultural style that was specific to time and place and was sometimes seen as deriving from the cognitively motivated desires of people to adhere to local norms of behaviour. The other was what the human behaviour had achieved, which was its function, and this could be understood as a facet of behaviour that all humans shared. Thus human behaviour appears to have resulted in certain material outcomes which could be recognised by the archaeologist and rendered comprehensible by reference to the functions that those outcomes had fulfilled.

Cultural traditions had no role in the New Archaeology's explanations for systemic change. For example, in his study of hunter-gatherers Lewis Binford argued that it was the way that subsistence demands were met by hunter-gatherers that was the key to his understanding of hunter-gatherer behavioural diversity, and whilst

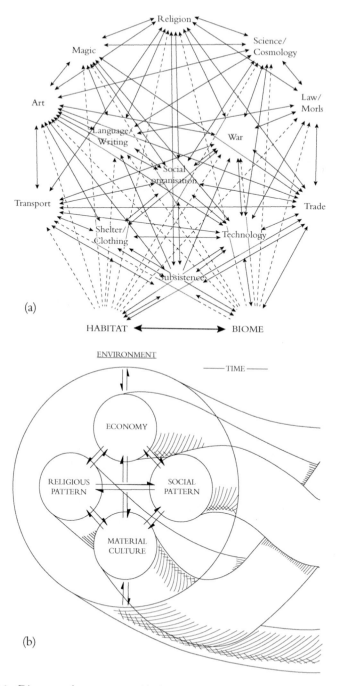

FIGURE 3.1 Diagrams that represent (a) the integration of different aspects of human activity (redrawn from Clark 1957, Fig. 25), and (b) subsystem states within a 'socio-cultural system' in 'dynamic equilibrium' with its environment (redrawn from Clarke 1968, Fig. 14).

this does not deny that aspects of cultural behaviour are represented archaeologically, these representations did not contribute to Binford's understanding of the historical development of these groups:

> I have never suggested that culture is not manifest in the archaeological record or that observable difference in the archaeological record might not have cultural significance. What I have suggested, however, is that behaviour is the byproduct of the interaction of a cultural repertoire with the environment. . . . Variations in the frequency with which certain culturally patterned behaviours will be executed is referable to the character of the environmental and adaptive situations in which cultural man [*sic*] finds himself at different points in time and space. (Binford 1973, 229)

It was upon the basis of the reasoning adopted by Binford that the ethnographies of hunter-gatherers could be read as if they attested to a form of life that was structured by the demands of subsistence adaptation. Consequently, it was from the perspective of their mechanisms of adaptation that the ethnographies of hunter-gatherers proved to be relevant to the archaeological understanding of hunter-gatherer histories. In his substantial, if somewhat confusing, volume *Constructing Frames of Reference* (Binford 2001), Binford argued that the ethnographies of 339 hunter-gatherer groups had enabled him to correlate their organisational components in terms of technology, biomass exploitation, population size, task and status organisation, and niche environments, and upon the basis of these correlations he could identify the processes that structured different 'system states'. What Binford meant by a 'system state' was never very clearly defined (e.g., Binford 2001, 165 & 211), although Amber Johnson, who had worked with him on his 2001 volume, treats these states as the rules (presumably of behaviour) that determined the variation between different adaptive strategies (Johnson 2014, 5). The patterns of archaeological residue are assumed to represent these rules, which had arisen from the necessity of a population, in possession of a particular technology, to adapt to various ecological constraints. There is clearly some circular reasoning here given that the patterns of material residues represent the execution of rules of adaptation, and the rules of adaptation are employed to explain the pattern of the material residues. As a consequence, archaeological analysis does not seem to tell us anything of any real interest because the rules governing the network of resources employed in an adaptation to the subsistence base were designed by that same 'base'. The particular ways that people might once have understood their world, and have acted on that world in light of that understanding, is therefore bypassed by the logic of this analysis. The New Archaeological perspective was that an understanding of humanity's diverse perceptions of the world was not only archaeologically impossible to reconstruct but was also irrelevant to the archaeological project, given that we can see how the various behaviours, utilising a particular technology, had adapted to their environment.

Binford accepted that the organising processes that he believed were recorded in the ethnographic cases of hunter-gatherers in various ecological settings would also have been amongst those employed in similar settings by post-glacial hunter-gatherers across Eurasia. He did not aim to offer direct ethnographic analogies for the interpretation of archaeological residues; his aim was instead to use the ethnographic data to establish the kinds of strategic processes of adaptation that were likely to be attested archaeologically. It was the strategies of hunter-gatherer adaptive variability that Binford reasoned must have enabled their transformation to agriculturalists (cf. Johnson 2014). In other words, these communities always had options, but those options were constrained by the physical correlations that existed between the available resources, the size of the population, the available technologies, and by the need to adapt and thus to survive. The recurring theme for Binford was that the various strategies by which the 'dynamic properties' of hunter-gatherer organisations were known must have arisen from a combination of their occupancy of different niche ecologies, and from the ways that the organisation of labour and the patterns of resource exploitation were designed to accommodate the 'packing' that resulted from increasing population densities:

> hunter-gatherers living at population densities below the packing threshold vary in their group sizes, subsistence bases, patterns of mobility, and labor organization, and they may live in a wide variety of habitats. None of these groups, however, whose populations are below the packing threshold are sedentary. Even among those groups that have exceeded the threshold, few are fully sedentary unless they are aquatic specialists.
>
> After packing occurs and mobility is severely constrained, affected groups position their labor units adjacent to resources and their sites are usually organized in terms of residential units. (Binford 2001, 438)

As in his earlier 1968 paper, Binford was keen to avoid simple, deterministic explanations for hunter-gatherer histories. Instead environments are treated as resources that provided certain niche options for their occupancy, and population densities provided both constraints and opportunities for the population systems that coped with those resources. To claim that here, as in his earlier work, a causal determinate is on offer to 'explain' the origins of agriculture would therefore be to mis-read the subtlety of his arguments. We are offered instead the causal conditions that were necessary for systemic change, including the available terrestrial and aquatic resources and certain levels of human population density. Whilst these conditions included those that were necessary for the development of agricultural systems, we might wonder whether they, by themselves, amounted to a sufficient cause for that transformation.

The three major organisational changes that attracted, and have continued to attract, attention in old world archaeology are those that were involved in the transformation from hunting and gathering to agriculturally based economies, the adoption of metalworking by previously stone-using communities, and the rise and subsequent collapse of city states and empires. We therefore need to understand why it has proven so difficult for the New Archaeology to establish the explanations that it sought for these kinds of transformation.

The new methodology

Clearly the New Archaeology needed a methodology that could achieve three things. It could establish the different kinds of behavioural organisation that were attested for by the material residues, it could describe the development and transformation of these types of organisation through time (the explanandum), and, thirdly, it could identify the general processes that explained why these organisations had undergone any observed changes (the explanans). The requirement to establish how these processes might have operated under particular historical conditions, where these conditions often appeared to be represented by the external environment, looked very much like the demand made by Hempel's characterisation of the ways that historical explanations should refer to the operation of certain covering laws. Even if the idea of historical laws was rejected, it was still assumed that general explanations could be identified for the ways types of behavioural organisation might have responded to certain kinds of changing environmental conditions. Indeed, the New Archaeology's tendency to converge upon, if not to actually adopt, Hempel's model for the laws of historical explanation arose from the shared assumption that history, as a process, could be understood as the working of mechanisms that brought into existence particular kinds of organisation, although exactly what those mechanisms were was never very clear. It was these structuring processes that some believed were governed by various covering laws or general regularities that determined the kind of historical trajectory that each kind of organisation would follow. The New Archaeology certainly did not presume that these processes would be discovered simply by the empirical study of material sequences. New Archaeologists accepted that they could not dig up 'how history had happened', but they could model the organisations observed by the patterns of residue, and the existence of the processes that had transformed these organisations might be modelled hypothetically as the result of theoretical work that drew upon various anthropological and historical analogies. The emphasis upon theorised historical processes being generally applicable in the workings of similar organisational systems implied that the theoretical explanations offered for the process of historical transformation could eventually be validated by further empirical research involving a similar kind of organisation. However, it remained unclear how this was to be achieved. In practice the testing of the various theorised explanations amounted to little more than demonstrating that the explanation offered seemed to be reasonable, given what was known of the organisational changes that were represented.

The example that was previously described and that sought to explain the development of megalithic tombs during the European Neolithic illustrates something of the way that this procedure was followed (Renfrew 1976). In countering the methodology of Cultural Archaeology, Colin Renfrew abandoned the comparisons of monumental architecture and artefact design and in their place he described the monuments in terms of their regional distribution patterns (Figure 1.2), modelling that distribution to represent the form of territorial organisation that he believed had been adopted by the early agriculturalists of western Europe. As we have seen, Renfrew then sought to explain why dispersed agricultural communities displayed an increasing level of territorial organisation (i.e. how the modelled organisation had come about) by claiming that a growing population, confronted by the restricted availability of land, developed patterns of territorial inheritance. Whilst the explanation for an emergent form of inherited territorial organisation might seem plausible, no empirical evidence was offered to validate the causal processes of population pressure on land resources that Renfrew had theorised as having existed (the explanans) (although see Renfrew 1976, 208–216).

It is important to notice that by modelling the residues to represent a particular kind of organisation, archaeologists were necessarily determining the way that they would explain the emergence of that organisation. Thus, by modelling the distribution of megalithic tombs to represent a level of territorial organisation, it was the latter, and not tomb architecture itself, that Renfrew's theory of evolving land tenure sought to explain (cf. Chapman & Randsborg 1981). This implies that archaeologists will assume the kinds of historical process that were at work when they model the relationships they believe existed between the material residues and human behaviour in the past. To take another example, in his study of the mechanisms that might have resulted in the development of complex societies Flannery (1972) proposed that the system comprised a hierarchy of subsystems:

> from lowest and most specific to highest and most general. Each subsystem is regulated by a control apparatus whose job is to keep all the variables in the subsystem within appropriate goal ranges – ranges which maintain homeostasis and do not threaten the survival of the system. Management of crop plants, for example, might be regulated by a lower-order control issuing specific commands; the distribution of harvests and surpluses (the 'output' of the latter subsystem) might in turn be regulated by calendric rituals or group leaders somewhere in the middle levels of the hierarchy. On all levels, the social control apparatus compares output values not merely with subsistence goals but with ideological values, the demands of deities and ancestral spirits, ethical and religious propositions – the human population's 'cognized model' of the way the world is put together. (Flannery 1972, 409)

In treating this systemic arrangement between subsystems as if the structure of the system operated to maintain its stability, a procedure that was supposedly achieved by monitoring, and thus by controlling, the through-put of energy and information, Flannery seems to adopt a managerial explanation for the origins of systemic complexity (Gilman 1991). This perception of the processes at work therefore avoids the suggestion that those holding higher-ranking positions within complex systems were more concerned with developing the appropriation of resources by that social elite than they were with managing the system for the betterment of its participants. As Gilman observes, '[t]he central difficulty of the managerial account of the development of hierarchical social systems is that it fails to explain why the elites inherit their privilege' (1991, 147).

The expectation that the historical processes affecting all human conditions would have organisational consequences is a common enough assumption, but it is a characterisation that has political implications because it leaves unexamined the question of what might drive 'historical processes' forward. By avoiding a critical examination of the relationship between our expectations concerning the forces that caused certain historical changes and the development of a methodology of recording, archaeologists have traded in taken-for-granted beliefs about historical processes. This is not a particularly radical observation; it simply restates Thomas Kuhn's observation that all science works within accepted bodies of paradigmatic assumptions. These assumptions define the ways that a coherent set of disciplinary practices operate in harmony with the objectives of analysis (Kuhn 1970 [1962]). Any paradigmatic change in archaeology will necessarily involve a different way of seeing things (Bradley 1997), resulting in changes to how things are described and the kinds of material that are taken to be of archaeological relevance (Kristiansen 2014), along with changes in our preconceptions concerning the nature of the historical process (Friedman & Rowlands 1977; Barrett 2014a).

It is our perceptions of how the past might have operated that drive our changing understanding of archaeological data. To take a relatively uncontentious example, the radiocarbon revolution (Renfrew 1973c), in which the chronologies of European prehistory were established independently of any of the proposed links between Europe, south-western Asia, and Egypt, was not simply a matter of the new dating technique rendering the assumed regional links proposed by cultural diffusion inoperative. Attempts to explain changes in material sequences, as the result of diffused cultural influences, had already been dismissed as an inadequate perception of the past by the time that the revised chronologies became established (Lyman et al. 1997). The 'revolution' in re-thinking long-established cultural comparisons was driven by the desire to model sequences of archaeological data as if they represented the ways that changing patterns of behaviour had been organised indigenously, instead of representing how the cultural motivations of those behaviours had been derived from influences that had emerged from elsewhere. The radiocarbon chronologies were thus seized upon as being fully understandable in terms of this new perception of the historical processes. The radiocarbon dates facilitated the development of an already existing desire to think about the historical processes in a new way; they did not drive that change in thinking, as Renfrew had implied: they enabled it (cf. Renfrew 1969a).

The intimate relationship between modelling the data and assumptions about the mechanisms of history has an important implication. An archaeological understanding of human history cannot be the same as that which has been developed either by the traditional, text-based, historian or by the anthropologist. Historians and anthropologists model very different kinds of data in their own studies compared with that of the archaeologist, including a substantial component of literary and verbal testimony from those who were, and who are, being studied. The much-cited limitation that the fragmentary nature of archaeological finds supposedly places upon the interpretation of the past arises not because archaeology is intellectually and methodologically weak, but from the misguided desire that archaeology should offer accounts of processes which mimic the accounts written by anthropologists and historians (cf. Smith 1955). It was the assumption that the material patterns recovered archaeologically represent the now absent conditions which would be more effectively studied by anthropologists that gave rise to such comments as those offered by the British anthropologist Sir Edmund Leach:

> do please recognise the limitations of the archaeologist. As soon as you go beyond asking 'What' questions, such as: 'What is the nature of this material?' and start asking 'How' and 'Why' questions . . ., then you are moving away from verifiable fact into the realm of pure speculation. (Leach 1973, 764)

The archaeological response to Leach's commentary should surely have been that the 'How' and the 'Why' questions of material change needed to be addressed archaeologically, rather than by archaeologists attempting to address these questions as if they were second-rate anthropologists, which they are not.

The historical condition

In what ways did Cultural Archaeology, and then the New Archaeology, think differently about the historical conditions that they sought to investigate? Both were concerned with explaining why sequences of material residue had occurred, and both recognised those sequences as if they were patterns of behavioural stability interspersed by horizons of change. The patterns of stability were demarcated chronologically and geographically as a time-span, or a region, or as a phase of material coherence (Willey & Phillips 1958, 22). These were patterns that the New Archaeology sought to depict as regions or periods of organisational coherence that had undergone change as the result of a growing adaptive instability (Earle & Preucel 1987), whilst Cultural Archaeology had modelled the patterns as if they represented the times and areas over which cultural rules of behaviour had been adopted, and that these might have changed as the result of externally derived influences.

In both cases it was at the perceived chronological and geographical boundaries demarcating the patterns of material coherency that archaeology was called upon to explain why change had occurred. The New Archaeology seemed to assume that the mechanisms for change were prompted by processes that were of a different order from those that had sustained stability, posing the need to explain why, if institutional behaviours had arisen to provide for an adaptive efficiency, those institutions had, at certain moments or at certain places, needed to generate change. Fred Plog introduced his *Study of Prehistoric Change* with the comment that '[f]or me, the archaeological record is a record of change. It holds limited potential for the understanding of the structure and functioning of societies in a synchronic frame' (Plog 1974, ix).

Colin Renfrew seemed to concur when considering the way that 'systems thinking' contributed to studies that concerned the 'natural regularity' of those systems, commenting that conditions of 'self-regulation, or homeostasis, . . . do not of themselves constitute an explanatory mode' (Renfrew 1982, 8). It was therefore change in material patterns that became the focus for archaeological explanations (Hill 1977; Plog 1974; Renfrew 1973b). Indeed, it appeared as if '[s]tability, apparently, just happens – it does not require explanation' (Shanks & Tilley 1987b, 34).

The challenge for New Archaeology was that if all historical conditions were represented by the available data, and if all explanations were assumed to be causal (Salmon 1982, 45), then the processes that had secured systemic stability, and the processes that caused change, must both be represented by archaeological data. Given this situation then how might the material be modelled to represent organisations that, under normal circumstances, achieved stability, but under other circumstances could bring about change? The answer to this puzzle was sought by the adoption of 'systems thinking' that distinguished between the system modelled by material cultural residues to represent the organisation of human behaviour, and the environmental system of 'natural' processes (Figure 3.1). Whilst the environmental system was certainly open to extensive modification by human behaviour, the two systems were necessarily treated as being semi-autonomous because each was reproduced, or so it was believed, by different processes. The material-cultural system was treated as if it were reproduced by institutional patterns of human behaviour, whereas the 'natural' system was reproduced by biological processes.

The material-cultural system and the natural-environmental system have each become entrenched units of historical analysis, partly by default and partly as the expression of a deeply held prejudice that the human world existed outside that of the natural world. It was from the late 1960s that 'environmental archaeology' entrenched this distinction by achieving its continuing status as a sub-discipline within archaeology (Outram & Bogaard 2019). The geographical scale over which the various material-cultural systems were modelled, as if human behaviour had exploited its 'natural' environment, varied considerably. The smallest scale perhaps was the single archaeological settlement site at the centre of a catchment of exploitation (e.g. Jarman & Webley 1975), whilst the largest was the regional system of exploitation and exchange (e.g. Flannery 1976, 131–223; Barker 1995). By the 1970s archaeological studies were produced that explored the ways in which changing human and environmental systems could be integrated into a single history of development (Bradley 1978).

In the case of the system, paths of 'feedback' were modelled as if they had operated between various subsystems that functioned to maintain either systemic stability or, under different conditions, systemic change (Renfrew 2005). The appeal of systems thinking seems understandable:

> [i]t is clear that if we are to have any adequate understanding of the world we live in, our knowledge must include knowledge of the organized wholes which we call systems, as well as knowledge of component parts of these systems. (Salmon 1978, 175)

It is therefore somewhat odd that environmental archaeology has not developed a systems approach towards its analysis of the interplay of different biological, chemical, and physical forces.

How might we envisage the 'organised whole' of which Merrilee Salmon wrote, as having been structured? Which parts, for example, are we to assign to the material-cultural and which to the environmental systems? How are those parts linked within the cultural system, and how is the boundary between the two kinds of system defined? Although Merrilee Salmon (1978) expressed her doubts as to the relevance of systems theories to archaeology, other commentators have been keen to accept that, by identifying the organisational systems the human activities had once maintained, they were able to provide an explanation for the conditions of systemic stability as well as being able to theorise the circumstances that had generated periods of systemic change.

In 1962, Lewis Binford had argued that archaeology should demonstrate the 'constant articulation of variables within a system'. A historical process that had resulted in a change in one variable relative to changes in other variables would supposedly generate the potential for the modification of the entire system (Binford 1962, 217). In Britain D.L. Clarke defined *process* as that vector which 'describes the series of states of an entity or system undergoing continuous change in time and space' (Clarke 1968, 42; cf. Figure 3.1b). Systems as a whole, rather than the isolation of single behavioural traditions (which had been the analytical focus for Cultural Archaeology), were therefore taken by the New Archaeology to describe the trajectories of stability and change represented by the patterns of material residue. It was the system that contained the mechanisms that both secured the stability and also engineered the changes that were observed in the material sequences.

The initial definition of the cultural system

Binford had proposed that the patterns of residues represented three 'operational sub-systems': technological, social, and ideological (Binford 1962). These subsystems supposedly enabled humans to adapt to their environments. With an acknowledgement to Leslie White (2007 [1959]), Binford asserted that the subsystems provided for 'the extra-somatic means of adaptation for the human organism' (Binford 1962, 218) and that they could therefore be treated as the interrelated assemblage of practices and technologies that had enabled people to work within particular environments. D.L. Clarke also referred to the cultural system as being coupled to 'the external environing system' (Clarke 1968, 83) and Fred Plog commented that '[a]t a minimal level, a system can be defined as two or more behavioral strategies linked to each other in such a way that a change in one is likely to produce a change in the other' (Plog 1977, 49).

Identifying the boundaries of each system, along with any internal subsystems, was regarded by Renfrew, and by others, as 'a matter for the analyst' (Renfrew 2005a, 261). This confirmed the view that systems analysis involved the building of simplified models of the more complex conditions of history, and that these models were taken to be represented by the residues of 'cultural' or 'natural' materials. David L. Clarke was at pains to stress 'the arbitrary nature of this kind of component description . . . to partially describe an otherwise extremely complex reality'. If the way that human behaviours were being characterised was indeed 'based on the prejudices of current opinion' (Clarke 1968, 102–103), then such prejudices were hardly likely to have been 'arbitrary' as Clarke suggested, but rather they expressed the largely unexamined assumptions, often expressed politically, about the processes which structured the historical condition. The various behavioural subsystems gained their historical reality by being represented by a set of residues (their record), and these subsystems were believed to have had economic/social consequences. These patterns of institutionalised behaviour have been studied by separate sub-disciplinary specialisations of material analysis, and it is important to recognise that these specialisations also define contemporary career trajectories within archaeology. Ancient organisational systems and their environments continued to be 'decomposed' by the New Archaeology into subsystems that were represented by different kinds of residue, and it was these that were made available for specialist analysis, before their systemic re-assembling by a process of 'synthesis'. This process has remained central to current archaeological practice. Kuhn's original observation is important here. Paradigmatic ways of working are far from being mere intellectual fashions; instead they are embedded in the day-to-day working practices of people's careers (Kuhn 1970). New Archaeology, by creating models that tied the patterns represented by different kinds of material, such as animal bones, to different adaptive strategies, such as kill-patterns, as way of characterising the past, then used those same systemic models to structure the working practices of the discipline, such as the specialisation of animal osteology. Thus, whilst we might believe that we have now broken with the intellectual programme of the New Archaeology, its working practices continue to structure the working practices of archaeology.

The principle stating that human systems were adapted to their environment is a tautology, in that any system of human activities that has existed over any period of time must have functioned (that is adapted) within the prevailing system of its environmental constraints (cf. Salmon 1978, 176). The challenge is surely to understand *how* a particular kind of human organisation had adapted to a particular kind of environmental condition, whilst the New Archaeology sought to establish *why* a system of adaptation might have changed. It is important to note that it was the entire human system that is here assumed to have adapted to its various environmental constraints, allowing that individual traditions of behaviour might have been adaptively neutral or indeed maladaptive. Lines of maladaptive behaviour could therefore be carried within a total system that was itself adaptive.

David L. Clarke's early examination of system analysis for archaeology began 'from the assumption that cultural [human] systems are integral whole units', and upon this basis, 'material culture, economic structure, religious dogma and social organization' were subsystems within the cultural system that was distinguished from an external environmental system (Clarke 1968, 43). Clarke took the historical process to be driven by the communication occurring between the elements within a cultural system that had somehow monitored the adaptive effectiveness of the entire system, although how that process of communication and monitoring might have worked in each particular case is difficult, if not impossible, to understand. The problem of mapping a particular category of archaeological residue against a single subsystem might arise where categories of behaviour resulted in more than one kind of functional outcome, but had generated a single kind of residue. For example, a behavioural tradition such as flint knapping required the procurement of stone, and might have serviced the needs demanded by hunting, butchering, and skin working. It could therefore be assigned to either Clarke's material culture or to his economic subsystem, or indeed to both. We might recall Clarke's own assertion to the effect that it was the investigator who chose how the material was to be assigned. Indeed, Merilee Salmon (1978, 180) objected that Clarke had not demonstrated that the material culture assemblage could even be assigned to a subsystem, for whilst technology, as a combination of human procedures and their material resources, might be regarded as a subsystem, material culture, simply as an assemblage of things, could not be assigned to any single subsystem. It followed that Merrilee Salmon expected subsystems to be defined by the particular ways they processed the inputs from adjacent subsystems, for example in the way that the economic subsystem processed the inputs of material, energy, and information in ways that were distinguishable from the processing of those same kinds of inputs by the 'religious' subsystem. However, whilst religious subsystems might have processed material by means of ritual procedures, and employed symbolic representations to do so, neither of which were expected in the operation of economic subsystems, food taboos that expressed various religious commitments might well have determined the procedures of the economic subsystem. The category of a behavioural outcome, such as the 'economic' outcome assigned by archaeologists to the economic subsystem, did not therefore necessarily match the kinds of 'inner' motivation that once drove those behaviours, such as the moral dispositions towards food-stuffs. This returns us to distinction between motivation (why people thought that they were doing something) and what the action actually achieved (its function).

It was the distinction between motivation and function that informed Binford's suggestion that ethnographic field work was 'traumatic' because the observer's beliefs about the motivations for behaviour were challenged by the testimonies of the people whom they studied and who 'behave differently, express different concerns, and express themselves and their motives in terms unfamiliar to the observer' (Binford 1987, 395). Binford's answer was to maintain the distinction drawn by Collingwood between the 'inside' and 'outside' of an event, and to distinguish between the inner 'understanding that must come from the informants' and the outsider's understanding that created the data of the field scientist who worked 'through pattern recognition studies to gain an insight into how the past was organised' (Binford 1987, 403). His principle was that archaeologists should adopt the etic or outsider's perception on human behaviour and that, consequently, whilst we might accept that human motivations derived from some inner (emic) source for these motivations, these can be excluded from archaeological consideration.

If we were to follow Binford's proscription then we would necessarily accept that the New Archaeology developed systems thinking as a way of modelling archaeological data in which material categories represent the consequences of different kinds of activity operating within the constraints of technological achievements and environmental processes. The 'inner' motivations for human actions remained unknown and unknowable to the archaeologist. Binford's thinking implied two things. First, material change was treated as the unintended and potentially long-term consequence of processes that, whilst motivated by an unknown and, for archaeology, an irrelevant cultural logic, attested to what people 'actually did'. Second, what people 'actually did' made sense to the archaeological observer when viewed against the needs that those actions had satisfied. Third, conditions that had operated in different cultural and historical contexts could, nonetheless, be treated as comparable in terms of their functional consequences. The focus for archaeology was therefore directed towards establishing what people had 'actually' done and not what they thought they were doing. It was in this way that the forces of historical explanation were abstracted from the stylistic details of the material residues and rendered comparable, thus discarding the details of stylistic practices that had once been so painstakingly recorded by archaeologists.

Given that the New Archaeology initially treated system dynamics as the transfer of materials, energy, and information between each subsystem, any fluctuations that might have occurred in these transfers between subsystems were assumed to have either been dampened by negative feedback, thus stabilising the system as a whole, or amplified through positive feedback to generate a change in the overall state of the system. The default position, for any system, was assumed to have been its adaptive stability, or 'homeostasis'. As Renfrew once put it:

> [t]his conservative nature of culture cannot too strongly be stressed. . . . [I]t is the natural tendency of culture to persist unchanged – apart from a small random drift which arises from the imperfect transmission of the cultural pattern between generations. It is change, any change, which demands explanation. (Renfrew 1972, 487)

The assumption that systems had 'naturally' tended towards a stable articulation with their environments meant that those procedures that archaeologists identified as having an 'economic' consequence were taken to be '[t]he primary human adaptation to the environment' (Higgs & Jarman 1975, 4; cf. Clark 1952). The principle that Binford and others established was that behaviours that had generated these 'economic' consequences worked with an adaptive logic to which the culturally specific motivations of the participants must have conformed. Binford could therefore be impressed by the way that it was 'the subsistence base' that had contributed to his explanations of hunter-gatherer variability (Binford 2001, 433). The emphasis given to economic outcomes as indicative of systemic adaptation was supported by the belief that the archaeological record of past economic processes was open to reliable interpretation simply because that record was the mechanical, and thus the understandable, consequence of human behaviour (Hawkes 1954). Thus, strategies of adaptation structured the system and were represented by the residues of economic outcomes. The archaeological problem became one of explaining if, and why, economies might have changed.

Systems thinking proved seductive to Anglo-American archaeology in the 1960s and 1970s. It provided a recognisable past by modelling systems that could be treated as if they were taxonomically equivalent to 'communities', 'societies', and 'a people', and ultimately to the nation state, a role which had once been assigned to the concept of 'culture'. Systems thinking therefore enabled the integration of well-established levels of sub-disciplinary expertise, designed to trace the histories of different kinds of material production, into an understanding of a single historical condition. By proceeding in this manner, systems thinking avoided the 'flattening' of behavioural diversity that was the consequence of a Cultural Archaeology that had characterised all material residues as the expressions of the same thing: a cultural tradition. Systemic analysis conformed to Binford's view that scientific explanations were those that demonstrated the 'constant articulation of variables within a system and the measurement of the concomitant variability among the variables within the system' (Binford 1962, 217). If the analytical variables of archaeology were artefact and monument categories representing systems of adaptive stability, then it followed that organisational change was most likely to have resulted from conditions of adaptive instability.

Whilst the analysis of the systemic organisation of human behaviour, operating within an ecological setting, was certainly prompted by Binford's 1962 paper, an earlier exploration of the systemic integration of human behaviours within particular ecologies had been undertaken by Grahame Clark in his *Archaeology and Society* first published in 1939 (Figure 3.1a; Fagan 2001, Fig. 5.3; Clark 1957, Figs. 25 & 49). It was the need to understand the ecological integration of human and animal behaviour in particular that had informed the direction taken by Clark in his analysis of the early post-glacial activity at Star Carr in modern-day North Yorkshire, U.K. (Clark 1954). Clark's analysis was important because, amongst other things, it reminded us that the spatial scale and location of a human system that is adapted to the demands of its environment must have been capable of a significant degree of flexibility as it tracked the seasonality of the available resources (cf. Clark 1952).

Historical explanations: from maladaptation to socially driven change

Modelling of archaeological data to represent earlier cultural and environmental systems was designed to enable archaeology to explain cultural change in terms of historical generalisations. The processes resulting in change seemed to arise from the relationship between the system of human behaviours and that of the environment, implying that change was generally prompted by a drift of the former towards its maladaptation to the latter. To illustrate the limited scope of this kind of analysis we will take two early examples designed to explain the origins of agricultural domestication in the Americas and in Eurasia.

Whilst the idea of a Neolithic or an agricultural 'revolution' that marked a break between hunting and gathering subsistence regimes and those of agricultural production – a 'revolution that transformed human economy' by providing 'control over . . . food supply' (Childe 1965, 66) – might now be regarded as an over-drawn distinction (Gamble 2007; Pascoe 2014), and whilst the 'bandwagon' of research into agricultural origins (Flannery 1973, 271) has slowed since the 1960s, the emergence in the late Pleistocene of genetically distinct populations of crops and animals that were maintained by systems of human management continues to be a significant focus of archaeological research (Barker 2006). In 1968 Kent Flannery and Lewis Binford both published studies that attempted to offer systemic explanations for the beginnings of plant domestication, in Mesoamerica by Flannery and in south-west Asia by Binford (Flannery 1968; Binford 1968). Both authors stressed that hunter-gatherer and foraging systems of procurement were not, as some had claimed, governed by regular crises in food availability, that hunter-gatherer population sizes were not therefore regulated by food restrictions, and that these populations were not teleologically directed towards the 'invention' of agriculture as a way of resolving an ever-present food crisis (cf. Cohen 1977). In short, hunter-gatherer populations were stably adapted to their various environments, as systems modelling would imply (cf. Lee & deVore 1968). The implication was that the processes resulting in stable adjustment must, under certain circumstances, have generated a trajectory towards the domestication of plants and animals. From the perspective of systems analysis, the challenge was therefore to establish the regional conditions under which the negative feedback mechanisms that routinely secured homeostasis within hunter-gatherer systems, might have tipped over into a cycle of positive feedback that amplified systemic change towards agriculture.

Early human settlement in the Southern Uplands of Mexico was treated by Flannery 'as a single complex system, composed of many sub-systems which mutually influenced each other over a period of over seven millennia' (Flannery 1968, 68).

The seasonality of resources across diverse environments, matched by cycles in the congregation and dispersal of human populations, and the scheduling strategies by which alternative resources were chosen for exploitation, were among the negative feedback mechanisms that Flannery proposed as being responsible for maintaining the stability of hunter–gatherer systems of procurement. These had ensured that 'populations never grew to the point where they could effectively over-reach their wild food resources' (Flannery 1968, 75). Positive feedback was however eventually triggered, in Flannery's view, by the cumulative outcome of unforeseen genetic changes in one or two species of plants. Whilst the exploitation of these plants 'had been a relatively minor procurement system, . . . positive feedback following these initial genetic changes caused one minor system to grow out of proportion to the others, and eventually to change the whole ecosystem of the Southern Mexican Highlands' (Flannery 1968, 79). These cumulative genetic changes resulted, according to Flannery, in making 'maize cultivation the most profitable single subsistence activity in Mesoamerica'. 'The mere combining of maize and beans in the diet of the southern highlands, ... was a significant nutritional breakthrough' resulting in a cycle of growth where 'the greater the yield, the higher the population, and hence the more intensive the cultivation' (Flannery 1968, 80).

Binford also proposed that, amongst hunter–gatherers, 'an equilibrium system can be established so that populations are stably regulated below the carrying capacity of the local food supply' (Binford 1968, 327). Binford's model allowed for two demographic systems to exist amongst hunter–gatherers, both of which satisfied the requirement for systemic equilibrium. These were: closed systems within which some redistribution of an increasing population occurred between groups but where cultural mechanisms operated to restrict population growth overall, and open systems where population increases were 'budded off' into daughter groups 'in areas which are not filled to the point at which density dependent factors are brought into play' (Binford 1968, 329). Thus, whilst Binford claimed that he sought to resist explanations for the domestication of plants and animals based upon environmental determinism, and whilst he also rejected claims that agricultural practices arose as the consequence of a food crisis amongst hunter–gatherers, he nonetheless set in place a model by which the differently structured population systems eventually encroached one upon the other. This resulted in the hypothesised expansion of populations into 'frontier environments' where 'in the context of such situations of stress in environments with plant and animal forms amenable to manipulation . . . we would expect to find conditions favouring the development of plant and animal domestication' (Binford 1968, 332). Fifteen years later Binford revised this model by emphasising the importance of hunter–gatherer territories for containing the information necessary to ensure adequate resource options. In developing his revised view, he asked '[w]hat would force a group of people to shift from a system based on an information bank (hunting and gathering) to one based on a labor bank (agriculture)?' (Binford 1983, 208 emphasis omitted). The answer, he suggested, was that the global rise in human population densities during the late Pleistocene had resulted in the 'packing' of the territorial ranges across which particular hunter-gatherer populations could operate, and with this packing came the loss of resource options available to those populations. As a result, an increased reliance on plant foods in place of large game might have been one option which, in some key regions, amounted to a move towards sedentism, along with the labour-intensive management of plant resources that resulted in the development of agriculture.

Neither Flannery's nor Binford's accounts provided us with an explanation for the development of agricultural practices in the regions that they discuss, if by 'explanation' we were expecting to be offered a causal, and thus deterministic, statement as to why agriculture had occurred. What Flannery and Binford did offer were passages towards conditions that *might* have encouraged the adoption of cultivation. These accounts might satisfy the expectation that an archaeological explanation should simply establish the statistical probability for the origins of systemic change (Salmon 1982; Mellor 1982), but the mechanisms that brought about that change remain undefined. The transition to an agricultural system could only have been achieved by the long-term re-organisation of human labour with all of its attendant conflicts and emergent solidarities. The transformation will therefore have redefined some of the ways that the distinctions of gender, age, and rank were recognised, and the attendant obligations of status would have impacted upon the controls and exchanges that were exercised by some, and contested by others. These will have involved the resources of people, animals, plants, and land. It was through the renegotiation of these profoundly important human relationships, rather than through an adaptation to a newly emergent environmental potential, that the trajectories towards agricultural systems will have been followed. But if the nature of archaeological data is to represent only those things that can be analysed (if the data themselves impose a limitation on what an archaeological analysis is able to 'see'), then we appear to be caught in the trap of knowing that the historical conditions that interest us, and were active in the processes of culture change, find no obvious representation in today's archaeological materials. How might we ever 'see' the complex processes of intercommunal relationships between people and things that must have been involved in the remaking of the roles of gender, age, and rank by which the transformation of hunter-gatherer communities into those of agriculturalists was brought about?

Archaeology clearly faces a significant challenge that was not adequately addressed by the New Archaeology. The ways that human relationships are structured, and described in terms of social relations, have always been entwined within the existing network of things (Latour 2005). The New Archaeology modelled the surviving material residues as if they represented different behavioural categories, but these things were part of the behavioural processes that we hope to understand. Treating them as the representation of those processes seems to be a less than adequate response to the analysis of the complexities that have been operating. Indeed, if we reject the claim that past categories of human existence, such as those that might be employed in anthropological accounts of contemporary societies, are represented by certain material residues, then there would seem to be little point in attempting to use archaeological data to mimic anthropological data.

We should perhaps remember that human behaviour has always been in a state of 'becoming' by means of the processes of construction, in which humans have grown, learnt, and embodied the mastery of becoming a certain kind of human. These procedures of 'becoming' have always been played out in a context that comprises other living and developing things, material things, and other humans. Some of these conditions have survived as the eroded residues that are recovered and studied archaeologically. Therefore, rather than assuming that categories of human behaviour are represented by particular material residues, with all the limitations that this introduces, we might instead develop an understanding of how the differences in the making of humans and their attendant material conditions could have changed, based upon the data that we have. This means that instead of considering past behavioural systems as machine-like organisations which, when prompted by problems of adaptation, could somehow reorganise themselves, we should consider the ways that complex systems of life and of things reproduced themselves over a period of time. It was the reproduction and the ongoing transformation of such systems that renders them archaeologically visible by means of the surviving residue of the conditions that they had inhabited. The current archaeological paradigm presumes to model this debris as if it represented the processes of systemic reproduction; however, the question of biological growth, development, and reproduction exposes the limitation of the representational paradigm. We should perhaps begin by enquiring: what would it have taken for the reproduction of these complex systems to have been achieved? The simple answer is that the reproduction of each system must have been achieved, amongst other things, by the biological reproduction, growth, and maintenance of the humans who learnt, and became capable of fulfilling, the roles that were required of them. This necessitated *inter alia* learning, employing, developing, or indeed failing to develop, the styles of behaviour that the New Archaeology had decided were expressive of cultural rules which not only lay beyond archaeological analysis, but were irrelevant to historical enquiry.

Conclusion

For all the fuss that accompanied its original formation (e.g. Hawkes 1968), the New Archaeology was nothing more than a new archaeological methodology. It accepted the ontological reality being studied by archaeology, which it neither attempted to question nor to change. That ontology was the sequence of material residues that had resulted from the histories of an earlier human presence. What the New Archaeology did do was to remodel that reality as a system of material outputs that represented the functional adaptation of different systems of human behaviour, with the intention that these ancient systems could be studied archaeologically, and their transformations explained. The New Archaeology demanded that archaeological methodologies should operate objectively and scientifically by:

rejecting the subjective assessment of specific cultural influences to explain material change; demanding that the material sequences be described quantitively; treating the material as humanly produced to satisfy certain systemic and functional requirements; and distinguishing human material cultural systems from the environmental contexts within which, and upon which, those human systems had operated. All these procedures assumed that human histories were determined by the operation of certain common and identifiable processes, an assumption that attracted a certain level of criticism (see Chapter 5; cf. Johnson 2010). However, if the point was to establish archaeology as the comparative study of how commonly organised systems of human behaviour had adapted to various natural environments, then the New Archaeology did design a methodology which achieved this end. The question is whether this is an adequate characterisation of the human condition.

4

A SOCIAL ARCHAEOLOGY

Introduction

In 1973 Colin Renfrew recast the modelling of archaeological residues to represent the operation of social systems and, by so doing, he provided a basis upon which the development of a 'Social Archaeology' might occur (Renfrew 1973d; cf. Renfrew 1984). Although this remodelling has often been treated as if it were a continuation of the programme of the New Archaeology, it had the potential to disrupt the earlier approach. This was because while the New Archaeology treated historical change as if it had arisen largely from the need of systems of human behaviour to adjust to changing environmental constraints, a Social Archaeology introduced the idea that social strategies were amongst the processes that brought about historical change. In other words, the move to a Social Archaeology shifted the focus upon the agencies of change from the mechanisms of environmental adaptation to the mechanisms of social competition.

Renfrew argued that a Social Archaeology would signal the need for archaeologists to engage with 'the things which distinguish human culture from that of other species, which are unique to human experience' and that these should be investigated 'as intensely as others, such as subsistence and technology'. Renfrew therefore implied that it was these *things* that were the products of the socially informed behaviour of humans (Renfrew 1973d, 6 & 7), indicating that social behaviour, if not in itself unique to humanity (Wilson 2012), gains a unique set of characteristics when it becomes the product of human behaviour. Amongst those characteristics is the human ability to further extend the 'extraordinary diversity' of the ways that life can be lived (Ingold 1994, 329), while the analysis that Renfrew and others offered remained committed to explaining the emergence of the general similarities that have also existed in the ways that life was organised. Both the particular cultural achievements of life, and the general patterns of life's systemic organisation continued to be taken to be represented by archaeologically recovered materials, and each was the product of lives that were lived 'socially', that is, among and with others.

Renfrew's commentary, along with the one that was offered by Redman and his colleagues (Redman et al. 1978), argued that the development of a Social Archaeology would extend the scope of archaeological reasoning. In place of the simple description and dating of past human cultural conditions (presumably describing the specifics of how lives were lived at certain times and in certain places), and the emphasis upon the organisation of subsistence economies as the means of environmental adaptation, Social Archaeology would mark a concern with the function of human activity when expressed through the existence of rank, status, and the workings of political institutions. These views were set against the pessimism that had been expressed by Margaret Smith (1955), Christopher Hawkes (1954), and Edmund Leach (1973) to the effect that the investigation of the archaeological residues to reveal the social strategies employed by extinct human communities lay beyond what was methodologically possible for archaeology to achieve.

Renfrew turned towards establishing a programme of Social Archaeology immediately after publishing the first full-length use of systems analysis in European prehistory (Renfrew 1972). The move implies that he regarded Social Archaeology as a more effective perspective from which to explain the processes driving long-term material change than the use of 'systems thinking' alone. While Renfrew still saw a Social Archaeology working as a generalising discipline of analysis (Renfrew 1973d), the important developments heralded by the move included the idea that the feedback processes within the social system did not need to be treated as functioning primarily to dampen change and sustain stability. Feedback could now be treated as the ongoing consequence of strategies that were driven by competition between the authority of some, and the submission of others: it was the social strategies of various agencies that might drive the broad spectrum of systemic change which affected systemic stability, growth, transformation, and contraction. It is therefore important to understand how the archaeology of social strategies began to disrupt the idea that archaeological materials could be modelled to represent behavioural systems that were adapted to meet various environmental constraints.

From an archaeology of adaptive systems to a Social Archaeology

Renfrew's concern throughout his work in the early 1970s was to show how a break in reasoning might be achieved from the archaeological tradition, once dominant in European studies of the Neolithic and Bronze Age, where the occurrence of cultural change was traced to the diffusion of influences originating in south-west Asia and the eastern Mediterranean (cf. Childe 1939). Renfrew needed to counter such arguments by identifying the indigenous mechanisms that might explain the development of the monuments and technological changes that defined

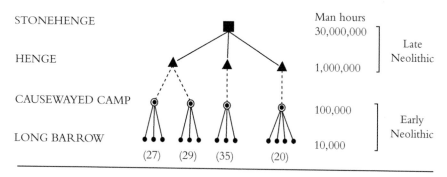

FIGURE 4.1 Renfrew's proposed 'socio-spatial hierarchy' of southern British social organisation in the late Neolithic (redrawn from Renfrew 1983, Fig. 3).

the prehistory of Europe. He therefore argued that a Social Archaeology meant that many of the material residues of these periods either represented the ways that the socialised actions of people indicated how past social systems had been organised (into such things as chiefdoms or states), or expressed the social values that were manifest in the production, circulation, and deposition of certain artefacts, or in the building of certain monuments.

Renfrew's initial use of a systems-based analysis was designed to explain the processes that had resulted in two things: the development of the Aegean Bronze Age (Renfrew 1972), and the sequential changes that had given rise to the emergence of the ranked societies of the Early Bronze Age in southern Britain (Renfrew 1973b, 539–558; cf. Renfrew 1969a). In both cases, Renfrew mapped the sequence of monument building, burial deposits, artefact production, and environmental changes in ways that seemed to reveal an emergent and centralising authority (Figure 4.1), and he equated that authority with the chiefdom type of organisation that had been identified anthropologically (Service 1962, 133ff.). He adopted one widely held assumption to explain the rise of chiefdoms: that they functioned to redistribute the various products of localised and specialised processes of production and ecological exploitation, and that the emergence of chiefdoms might therefore be treated as a systemic response to these processes of production. The social system was therefore still treated as a form of adaptation, although the proposal for the emergence of chiefdoms explains neither the development of specialist producers, nor how chiefs achieved their positions of political domination. As Renfrew himself noted: '[i]n such explanations there is often opportunity to wonder what caused the cause' (Renfrew 1972, 480).

Renfrew was responding to Leach's criticism (see page 47), in which Leach had asserted that archaeological attempts to explain social change were nothing more than a move 'into the realm of pure speculation' given that the social processes had been played out in such a way that, whilst 'the rules of the game are laid out in advance . . . the ways the game is played out is unpredictable' and that there 'are always an indefinitely large number of alternative ways in which particular social systems might be adapted to meet particular ecological and demographic situations' (Leach 1973, 764 & 767). Renfrew countered that much of Leach's argument was irrelevant to the archaeological project simply because it was possible to use archaeological data to understand the physical consequences of various social realities, even if it was not possible to access the cognitive motivations of the practitioners who had belonged to those realities (Renfrew 1977).

Renfrew's 1972 study of the southern Aegean and Cyclades had been the first detailed publication of systems analysis in archaeology and it was directed towards providing an explanation for the third-millennium changes that witnessed the birth, and then the growth, of the first European civilisation in the Aegean in the second millennium BCE. The emergence of this European civilisation therefore arose, according to Renfrew, not out of influences from the east, as Childe had proposed (Childe 1958, 7 & 78ff.), but out of the indigenous interaction between subsistence procedures that had adapted to a specific soil regime, the available technologies, the traditions of behaviour in the use of symbolism, and the exploitation of trading contacts, all of which were integrated though processes of social exchange (Renfrew 1972, 22–23). In other words, change arose as the result of feedback between different social strategies within the regional system, and Renfrew rejected the idea that any single factor, such as the generation of a food surplus, 'can of itself produce changes in the structure of the culture. For a "take-off" at least two systems must be changing and mutually influencing their changes' (Renfrew 1972, 39).

It was after surveying both the material sequences and the development of the hypothesised subsystems that Renfrew identified the social processes that could have driven the rise of the palace economies. One of these was the developing subsistence strategies of the Neolithic. Given the challenging soil conditions of the southern Greek mainland, these subsistence strategies were transformed by olive and vine cultivation, 'opening the possibility of production specialisation in single commodities' (Renfrew 1972, 280; cf. Halstead 2004). Another process was the long-term development of metallurgy that had occurred in the context of the enhanced trade networks of the Aegean, sustained by the developing naval architecture of the third millennium (Renfrew 1972, 444 & 451). The latter was driven by the need to satisfy the competitively charged search for exchange relationships and for access to items for display. The palace economies of the second millennium thus emerged, in Renfrew's account, because of the third-millennium developments in subsistence cultivation, craft production, and trade, all of which were integrated through 'the human inclination to give a social and symbolic significance to material goods' (Renfrew 1972, 497). The 'multiplier effect' that had driven change was the result of the forces of social competition in the second millennium:

> [t]he finery of the Minoan palace, the treasures of the Mycenaean Shaft Graves, the golden drinking cups of Troy, were not conceived solely for the material well-being of those who enjoyed them. They were produced

also to signify the wealth of the owner, and to reinforce that impression by extravagance as well as by opulence. (Renfrew 1972, 498)

European civilisation was a stage in social evolution that had emerged through a system of processes that were integrated as the result of socially motivated actions.

Social strategies had become archaeologically visible in Renfrew's analysis of the Aegean sequence, and a year later in his published review of the Neolithic and Bronze Age in southern Britain, in two ways. First, the indigenous systems of behaviour were organised according to a logic which seems to have involved an increasingly centralised authority capable of co-ordinating and directing labour in the building of monuments (Figure 4.1), and the management of the redistribution of specialised produce. Second, exchange systems had extended in scale beyond those demanded by the needs of a regional population for a subsistence base, and this introduced into archaeology the need to deal with the notion that human behaviours were driven by ideas of social value and choice, rather than simply by the needs of survival. In his Aegean study these social processes contributed to the positive feedback mechanisms that Renfrew had claimed to identify. Thus, the palaces of southern Greece and Crete were taken to have functioned as the centres of elite display, agricultural storage, and economic redistribution. Although Renfrew would come to doubt his initial attachment to the model of a redistributive economy as applied to the palaces (Renfrew 2004, 266), the equation of an emergent elite with a redistributive function was one that became widely employed in the early 1970s to explain the emergence of social hierarchies. This followed upon Service's suggestion that the social institution of chiefdoms functioned to redistribute, and thus to integrate, the labours of specialist producers who had operated across a diverse mosaic of ecological resources (Service 1962, 134; cf. Pauketat 2007). This model of a chiefly function was demolished by Timothy Earle (1977), who was able to demonstrate that Hawaiian chiefdoms did not integrate ecologically diverse regimes of production, but instead dominated a region's production to ensure that they could extract the 'wealth finance' necessary for various forms of elite activity. Clearly a distinction existed between modelling the rise of chiefs to fulfil the role of what Gilman (1991) had dismissively referred to as 'managers' who had supposedly integrated an increasingly diverse subsistence system, and their emergence resulting from an ability to exploit a portion of the productive output of others. It is not simply that a Social Archaeology provided very different images of the historical processes as a way of explaining the emergence of social institutions, but that the function of a once existing political institution does not explain the processes that had resulted in its inception: chiefs might, in some cases, have functioned as managers but this does not explain how they gained their power originally. Thus, whilst we might choose to regard a functioning social system as facilitating a form of stable adjustment to its environmental conditions, any social distinctions that structured the system must have originated in the development of cultural ideas of the differences between people and between things, as well as in the relations of power existing between different groups exercised by claims of authority and the demands of submission. The problem facing a Social Archaeology was that, having modelled the material as if it represented a system of functioning relationships, archaeology was still faced with establishing the mechanisms that had structured the emergence of that system. Given the contentious nature of the understandings that are offered for the validity of today's political systems, we might wonder how archaeology was to negotiate these conflicting issues in relation to extinct systems of human behaviour.

It was the suggestion that chiefdoms, as a distinctive type of organisation, could be distinguished archaeologically 'by the presence of centres which co-ordinate economic, social and religious activities' (Service 1962, 143) that resulted in the proposal that the sequence of earthwork 'centres' in southern Britain, culminating with the final stone-built structure of Stonehenge, was the record of emergent chiefly polities that had arisen as the result of an increasing centralisation of power during the Neolithic and Early Bronze Age (Renfrew 1973b, 539–558). The brief study of the southern British material offered by Renfrew was of a very different character from that of his much more extensive study of the Aegean (Barrett & Boyd 2019). The purpose of the British study was simply to demonstrate that the patterns identified in the archaeological record could be modelled to correlate with a list of some twenty features that both Marshall Sahlins and Elman Service (Sahlins & Service 1960; Service 1962, 133–169) had emphasised as characteristic of anthropologically attested ranked and chiefly systems of social organisation (Renfrew 1973b, 542–543). The emergent polities were thus presented in terms of organisational systems, although a system-based analysis of feedback mechanisms that might have been expected to explain the proposed developments in the social and economic system, was not offered. In addition, only very slight evidence was offered for ecologically specialised production processes that might have been integrated through a proposed redistribution system (Renfrew 1973b, 554–556). It was perhaps in the course of preparing the Aegean and southern British cases that Renfrew had become convinced that the indigenous systems that he was studying could be best characterised as social systems, thus allowing for the active role of cultural values to contribute to the explanation of systemic change. When, nearly twenty years after Renfrew's paper had been published, Richard Bradley offered another view of the historic development of the supposedly 'chiefly' societies in southern Britain, utilising the more refined chronologies that had by then become available, he made no reference to feedback mechanisms between subsystems. Instead the idea of feedback between subsystems was replaced in Bradley's model by notions of socially inscribed control over subsistence products and ritual practices, and the polities were now depicted not so much as integrated systems but as theatres of production over which different forms of political authority had competed (Bradley 1991).

It was with models of inter-regional exchange that, by indicating contact between different regions and different social systems, the basis for a possible challenge to Renfrew's argument against diffusionist explanations for material change began

to emerge. Diffusionist arguments depended, after all, upon inter-regional contacts in which dominant cultures tended to cause cultural change in those regions
that lay on their periphery, and such contacts, when offered to explain material
change, were often claimed on the basis of the subjective assessments of similarities in cultural materials. Such contacts, if substantiated, might therefore indicate
the paths of possible cultural influence, and Renfrew was careful to demand that
any claim for inter-regional contact be supported by the physical sourcing of the
raw materials used, rather than by comparisons of artefact styles, commenting that
'[a] proper interpretation depends upon the scientific characterisation of the material' (Renfrew 1969b, 151; cf. Renfrew 1975). He did allow, without necessarily
accepting in his own work, the 'careful comparison of artefact forms to establish
resemblances so close that they cannot be fortuitous' (Renfrew 1972, 441), and
he argued that the actual movement of materials and inter-regional contacts could
be mapped objectively by archaeological analysis, and that different mechanisms
of exchange between places of production and consumption could be identified
(Renfrew 1975). He was therefore keen to demolish previous attempts to claim
regional interaction and cultural influences based upon what he regarded as vague
visual comparisons of material similarities (Renfrew 1969a), as well as doubting
claims that similarities in the techniques of production, which might have been
fortuitous, were also strong enough to sustain suggestions of inter-regional influences (Newton & Renfrew 1970). Renfrew's analysis of the artefact sequences of
the southern Aegean led him to argue that whilst limited contacts between Crete
and the eastern Mediterranean could be substantiated for the third millennium,
evidence of wider links across the eastern Mediterranean did not exist and 'no
objects of west Mediterranean origin have been found in Aegean contexts dateable
to the third millennium B.C.' (Renfrew 1972, 444). The apparent isolation of the
Aegean within the broader eastern Mediterranean at the end of the third millennium stood in contrast to the increasing development within the Aegean itself of
an 'international spirit' that united the southern Greek mainland, Crete, and the
Cyclades in this same period and had 'transformed what were hitherto essentially
independent cultures in different regions of the Aegean into a complex of related
units, whose individuality although at first distinct became gradually less marked as
the bronze age continued' (Renfrew 1972, 451).

The general image that was being evoked was that of social change being
achieved by the indigenous development of an authority that, by means of the
exchange relations that had moved people, materials, specialist products, and information within an expanding polity, was able to weld together larger political,
social, and economic units. Widespread contacts from beyond these emergent polities, and which in the case of the Aegean were marked by the procurement of Baltic amber which was deposited in some of the 'princely burials of the Mycenaean
civilisation', resulted from long-distance chains of prestige exchange that appeared
to lack social consequences (Renfrew 1972, 467–468). It was as if the existing
elites participated in this form of exchange, but were not themselves created by it.

Political, social, and economic development, including the rise of the Bronze Age civilisations of the Aegean, was therefore an indigenous development rather than one that arose as the result of external political domination:

> in terms of this model the decisive factor for the development of Aegean civilisation was the development of a redistributive system for subsistence commodities. This emerged as a consequence of the intensive exploitation of a new spectrum of foodplants, notably tree crops, yielding a new diversity in produce. (Renfrew 1972, 480)

Social structures

The methodological problems that have accompanied the attempts to build a Social Archaeology might be best illustrated by the ways that the term *structure* has been used, both as a noun to describe an arrangement or organisation, and as a verb to describe a process (as in 'to structure'). In the former case a social *structure* describes the more general arrangement of institutions, such as those functioning within a chiefdom that is an arrangement of status differences linked by the downward pressures of obligation and authority and by the upward movement of tributary materials. Such an arrangement holds out the possibility of being unambiguously represented by the pattern of archaeological residues, as illustrated by the late third-millennium settlement hierarchy on Crete (Renfrew 1972, Fig. 14.14). It therefore appears as if the patterned range of settlement locations, sizes, and their supposed functions could be treated as if they offered the representation of the social structural complexity of the regional system (Flannery 1976, 195).

The second use of *structure* as a verb indicates the ability of an agency to bring an arrangement into existence or to transform an existing arrangement. Such an agency would require an existing facility, the material conditions of its existence for example, for it to either reproduce existing structural arrangements between things and people, or for it to transform those relationships. These 'structuring structures' expressed the practical intention of an agency to achieve certain ends (Bourdieu 1977) and would have involved, on the part of the human agents concerned, the interpretation of the conditions occupied, and the aims of the strategies that were employed.

The conditions that are studied anthropologically, are conditions that are replicated by agents who work through their own lifetime projects to reproduce, and possibly transform, the social and material conditions to which they belong. This process of replication is achieved by the human agents' abilities to draw upon a body of material resources and traditional practices, along with their own dispositions and abilities to act, given the various constraints that might act upon them. These subjectivities would seem to stand in contrast to the fossilised patterns of social types that archaeological studies reveal as being represented by the patterns of archaeological residues. The disciplines of anthropology and of archaeology were distinguished by Renfrew who proposed that an anthropological understanding of 'a society' was of the structure 'as its members see it' whilst an archaeological perception, 'lacking access to direct verbal testimony', utilises the available residues to gain a knowledge 'of the operation of certain aspects of the society' (Renfrew 1977, 90 & 91). From this view, the archaeological account of a social structure must 'centre upon specially patterned interactions which are indicative of [its] organisation', a cultural system whose 'interactions with the environment [are] seen as input or output to that . . . system' (Renfrew 1977, 98 & 108). Archaeology appears to model the social 'polity', which is defined as the highest order of social organisation (Renfrew 1977, 105), as if its organisation was represented by material residues. The problem for archaeology is that each polity was reproduced historically by the practical expression of the world as it was seen and lived in by the agencies that inhabited it. If an understanding of these subjective processes of 'structuration' was only available to anthropologists who could access a verbal testimony of the members of other communities, then this would seem to preclude an archaeological understanding of the processes by which social organisations were reproduced.

It is important to re-emphasise at this point that archaeology, like anthropology, seeks *our* understanding of the lives that others once lived. This is not the world 'as they saw it' but the world in which their actions make sense as seen by us. We own, and are responsible for, our understandings of others. This does not mean that we are free to colonise those lives with ideas as to how we might interpret those same conditions, nor does it mean that we are bound to attempt the impossible, namely to see the world as they saw it. What it does mean is that we should attempt to recognise the options that those others had to enable them to respond to the conditions in which they lived and which we glimpse in the surviving fragmentary residues studied archaeologically. To do this in a self-critical manner will mean that we make our assumptions explicit. The structuring of the social system was therefore achieved by agencies that were able to direct their own interpretation of the conditions which they inhabited towards either the replication of those conditions, or towards their transformation. It is by seeking to understand the basis upon which the roles of the various agencies of history become comprehensible to us that archaeology aims to build its understanding of the ways that those various agencies once operated, without having access to the verbal testimony of those agencies.

Social typologies, social practices, and world systems

Renfrew's perception of the social realities of the past was that they operated as a series of autonomous polities (Renfrew 1977). It was these polities that supposedly contained the social mechanisms for their own historical development, transformation, and collapse (Renfrew 1979). The claim that a social system could be analysed as if it had operated as an isolated polity was questioned during the 1970s. Immanuel Wallerstein introduced the concept of a modern world system in his study of 1974 which explored the ways that the emergence of the European trading empires had, from the sixteenth century CE, dominated and transformed the economies of the so-called third world into service economies for European states (Wallerstein 1974). Alongside this, the discipline of anthropology entered into something of a crisis with the realisation that the isolated groups of 'primitive peoples' that formed the basis for its empirical studies, and which had sometimes been treated as if they were the relict survivals of ancient peoples, were in fact not only thoroughly modern but were contained within, and structured by, systems of colonial domination of which anthropology may well have been a part (Ekholm 1977 & 1980; Friedman 1994; Kuper 1988). Both the historical work of Waller-stein and the critical studies of anthropology were therefore set firmly in the context of modern systems in which the historical development of European states, the new world, and the impoverishment of much of the so-called third world were all contained. The challenge set by this 'world systems' perspective was whether the historical trajectory followed by any polity, be it modern or ancient, was unlikely to be understandable unless that polity was seen to be part of a global system of relationships. Friedman argued that:

> [a] viable way out of this impasse is to start conceptually with social repro-duction rather than social institutions. . . . Cycles of reproduction are not necessarily bounded by individual societies, . . . they provide the total frame-work for the analysis of cumulative social process and social transformation. (Friedman 1994, 7)

The focus upon social reproduction concerns the ways that a system of institution-alised relationships was structured over time. The problem was that the historical trajectory of the local system, or polity, depended upon resources that derived from beyond the polity itself. The polity was therefore seen from this perspective as the localised element of a much larger system. Early archaeological examples of the way that such processes of structuring might be understood were provided by Susan Frankenstein and Michael Rowlands's analysis of the long-term develop-ment of central European Iron Age society (Frankenstein & Rowlands 1978) and by the Bronze Age practices of grave deposition that were traced across modern-day Denmark by Kristian Kristiansen (1978). Frankenstein and Rowlands studied the development of the enclosed *Fürstensitz* of the late Hallstatt period in central Europe, such as the Heuneburg, with its evidence for production, and the elabo-rate grave series (*Fürstengräber*) that occur in the landscapes around the *Fürstensitz*. They argued that these sites were indicative of a system that did not develop inde-pendently of their contemporary exchange relations with the Greek colonial settle-ments that had been founded on the northern Mediterranean coast to the west of the Italian peninsula and around the mouth of the Rhône. Instead of treating the central European system and that of the Greek colonies as two independently evolving systems linked by trade, Frankenstein and Rowlands argued that these were two components of a single world system. In this model the development of social differentiation represented by the *Fürstengräber* grew and then diminished as the result of the elite's shifting control over the importation of exotic materials which increased their expansion and control over local debt obligations. Meanwhile Greek mercantile activity expanded by procuring raw materials and slaves via the enhanced political structures of central Europe. In a broadly similar way Kristiansen traced the historical contrasts within the regional agrarian systems in Denmark, with their differential ability to maintain agricultural productivity, as explanations for each region's ability to sustain the political structures it required to procure the exotic metalwork from central Europe. It was these imported metalwork items that were employed in the competitive display that occurred during funerary rituals (Kristiansen 1978).

The archaeological recognition of the flow of prestige materials into indigenous exchange networks, with the emphasis being placed upon systems of prestige exchange and conspicuous consumption, and that drew upon anthropological models of gift giving and ritual display, differed from the emphasis that Wallerstein had placed upon the bulk appropriation of the raw materials and labour products from increasingly impoverished colonised communities by the capitalist core economies. Consequently, doubts were expressed concerning the wider applicability of the world systems model, with its emphasis upon bulk shipments and capital accumulation, compared with the operation of pre-capitalist systems with their emphasis upon prestige objects and ritual consumption (Schneider 1977). Given these doubts, archaeologists may have been too hasty in applying the language of the world systems model, originally formulated with reference to the modern world, and with its terminology of cores of wealth accumulation and impoverished peripheries, to the prehistory of Europe (Harding 2013). Nonetheless there are two important lessons for archaeology in its encounter with this model. The first is to question the assumption that the histories of local social systems can be treated as if they were necessarily autonomous, rather than being segments of larger systems involving the production, circulation, and consumption of materials, information, and values, and to do this without necessarily re-introducing diffusionism as an explanation for material change (Kristiansen 1998). If this first point is to be accepted then the second lesson is the need to develop the analytical procedures that can build an understanding of how the flows of materials, information, and values might have been appropriated and utilised in a number of systems by examining the different ways that they were employed, and how these processes of appropriation and use can be understood archaeologically (Barrett 2012; Barrett & Boyd 2019, 165–169). It is to the ways that archaeology has addressed this second lesson that we must now turn.

The problem with anthropological analogies

The New Archaeology had begun to be referred to as 'Processual Archaeology' by the end of the 1960s (Flannery 1967, 119). It was a renaming that acknowledged the aim to identify the *processes* that had brought about the systems of behavioural and organisational change amongst humans. By treating the patterns of archaeological residues as if they represented the ways these social activities had once been organised, the archaeological challenge was expressed as the need to establish the social processes that had structured those organisations, rather than have explanations that relied upon processes of environmental adaptation. With this in mind, archaeologists turned to theory for guidance. Theory is generalising in its scope, and it was in theory that the processes that were assumed to have structured different forms of social reality could be described. Matthew Johnson has defined archaeological theory as 'the order we put facts in' (Johnson 2010, 2 emphasis omitted), implying that theoretical work has the task of establishing the processes that structured the different kinds of social order that are represented 'factually' by the patterns of residue.

With the goal of establishing theories that explained the evolution of a type of social system, it is unsurprising that the anthropological works of Service (*Primitive Social Organisation*, 1962) and Fried (*The Evolution of Political Society*, 1967) should have become points of archaeological reference (Chapman 2003, 34–38). The attractiveness of both books was not only that they provided definitions for different types of social and political system, but they also offered an evolutionary path that linked sequences of types that ran from the simpler systems, structured on the basis of familial ties and associated with hunter-gatherers to the more complex, bureaucratically dominated systems of the state (cf. Sahlins & Service 1960). The archaeological use of anthropological analogies appeared to be justified simply because archaeological residues represented the types of social organisation that anthropology had also identified. This way of thinking therefore empowered the search for the general processes that might explain the rise and transformation of both the anthropological and the archaeological cases. Anthropological sources therefore appeared to offer archaeological theory the processes by which to explain systemic change. Perhaps it is because of these deeply embedded assumptions that archaeologists have been unable to follow Marvin Harris's appeal that they should 'shrive' themselves 'of the notion that the units which [they] seek to reconstruct must match the units of social organization which contemporary ethnographers have attempted to tell [us] exist' (Harris in Binford & Binford 1968, 359–360). After all, what other 'units of social organization' could be productively represented by archaeological data and theorised as the product of anthropologically derived models of process, once archaeology was locked into this kind of reasoning?

By employing social evolutionary narratives and anthropological analogies, archaeology has ensured that the social system, perhaps described as a polity, has remained the standard unit of analysis. The evolution of these systems is modelled as resulting from the accretion, over time, of the basic elements of social reproduction (e.g. Fried 1967, 51–107). These sequences inevitably arrive at an end point marked by the formation of state systems and empires as the height of evolutionary development. It is a view of history that draws heavily upon the European experience (Feuchtwang & Rowlands 2019).

It is important for us to be aware of patterns and regularities observed in the archaeological residues, and assumed to have been the result of historical processes, but which are no longer understandable from the currently adopted perspective. Attempting to explain these patterns is an example of where the aid of anthropological analogies has been sought and where theoretical archaeology has been developed. Most obviously these patterns include those that were once mapped to describe regions and periods of cultural uniformity and thus regions and periods of shared cultural behaviour (Childe 1929, v–vi; Roberts & Vander Linden 2011a). Change in these cultural sequences was once explained as having resulted from the diffusion of ideas and the migrations of people (see Chapter 8). As we have noted, such explanations have now been rejected, and the patterns of cultural similarity have been treated as if they are of little historical consequence (cf. Renfrew 1977, 94–95).

We can return again to the example of one such pattern, namely the distribution of Neolithic megalithic tombs around the Atlantic and Baltic margins of Europe. Once treated as indicative of migrations and of contacts between regions (Daniel 1963), now these monuments are treated as indicative of local practices concerned with control over limited resources (see page 11; Renfrew 1976; Chapman 1981). Shanks and Tilley (1982) offered an analogy to explain this phenomenon of tomb building that was anthropologically derived. It claimed that the social relations of agricultural production had given rise to a political order in which the authority of community elders, upon whose inherited labour-products the ongoing well-being of social reproduction had depended, was projected into history, and consequently legitimated, by reference to an ancestral line of inheritance (Meillassoux 1972). Claude Meillassoux, who had developed this idea, utilised the reasoning of Marx by arguing that hunter-gatherers who, by extracting the necessities of life directly from the land, had engaged in a form of 'instantaneous' production the products of which were shared without further reciprocal obligations, stood in contrast to agriculturalists whose social obligations were structured by a productive reality in which:

> [t]he members of one agricultural party are consequently linked not only to one another during the non-productive period of work, but also to the working party that produced the food during the previous cycle. Time and continuity become the essential features of the economic and social organisation. (Meillassoux 1972, 99)

Relations of indebtedness and authority were therefore theorised as being structured differently in the two contrasting cases of social reproduction. Hunter-gatherers might see 'the forest' as a divine and 'giving' presence and as a parental figure (Godelier 1977a, 5; Bird-David 1990), whilst agriculturalists might recognise their dependency upon, and thus an authority arising from, the labour products that they had inherited from previous generations. It was these lines of obligation whose authority seemed to reside with 'the dead ancestors' (Meillassoux 1972, 99). It might well have been possible that ancestral rites structured behaviour in the lives of the agriculturalists of the Neolithic of western and northern Europe, given the existence of monuments that contained human mortuary remains. Indeed, it is an argument that has been further elaborated upon by comparing the form of some of the Neolithic monuments with the mortuary remains housed in the stone monuments of central Madagascar (Bloch 1971). The formal comparison between Malagasy and European use of stone has now been further extended, perhaps to breaking point, by the expedient of claiming that stone used as a building material was likely, by virtue of its 'hardness' and 'permanence', to represent a structural concern with the timeless ancestral presence in contrast with wooden structures representing the impermanence (decay) of life (Parker Pearson & Ramilisonina 1998). However, all such arguments express, at most, the possibility of what might have ordered (or structured) human behaviour. It is equally possible that instead of projecting the political debts of the living into an ancestral past during the European Neolithic, the dead had remained as active members of the community, and that their presence was maintained by the circulation of their physical remains, as well as by the inclusion of these remains into monuments built to enhance various places within the landscape (see pages 134–138). The claim that an ancestral presence provided a form of political legitimacy among the communities whose behaviours are recorded archaeologically is therefore sustained, not so much by references to archaeologically derived data, but by the elegance of Meillassoux's model. Perhaps this elegance is enough for its acceptance, although I am not at all sure. Indeed, I am not sure what exactly this adds to our *archaeological* understanding of the early agriculturalists of western Europe. The ancestral motif remains highly generalised within the archaeological case (Whittle 2003, 124–128; Crossland 2014, 13–15), and it adds little more than some 'cultural colour' to the archaeological material. Unfortunately, referring to human bones as representing ancestors rather than the dead (Barrett 1994, 40–67) might imply that archaeology can claim to know more than it can actually deliver by reference to its own data (Whitley 2002).

By working with the presumption that types of social system (i.e. polities) can be identified as having existed both in the past as well as in the present-day ethnographic record, archaeological analysis has tended to proceed in one of three ways. First it has drawn upon the idea that the same type of social organisation will share common structural principles, including claims in which hunter-gatherer and early agriculturalist systems are not only distinguished by the social organisation and the technologies involved in production, but also by assumptions concerning the political and spiritual sources of their respective populations' well-being (Godelier 1977a & 1977b). Second is the assumption that the various social types can also be arranged to describe stages in an evolutionary sequence, for example in the ways that early state systems are assumed to have evolved from a prior form of chieftainship (but see Yoffee 1993). This would seem to imply that social evolution described a process involving the accretion of earlier independent systems into a single form of organisation, thus appearing not only to have involved an increase in both the vertical and horizontal distinction of roles, but also the geographical expansion in the scale of the system (Flannery & Marcus 2012). Finally, the evolutionary assumption also supports the belief that types of organisation that are functionally similar will nonetheless display considerable variation in their cultural expression (cf. Laland & O'Brien 2011). What such analogies do not do therefore is to offer us an understanding of the processes that were involved in generating the dispersed pattern of monumental types across the region of Atlantic and Baltic Europe (but see Schulz Paulsson 2019).

Despite claims to the contrary, the anthropological narratives of social dynamics do not explain the patterns that are recognised in the archaeological data. Indeed, we might conclude that the apparent consistency in the patterning of the residues, such as the so-called collective tombs of the Neolithic, is a phenomenon that is neither explained by Renfrew's earlier model of territorial adaptation (see page 12), nor by the more recent uses of an anthropological analogy. This use of analogy has claimed to understand why the social strategies represented by mortuary practices were executed in and around the Neolithic tombs of Atlantic and Baltic Europe (Shanks & Tilley 1982). It is an analogy that has avoided Renfrew's earlier suggestion that the monuments functioned to map the inheritance of land-rights amongst the earliest agricultural communities, suggesting instead that the monuments were erected to facilitate rituals arising from a politics dependent upon an ancestral authority. However, the suggestion has been made without attempting to explain why these strategies only found expression across the Atlantic margins of Europe (cf. Hodder 1990, 178ff.). This is a theme to which we must return (pages 134–138).

Conclusion

The aim of the New or Processual Archaeology was to identify the causal conditions that might explain the changes in past dynamics, as represented by the relatively static sequences of archaeological finds. The causal conditions sought were those that were generally applicable to the historical trajectories of certain types of organisation under variously specified environmental conditions. These changes were described by the sequential changes in the ways that human behaviour had been organised, rather than in the ways it had expressed itself according to style and cultural form. As a result,

> the explanation for any given change must . . . lie in a complex combination of environmental circumstances, of the structure and organisation of the society in question, of its interactions with other societies, and with very general properties and potentialities with man [sic] himself. (Renfrew 1980, 294)

Two questions are posed by this approach. Is this an adequate understanding of human history, and do the approaches that were employed by the New, Social, and Processual Archaeologies in the latter half of the twentieth century, deliver what was promised: the explanation of 'culture change'? For this to be explained by reference to the processes described by a Social Archaeology it seems necessary to accept not only that history worked through a limited number of processes within a particular form of social organisation to generate change within that organisation, but that the consequences of human behaviour within those organisations also worked, for most of their history, to sustain the stability of those systemic forms of organisation, and thus stability in the identity of cultures. Change in the traditions of human behaviour was therefore regarded as unusual, and consequently demanded an explanation. Human behaviour was defined, for most of its history, by two kinds of output, by its material products (the surviving remnant of which formed the archaeological record), and by its functional role in sustaining systemic stability through the relationships of feedback between different kinds of behaviour. The problem we then confront is the vagueness at the very point at which we have been led to expect an explanation for change. For an approach that was supposed to explain change in the systemic organisation of human behaviours, nothing is actually explained as to how changes in any such behaviour is ever negotiated. Instead we appear to be offered a series of theorised speculations that carry us from one system of stable adjustment to the next, and in which that systemic stability 'just happens' (Shanks & Tilley 1987b, 34). It is little wonder that Shanks and Tilley had such trouble attempting to critique the process (1987b, 34–36), for there is nothing here to critique. We might suppose that this handling of human history is inadequate.

We find such an unfortunate level of vagueness in the narratives concerned with social transformations, at the very point when we might expect clarity, because the means by which humans constructed the various traditions of behaviour by which they have lived, have always depended upon the ways that they have understood the world within which they could act. If traditions of behaviour changed then we might presume, as we have already indicated, that the ways that the world was understood were themselves unstable and thus capable of change under certain circumstances. If Processual Archaeology sought the causal conditions for change then it would be necessary for it to offer an understanding of how humans might have gained those understandings of their world. But having relegated such understandings to the 'internal' conditions of perception that lay beyond archaeological access, such a course of analysis did not appear to be an option.

A Social Archaeology formulated by the requirement that archaeological residues be modelled to reveal how various forms of social reality had been organised, has reached a dead end. All that it can offer us is a series of alternative arrangements, some admittedly more likely to have existed than others, but all largely speculative and each accompanied by the option that we should 'take it or leave it' depending upon which particular model of human society we wish to adopt. The choice is therefore prejudiced and it is political (McGuire 1993), and whilst we might expect to be able to evaluate the options, we are denied access to any empirical data that might sustain such an evaluation.

5

FROM FUNCTIONALISM TO A SYMBOLIC AND STRUCTURAL ARCHAEOLOGY

Did anything change?

The move away from attempts to establish possible laws of cultural development came with the emergence of an 'Interpretive Archaeology' (Tilley 1993; Hodder et al. 1995). Earlier doubts about the analytical programme offered by the various forms of New, Social, or Processual, Archaeology had certainly been expressed (e.g. Tuggle et al. 1972), but it was within British archaeology that an attempted alternative was outlined with the publication in 1982 of the edited *Symbolic and Structural Archaeology* (Hodder 1982b; cf. Tilley 1989, 185). Hodder claimed that the essays he had collected in that volume actually extended the programme of the New Archaeology and whilst the ideographic and particular nature of historical conditions now needed to be emphasised, he accepted that generalisations were still likely to emerge to explain the historical existence of various social institutions (Hodder 1982c, 13). Nonetheless Hodder's stated aim for the book was to 'resolve the culture/function dichotomy' and to 'reintroduce historical explanations as a legitimate topic of concern in archaeology' (Hodder 1982c, 5). This appeared to move archaeology away from the desire to establish the general processes, let alone laws, that might provide for historical explanations, and to open up the possibility for a more varied interpretation of particular historical conditions. The revised archaeological agenda was driven by the expectation that human history was not structured by any generally operating processes of change but was the product of the diverse strategies of cultural construction that had been employed in various ways by the members of particular forms of social organisation. The effectiveness of these strategies was seen to have been contingent upon the particular contexts in which they had been mobilised. To this end Hodder dismissed the systemic approach of the New and Processual Archaeology as being incapable of understanding change in the histories of human behaviour in any terms other than those resulting from the need of human practices to adapt to, and thus to function within, trajectories of environmental change. The result, in his view, was that systemic change could only be treated as if it had been environmentally determined, a perception that seemed to miss the emphasis that Renfrew had placed upon possible social strategic drivers of change. However, as Hodder noted, the concept of function implied that a purpose existed for actions that also carried a cultural value or meaning which was particular to the context in which those actions were executed:

> [a]ll actions take place within cultural frameworks and their functional value is assessed in terms of the concepts and orientations which surround them. That an item or institution is 'good for' achieving some end is partly a cultural choice as is the end itself. (Hodder 1982c, 4)

These cultural judgements are ones that would have been understood and employed by those who had once operated within the cultural context that is being studied (an emic perspective), rather than perceived from the perspective of the external observer (an etic perspective). This captures something of the thrust of the 'interpretive turn' in archaeology. It demanded that the cultural judgements and expectations of the human agents, who were regarded as being responsible for making the historical trajectories represented by the sequences of material, needed to be incorporated into an archaeological understanding of those historical trajectories. The problem however remained: how was this to be achieved?

Hodder claimed that any consideration of the cultural conditions under which meanings and values had been recognised as embodied by things, necessitated an archaeological engagement with a theory of practice (cf. Bourdieu 1977 & 1990). The challenge for Hodder was to establish how such an archaeological theory of practice could be formulated to enable the move beyond the modern archaeological description of material conditions, and to arrive at an understanding of the historical and cultural significance once attached to those conditions. If archaeological descriptions achieved nothing more than being the representations of enculturated practices, such that a burial deposit simply represented the practice of how the dead were once treated, without any implications regarding the role of death and of the dead within that particular historical context, then how was archaeology to provide for an understanding of the practices that constructed that particular notion of death?

Hodder certainly accepted that the patterning in the archaeological materials had originated in human practices that had drawn upon certain cultural rules, and that these rules were then rendered visible by the material residues. However, this sounded suspiciously like the cultural archaeology that the New Archaeology had rejected. Hodder then asserted that the rules employed in such practices could not have existed simply in the brains of practitioners, and he suggested that this brain-centric view of culture arose from the structuralism of Lévi-Strauss, which Hodder implicitly rejected. Instead, he argued, cultural rules were routinely reworked or renewed in the practices by which the existing cultural resources (the things that had embodied a cultural significance for the practitioner) had been encountered, used, and re-arranged (cf. Giddens 1979, 1981, & 1984). The implication was that the cultural rules that guided human behaviour were not simply stored internally and thus cognitively, but were also embedded in the material contexts of human existence and thus experienced through ongoing practices. Practices were therefore enacted as a relationship between people and things, and this points us towards Hodder's more recent ideas concerning the ways that human practices are entangled within, and are thus structured by, existing material realities (Hodder 2012). This argument was only formulated in the very vaguest of terms at the time of its initial outline in 1982 and, as a result, it remained unclear how the structural principles that had aligned institutional patterns of human behaviour had actually operated, and how they could be identified archaeologically (Giddens 1984, 376; cf. Barrett 1994). It was this lack of clarity that resulted in the failure to wrestle a theory of practice away from the grip of a cognitively-based structuralism, a failure that has hastened the rise of a so-called 'cognitive archaeology' (Abramiuk 2012). It is in the arguments of a cognitive archaeology that we find the tendency to revert to the view that cultural practices, and the consequential arrangement of things, were meaningfully constituted because those practices, and those arrangements of things, expressed an 'in the head' concept of cultural order. Meaning, in other words, was assumed to arise in the human mind before it is then transcribed onto things, as Marx had argued in his comparison of the architect and the bee (see page 24). In the latter part of his opening chapter, Hodder (1982b) began to confront, without necessarily solving, the challenge that has remained basic to the discipline of archaeology: how might we understand the relationship between the histories of human existence and the existences of other material things?

It was with the publication of the 1982 volume that everything changed and yet nothing changed. What did change was the archaeological treatment of human behaviour, now widely regarded as an expression of belief, rather than as the mechanical response to environmental stimuli. What did not change was the demand that ancient human behaviour, and thus the archaeological residues arising from that behaviour, should be explained by reference to some underlying cause. The nature of the cause that was assumed to have determined human behaviour had simply now shifted. No longer conceived as the environmental or social stimuli that were external to, and had acted on, the human subject, the cause of behaviour had become the schemes that were internally (cognitively) conceived prior to their execution. It was these cognitive causes that now acted on the subject.

The idea that human behaviour is to be explained by reference to cognition introduces an obvious problem for archaeology. If explanations are to be understood in terms of the cultural beliefs that supposedly motivated human behaviour, and if such beliefs were historically and culturally specific, then it would be difficult to see how those beliefs could be recovered simply from the material residues alone. One way of side-stepping this problem was to return to the expedient of using an anthropological analogy to draw out the lessons that could be learnt from the source of the analogy (a contemporary living system), and to employ those lessons in the archaeological case. Alison Wylie (2002, 136–153) has reviewed the uncertainties that have accompanied the widespread use of analogical reasoning in archaeology, and she makes the important point that the use of analogy is not simply a matter of tracing similarities between different cases, but rather a matter of establishing the basis for the inferential reasoning that is being followed (cf. Fahlander 2004).

There are in fact two kinds of analogy that transfer information from anthropological sources into archaeological target studies. Formal analogies occur when an assemblage of things indicate that the same mechanical processes are recorded archaeologically that are attested ethnographically, resulting in predictions being drawn from the latter and applied to the former in ways that might then be evaluated. For example, in his classic study of the so-called 'smudge pits' that have been recorded archaeologically in the middle and lower reaches of the Mississippi River Valley, Binford (1967) compared the archaeological signature of these pits in terms of their shape, positioning within settlements, and the nature of their fills, with mainly nineteenth-century ethnographic accounts of the use of fire pits for the smoking of hides. On the basis of the correlation between the ethnographic accounts and archaeologically attested processes he proposed that additional associations, noted ethnographically, should be expected in the archaeological context (Binford 1967). Analogies such as this are therefore designed to provide for, and could be tested by, a more detailed archaeological evaluation of the material record.

The more contentious form of analogy is that which claims to extend the archaeological understanding of the factors that structured the complex associations of human institutions, material culture assemblages, and environmental resources by means of data from anthropology. These analogies return us to the claim that the archaeological subject and the anthropological informant both share a 'basic' structuring principle that determined the organisation of their behavioural characteristics. An example of this kind is found in the work of Binford that was discussed in Chapter 3 (page 43). Here the claim was that subsistence strategies based upon hunting and gathering warranted the archaeological use of anthropological data from similar but recent subsistence economies. This treats hunter-gatherer subsistence practices, operating within similar environmental constraints, as being basic to the organisation of other social institutions. It was upon this basis that the comparisons between the two were justified (cf. Binford 2001). The claim seems to have been widely accepted, in part because of the apparent 'simplicity' of the subsistence strategies that articulate hunter-gatherer practices with a seeming directness towards the available environmental resources: 'For these societies it is often implicitly believed that fewer variables come into play, therefore presenting a more understandable system for interpretation' (Redman et al. 1978, 6).

The impact of these two types of analogy has been significant, resulting in something of a revolution in hunter-gatherer studies. This revolution in thinking has derived from ethnographies that have overthrown the assumption that hunter-gatherer subsistence was structured by, and dependent upon, male activity that concerned big-game hunting and that resulted in the surviving residues of animal bone. Ethnographically attested hunter-gatherer subsistence appears, by contrast, to depend more upon the female gathering of plants, shell-fish, and small game, the residues of which are unlikely to be well preserved archaeologically (Lee & DeVore 1968). In addition, the archaeological assumption that hunter-gatherer existences had been precariously balanced by the routine pressures of subsistence demands being placed upon human labour-time has also been called into question. There are obvious dangers in the general application of such analogies. Broadly applied they create an a-historical image of human existences under conditions that are, and have been, far more varied than the generalisations might imply (Smith et al. 2010). We should also remember that it was the lives of hunter-gatherers that achieved at times some quite dramatic and quite specific historical outcomes, such as the colonisation of most of the earth's surface (Gamble 1993), and the emergence of post-glacial agricultural systems in Eurasia, Africa, and central America (Barker 2006). It would seem unlikely that these historical trajectories resulted from the timeless adaptive processes that are inherent to all human activities.

Causal explanations for the patterns of residue are often sought to account for the conditions that might have 'structured' the activities that gave rise to those patterns. It is these structuring conditions, whether they derived from the subsistence base, or from other relations of social reproduction, that have been treated as grounding the analogies drawn between archaeologically and anthropologically attested examples. This has resulted in 'the displacement, for some, of historiography as a defining feature of archaeology in favour of generalization about features of human society' (Olsen et al. 2012, 185). Obviously some generalisations about humanity must exist, for without them it would be impossible for us to understand each other. This remains the case even if these general conditions might also give rise to cultural practices that render others incomprehensible, difficult and, indeed, dangerous to know. But does archaeology make any unique contribution to this understanding of others? If our understanding of other people depends upon identifying the prior structural conditions that drive human motivations, then surely the social sciences, with their access to the testimonies of living peoples, offer a far more secure basis for analysis than a discipline whose data sets comprise an eroded material residue? Perhaps the archaeological contribution to a wider understanding of humanity lies in our questioning the path that the discipline has traditionally invited us to take, which is to work back from the residues to the activity in the hope of establishing the structural conditions that once motivated that activity (cf. Olsen et al. 2012, 186).

The meanings of things

From the perspective of the pragmatist philosopher Charles Saunders Peirce things only have meaning relative to an interpretant. It would be easy enough, in this light, to jump to the conclusion that things can only have meaning relative to a *human* interpretant. This anthropocentrism would be misplaced, simply because other forms of life also respond to the ways that they see and experience things (Nealon 2016). As others have argued, things emerge as particular kinds of thing through the process of interpretation. Those particular kinds of thing then have certain consequences in terms of the behaviour of the agency that characterises them. The implication is that any reference that is made by archaeologists to the 'meanings of things' remains empty until we are given to understand the practices of an interpretant whose relationship with those things brought such meanings into existence.

The complex ways in which things were understood and used, relative to people, have often been falsely characterised by the archaeological assumption that the pattern of things encodes the meanings that were expressed in their creation. It can be easily overlooked that the interpretant, in the case of an archaeological interpretation, is of course the archaeologist herself, and archaeologists do tend to assume that the meanings that they see in the material were those meanings that had originally been inscribed into that material by others. It has been but a short step to extend this kind of reasoning to treat the archaeological interpretation of materials as if it were analogous to the reading of a text (Buchli 1995).

This treatment of things-as-texts was originally developed from the perspective of the model for language use that was developed by Ferdinand de Saussure (Saussure 1974; Miller 1982). Saussure had treated a linguistic representation as if it was expressed as the consequence of a cognitive experience, and was formulated through the use of a sound/word order. This system of communication therefore comprised two elements: a conceptual element (the signified), and an expressive element (the signifier). Notice that in Saussure's scheme what is represented by the signifier is not the thing itself (the referent), but the language user's conceptual registering of that thing, the signified (cf. Kirby 1997). Notice also the chronological primacy that is awarded by this scheme to the cognitive element which the signifier then expresses. In this way an inner awareness, or cognition, is taken to precede expression, and the external world of things has slipped from view.

In the theory of language developed by Ferdinand de Saussure there is no necessary or mechanical link between an individual word (the signifier) and an individual concept (the signified) employed either by the speaker/author or by the listener/reader (Saussure 1974). The link is constituted instead by the conventions that a language user learns during their growing familiarity and competence with the pattern of sound differences that make up words (signifiers), and the differences in the world of things as they are experienced. It is this pattern of sound differences that is mapped against the differences in the things that are experienced physically and captured cognitively (the signified). In this scheme it would appear that the cultural work of classifying things is something that is indeed done cognitively. It is cognition that appears to group and to contrast the body's physical experiences of things and to assign various values to them (such as good things *vs* bad things, or hot things *vs* cold things). One consequence of this reasoning is that it distinguishes the processes of human cognition from the ways that other forms of life operate in the same environments as humans. The special status of humanity appears to be secured because humans have the cognitive ability to make sense of the world in terms of a cultural order. Animals on the other hand are assumed to respond to the world by instinct, whilst plants are assumed to merely respond to different environmental conditions and stimuli (Nealon 2016). There is no commitment in such reasoning to the idea that any forms of life other than humans might develop through their own interpretations of the world (but see Godfrey-Smith 2017).

The grammar of a language (i.e. the scheme that structures language use and facilitates the creation of meaningful speech acts) was distinguished by Saussure from its actual use in speaking (which might, sometimes, appear to be 'non-grammatical'). This distinction resulted in Saussure claiming that analysis should focus upon a language's grammar (*la langue*) rather than upon its more idiosyncratic use in speaking (*parole*). This turn away from the analysis of practice (speaking) encouraged the 'structuralist turn', because it was the supposed grammar (the structure) that 'underlay' and thus determined the possibility of meaningful verbal expression. It then appeared as if a case similar to that of language use could be made for other aspects of material practice.

We should remember that we have all learnt to speak by actually trying to speak, rather than by learning the grammar of our language, and we have all learnt to live amongst things by means of experiencing their use, and misuse, rather than by learning how to live from some kind of cultural manual. We have therefore learnt through practice. Practice theory concerns the ways that humans actually live and learn by means of their engagement with, and recognition of, the realities within which they live (Bourdieu 1977 & 1990), and these realities include the need to communicate with, and to be recognised by, others (Tomasello 2016). This kind of approach should lead us to doubt not only the attempt to use the Saussurean model to illustrate the way that language use might develop, but also its use to explain the reproduction of material culture. This brings us to the confusions that have arisen in archaeology as the result of the analogy that has sometimes been drawn between the use of language and the use of material culture. It is this confusion that has been amplified by the different ways that the term *structure* can be used. As we discussed in the previous chapter (see page 66), the term *structure* can be used either as a generative verb (to structure, as in 'to bring to order'), or as a descriptive noun (a structure, as in 'an arrangement').

An assumption of the Saussurean model is that the effectiveness of language-use obviously depends upon the expectation that its user will be understood. In other words, language use is one way of constructing a social existence in which a growing linguistic competence aligns the practitioner towards an existing and developing network of interpreters who are themselves also communicators. But if language use is simply treated as one form of behaviour among others, then we could also allow that it is behaviour, recognised by others, that constructs a social existence. Behaviour is itself directed towards, and is recognised with reference to, certain material conditions. We therefore arrive at the principle that a social existence emerges through the behaviour of bodies that are recognised by others as operating comprehensibly with reference to material conditions (Latour 1993 & 2005).

It was from the structuralist perspective developed by Levi-Strauss that things appeared to gain their meaning by their juxtaposition with and contrast against other things. The classic example of a structuralist analysis in archaeology is that of the parietal cave art (cave paintings) of Palaeolithic date undertaken by Leroi-Gourhan (1964). Leroi-Gourhan analysed the spatial distribution of animal imagery on a large number of cave walls, claiming that the images of horse and bison dominate in two clusters in a spatially distinctive ordering that is variously accompanied by images of subsidiary animal species, along with what Leroi-Gourhan and others have interpreted as the occasional, and admittedly very ambiguous, engendered signs for male and female. The somewhat uncertain conclusion that was reached by Leroi-Gourhan (Lewis-Williams 2002, 60–65) was that the Palaeolithic mind perceived the world as if it were structured by two distinct engendered qualities, and that it was this structure that symbolically generated the horse:bison assemblages of images. Bison images, for example, do not therefore 'mean' bison but were part of the representation of the cognitively engendered order by which the world was believed to have been structured.

Doubts about the treatment of material culture as if it had encoded meaning in this way arose initially from the observation that the making and using of things is quite unlike the making and using of sound-words. A hand-axe is created mechanically, fits into the hand in a certain way, feels heavy, hard, and cold, whilst the words that signify it do not do this. Material things therefore embody a form of physical resistance in their making and in their use that is largely absent from the making and use of words. However, the problem that accompanied the interpretive turn in archaeology went well beyond reliance upon a dubious analogy with language-use. We must now return to our underlying concern: the extent to which archaeological interpretations of a historical residue could ever reveal the ways that the material, and social life in general, had been knowingly constituted.

The challenge that a structuralist analysis presents to archaeology may be illustrated by reference to the interpretation of a surface of northern European prehistoric rock art. In considering such a surface we might well be tempted to regard the figures as the self-evident representations (signs) of actual human figures, carts, chariots, ships, ploughs, weapons, and so on. This would assume that those who had decorated these surfaces did so simply by referencing the shapes of those same things that had existed in the world around them. However, from a Saussurean perspective, the sign is only arbitrarily related to the *concept* of the referent (the actual thing). The structurally coherent relationship is the one that generates the signifier (the external expression) from the signified (the internal concept). Consequently, given that the 'outer' world of things might well have been transformed by being 'internally' conceptualised as the manifestation of an underlying sacred order, then that sacred order might be expressed metaphorically by the images deployed, in a similar way to Leroi-Gourhan's treatment of Palaeolithic cave images. Values such as virtue, authority, the divine, the under-world, or concepts of social distinction might then have been symbolically represented by the order of the images (Tilley 1991 & 1999). This is similar to the way that the reordering of skeletal remains in the western European Neolithic was treated archaeologically, as if it were the symbolic dissolution of the individual being and its re-articulation as part of an ancestral community (Shanks & Tilley 1982). Our carved rock surface *might* have represented, symbolically, a coherent scheme of order uniting various metaphysical forces and moral values. If this was indeed the case, then gaining an archaeological understanding of that order without the benefit of a culturally knowledgeable informant would seem to pose a considerable challenge, to say the least. Archaeological attempts to interpret what things might have originally represented must, as the consequence of this reasoning, be uncertain, ambiguous, and open-ended. We might therefore feel some sympathy when Olsen complains that:

> Scandinavian rock art, just to take a random example, [is where] one will find that a boat, an elk or a reindeer can be claimed to represent or signify almost everything – ancestors, rites of passage, borders, totems, gender, supernatural powers, etc. – apart, it seems, only from themselves. A boat is never a boat; a reindeer is never a reindeer. (Olsen 2012, 22)

In 1982 the anthropologist Ernest Gellner published an essay that was directed at an archaeological audience and which drew a distinction that Gellner recognised between the generative structures that were the object either of *structuralisme* with the 'scent of the Left Bank' that 'is forever attached' to it, or of the 'solid, earthy, blokey . . . humdrum' version of *structuralism* that described a cultural order in the anthropological tradition of structural functionalism (Gellner 1982). One major distinction between the two traditions, Gellner argued, appears in their treatment of culture, which in the case of *structuralisme* arises from the belief that things have an essence that is hidden but can emerge into open view in the patterns and regularities of material experience. This is very much the *structuralisme* of Lévi-Strauss and Leroi-Gourhan where, for the latter, the engendered essence of the Palaeolithic world emerged during a human and culturally moulded experience of it. It was supposedly this world that was symbolically represented by animal imagery. This contrasted with, in Gellner's argument, a structural concern with the organisation of small-scale societies, where culture was seen to operate as a set of arbitrary tokens that 'were required to identify this or that category of people, this or that ritual occasion' (Gellner 1982, 104). The latter understanding of culture is that it functioned as a secondary 'colour' to social structure, a perception that culture was somehow a 'secondary' veneer upon actions, a view that we might most easily equate with the approaches developed within the New, and then by Processual, Archaeology. The important observation, which Gellner then made, is that of the two perceptions of structure, the former (*structuralisme*) is an 'emic' perspective available to those living a particular form of life, whilst the latter (*structuralism*) is the 'etic' view achieved by an external observer (Gellner 1982, 112).

In light of Gellner's commentary, the break that an Interpretive Archaeology attempted to make from the demands of the New or Processual Archaeology was marked by the attempt to see the world from the perspective of those who lived the lives that were represented by archaeological materials, rather than the New Archaeological attempt to explain those lives as the product of some kind of determinate condition that had operated 'behind the backs' of the participants. It is perhaps for this reason that Interpretive Archaeology has found such a resonance with the concepts of human agency and post-colonial theory, simply because both these concepts recognise the rights and the responsibilities that others carry in determining the paths that are traced by their own lives, without being over-written and recolonised from the outside by our 'etic' narratives of 'explanation'.

Following a rule

Up until now archaeology has not prioritised an understanding of what makes the regularities in human behaviour possible. Instead it has claimed that its purpose is to know what structured or determined those regularities. It has been upon this basis that archaeology has sought to *explain* the regularities of behaviour as the result of external stimuli or internal motivations, treating either of these as the response to those external stimuli, or as the expression of internally cognised meanings. An alternative way to think about how we might gain a historical *understanding* of any period is to ask what made an individual's behaviour in that period, practiced amongst that of others, meaningful. It was, after all, the ability to *live meaningfully* in ways that could be understood by others that rendered a way of life understandable. What made this way of living possible by making people understandable to others? The point is not that material culture was 'meaningfully constituted' (as if it were made to represent some cognised meaning), but that different forms of life were lived meaningfully amongst that material culture. Life was, and is still, structured by its reference to things. It was life, not things, that was meaningfully constituted.

In his reflections on the regularities of behaviour that attest to 'following a rule', Ludwig Wittgenstein demonstrated that if such rules were privately formulated (that is, if they were indeed the creation of, and remained the product of, an individual's thinking alone), then any sequence of behaviour, however bizarre, could be explained as if it were rule-bound.

> This was our paradox: no course of action could be determined by a rule, because every course of action can be made to accord with the rule. . . . What this shews is that there is a way of grasping a rule which is *not* an *interpretation*, but which is exhibited in what we call 'obeying the rule' and 'going against it' in actual cases. (Wittgenstein 1968 [1953] §201)
>
> And hence also 'obeying a rule' is a practice. And to *think* one is obeying a rule is not to obey a rule. Hence it is not possible to obey a rule 'privately': otherwise thinking one was obeying a rule would be the same thing as obeying it. (§202)

To follow a rule is therefore to act in ways that others recognise, and such a recognition can only occur within the material context in which the rule-based action is executed.

Following a rule might therefore be better described as a *practice* (Arrington 2001, 129ff.), as if it were a matter of proceeding from one step to the next, a performance that is the ongoing reinvention of how to behave aright. Such a procedure might be described as a routine. Proceeding aright is a judgement of how to take the next step; it is necessarily shared and thus it is socially accountable. Following a rule is therefore to be assessed as such by those who claim a shared understanding of a procedure, it is not something that is asserted by the individual. It is under such a condition that others will respond to express the extent to which they find the agent's behaviour recognisable, and either acceptable or unacceptable. The agent can evaluate themselves whether they have proceeded aright, and sense the degrees of deviancy that might be tolerable. They can do this by monitoring the reaction of others.

Like all life, human life develops through access to the necessary resources of sustenance and protection, a relating to things that is the practical realisation of the qualities of those things. Human life is distinctive in its fragmentation into different kinds of humanness (Barrett 2014a). These various kinds of humanness are performed as different responses to the qualities of things, resulting in the allocation of spaces and resources differentially across a population. In this way the different manifestations of quality become recognisable by experiencing the networks of things, spaces, and people.

Wittgenstein sought 'to bring into prominence the fact that the *speaking* of a language is part of an activity, or a form of life' (Wittgenstein 1968 [1953] §23). This is indeed so, but speaking (the making of words) is normally expected to formulate a meaning relative to the context of the utterance, and this is only part of *all* the activities that are performed amongst the historical conditions and that made a particular form of life possible. It is surely remarkable that the important work that has extended Wittgenstein's philosophy into the social sciences has been undertaken with, at best, minimal reference to the ways that human agency is made out of a socially common revelation as to the qualities of physical things (Winch 2008; Bloor 2002; Gunnell 2014). A language lives not just because we speak it but because others hear and begin to understand what we are saying. And this is just one aspect of an activity that becomes understandable because it is directed towards things in ways that others might be expected to comprehend.

The argument that I am attempting to develop here is likely to fail to meet the expectation that archaeology's aim should be to establish the kinds of causal conditions that have resulted in human communities organising themselves in particular ways. However, to follow a rule, that is to live within a material and traditional context in ways that made sense to the self and to others, means that an understanding of the qualities and values of things was expressed by the practices that others were able to assess. By so doing, certain material conditions that supported understandable forms of social life were reproduced and developed institutionally (cf. Bloor 2002, 27ff.). These are therefore self-organising systems and there is nothing deeper, no ultimate and determinate cause to uncover. Our aim is to do no more than to grasp something of an understanding of how these systems of meaningful behaviour formed and were sustained, and thus how other forms of life other than our own were once possible before they passed into history.

The question of human exceptionalism

Up to this point we have been concerned to follow the traditional emphasis that archaeology places upon the identification and the consequent analysis of material residues. This has ensured that archaeological residues are identified as being of interest because they are believed to represent, and thus inform us upon an earlier human presence. It is for this reason that archaeology has studied things, and initially this study appears to have enabled archaeology to get at the 'Indian behind the artefact' (Braidwood 1958, 734), before moving to model 'the system behind both the Indian and the artefact' (Flannery 1967, 120). Two problems have accompanied this treatment of things as the representations of people's actions. First, and most recently, doubts have been raised concerning the ways that materials have been treated archaeologically as if the importance of those things was limited to their role as the representations of the human presence. The second problem concerns the largely unexamined assumptions that have underpinned the reasons offered for the changing patterns of human behaviour. The latter problem consumed the efforts of theoretical archaeology at the end of the twentieth century, whilst the issues surrounding the status of the material itself have now emerged as a more recent concern (Harris & Cipolla 2017). Fundamental to this latter concern is the distinction that is traditionally drawn between living things (with the archaeological emphasis upon humans) and non-living materials.

The distinction drawn between these two states of existence permeated all archaeological analysis throughout the twentieth century. It is upon this distinction that material residues have been widely treated as a record of humanity's presence in its various historical forms of organisation, its patterns of behaviour, and its impacts upon the wider environment. Put simply, humans acted on material conditions that were otherwise passive and the traces of those actions, inscribed upon the material, are recovered archaeologically. The result of this reasoning has been to build an archaeology that is clearly anthropocentric in its focus: things are archaeologically significant because they represent people's behaviour. Recent objections have called into question this way of treating all things, as if the existence of non-living things (as well as the remains of plants and animals) only mattered because they provided a way to reference the human presence. Surely, so the argument goes, the reality of all things has always existed and it is one that extends well beyond their relationship to the human subject. Consequently, it is misleading for archaeology to assign things to such human categories as 'prestige objects' in ways that do not appear to recognise their larger reality (Webmoor 2007). Olsen has expressed his own dissatisfaction with the dominance of the current humanistic archaeology and its reading of the material in representational terms. He writes:

> I am tired of the familiar story of how the subject, the social, the episteme, created the object; tired of the story that everything is language, action, mind and human bodies. I want us to pay more attention to the other half of this story: how objects construct the subject. (Olsen 2003, 100)

Paying attention to the 'other half of the story' has involved drawing upon a diverse range of approaches that share the common recognition that all past realities have comprised complex relationships between all the things then existing (Jervis 2019). In a radical move this position denies the distinction between living and non-living things. It states that all things are 'vibrant' in their various ways (Bennett 2010) and all such things existed together in the historical conditions that are examined archaeologically. These existences ranged well beyond the traditional priorities of the human presence, which archaeology has attempted to 'see' in terms of the human actions that resulted in a material record. The past therefore included that mass of things of which humanity was but a part, and this includes the things of which that humanity was either unaware at the time or, at most, only partly aware, and all things carry properties that are withdrawn and unavailable to human perceptions. The immediate challenge posed by this turn towards things-as-things, is that archaeology should now become a discipline that is concerned with the reality of the past as a manifestation of all things, rather than remain focused upon the past as it if it were constituted as a human past. Matthew Edgeworth has suggested that the recent turn towards things is underpinned by the desire to get beyond an understanding of things merely in terms of their 'correlation' with the human presence (Edgeworth 2016, 93). Correlationism insists 'that we can never grasp an object "in itself", in isolation from its relation to the subject' (Meillassoux 2008, 5). But what might archaeology gain by adopting a stance against correlationism, and by so doing acknowledge the need to understand the reality of all things as they have existed?

There is clearly the potential for considerable confusion here. Let us therefore start by accepting that archaeological materials, as an assemblage of material relationships, have only ever been part of the wider assemblage of relationships that enabled various categories of materials and various forms of life to come into being (cf. Latour 2005). The demand that we should establish what is, and what was, 'really real', as opposed to those things that were made real by and for humans by means of their actions, experiences, and perceptions, might be referred to as marking a turn towards a 'new materialism' in archaeology (Olsen et al. 2012). We need to distinguish between this 'turn' and a concern with ontological statements that are taken to be statements about the reality of actually existing conditions (Ribeiro 2018a). The question here is whether ontological statements are believed to concern statements about the world, independently of human perceptions of how that world is, as in 'there is only one world, despite there being many ways of living in it' (a single ontology), or whether we accept that because diverse human perceptions were, and are, part of reality, this therefore helps to sustain the idea that there are many different realities and thus many different ontologies (Alberti 2016). I assume that recent calls for an 'ontological turn' in archaeology are a call to adopt the latter position.

A further possible confusion is that the new materialism, and the concerns with issues of ontology, are both distinct from the questions that are raised by archaeology's traditional analysis of things. The latter is a question of epistemology, it concerns the ways that things have been treated as a way of establishing an archaeological knowledge of the past. My point here is that epistemological procedures must be designed with reference to what it is that we want to know. The differences of the approaches that we have traced in this and in previous chapters have concerned archaeologists wanting to know the ways human actions were organised and, optimistically, to establish what might have motivated those actions. My argument is that contrary to these common approaches, archaeology should want to know how varieties of humanness constructed themselves. How we therefore know the world, and how that world is in reality, are not one and the same thing (Bhaskar 1997).

Conclusion

Archaeology is certainly a discipline of things (Olsen et al. 2012), but it is a discipline of things that operates *with the specific purpose* of understanding how human histories became possible within particular material contexts (Barrett 2014a & 2016). I argue, therefore, that the ontological move that archaeology needs to take is one that treats the things that we study as a way of understanding how forms of humanness gained their particular historical existences. That they did this by reference to the things amongst which they grew and developed (cf. Hodder 2012) renders the process open to archaeological investigation. This returns us to Olsen's desire to understand 'how objects construct the subject' (Olsen 2003, 100), and it starts by maintaining the duality between the subject and the object, between forms of life and things. However, it inverts the argument traditionally maintained by archaeology. We treat things as making forms of human life, rather than treating those things as if they were merely the products of human actions. The duality that distinguishes between humans and things is thus maintained in this epistemology but not, as Harris and Cipolla appear to think (2017), because thinking in dichotomies is a pathological characteristic of modern thought. Instead it is the historical construction of that duality, by means of the emergence of various forms of humanity within given material contexts, that is the historical process that archaeology is attempting to understand (cf. Hodder 2012, 10).

6

THE EVOLUTION OF ECOSYSTEMS

Introduction

My aim is to break from the current archaeological consensus. This consensus accepts that archaeological materials result from processes associated with the behaviours of an earlier humanity, and as such they should inform us about those behaviours. The processes that structured the organisation of these behaviours are treated as if they ranged from the need for humans to adapt to changing environmental and social conditions, to the desire to express a cognised order among the things that those humans used and produced. The ultimate aim of the current consensus is to explain why the patterns of the recovered material remains, and thus the organisations of past human behaviour, changed historically and geographically. Various traditions of archaeological theory and methodology have been developed to enable this kind of investigation.

It is a consensus that treats human behaviour as the variable requiring investigation, rather than investigating the possibility that humanity is itself the historical variable. Humanity is therefore treated as a constant, but one that has operated historically by means of different behavioural traditions. Archaeology has thus sought to explain the variation in behaviour as if it had been prompted by various stimuli acting upon a single kind of humanity, and history becomes the history of different kinds of behaviour and their various stimuli. But what if the history of humanity is written to trace the paths followed by radically different forms of humanness? The contrast is between humanity as a constant, and humanity as fractured into different forms of humanness; that is, the contrast is between a humanity that has responded to different kinds of stimuli, and the forms of humanness that created themselves by interpreting the different worlds in which they developed (Graeber 2015).

If a Middle Palaeolithic flint knapper did indeed sacrifice a mouse as Childe envisaged (Childe 1956, 171; see page 33), before working on a flint nodule, then that sacrifice would have had the function of securing, for that knapper, the success of their flint working, and the mouse would have been a very different kind of rodent than the one that is known to us today. If we claim, as did Childe, that we now know that such a sacrifice was an unnecessary precursor to the successful working of the nodule, then that would be to claim that the world 'out there' is the same world for us as it was for that knapper who had operated upon that same world, but who had done so through a kind of cultural distortion, and that our knowledge of that world therefore supersedes hers. Mice, from this perspective, have always been 'just mice' as we now define them, even if we also happen to be less than proficient at flint knapping. Eduardo Viveiros de Castro has described another world which is inhabited by many different persons that are embodied in a variety of different physical forms, each of which sees the world from their own perspective (1998 & 2017), and he recognises that:

> it is unlikely that any nonmodern cosmology can be adequately described either by means of such conceptual polarities [*as the modern polarities that distinguish between nature and culture*] or as a simple negation of them (as if the only point of a nonmodern cosmology were to stand in opposition to our oppositions). (Viveiros de Castro 2004, 464 insertion mine)

Those others did not exist for our amusement, but we might, in all humility, learn something of ourselves from the kinds of persons that they were, and the worlds in which they had lived.

Childe's mouse-sacrificing flint knapper would certainly have experienced some of the same forces that we also experience – the ways that flint fractures as the result of percussion, for example – but the effectiveness of the flint-knapping process will have been experienced in ways quite different from own experiences today. Doubts concerning the claim that the one real world is overlain by various cultural representations (the distinction between the timeless constancy of things and the variability of human thoughts about those things) have recently been reviewed by Harris and Cipolla (2017). Their questioning of this view seems to result in adopting one of two alternative analytical procedures. The first abandons the idea that we are investigating the ways that humans like us once interpreted, or acted upon, the same material conditions that we also confront but in ways that differ from our own interpretations of that same world. Instead it accepts that multiple worlds must have existed to enable different kinds of humanness to develop. Whilst not agreeing with this position as it has been employed in some anthropological studies, Ingold has characterised it as one in which the:

> [w]ays of knowing the world . . . are inseparable from ways of being in it, and what these ways bring forth are worlds in themselves that can be neither reduced to elementary constituents common to all nor sublimated into superordinate structures of thought. (Ingold 2016, 302)

The second procedure is to claim that archaeology is simply the study of the surviving assemblages of things that actually exist for us. While these things once included various forms of humans amongst their number, and while we might use these things to write history, there is no inherent need for their existence to be legitimated by a correlation with that prior human existence (Olsen 2013). The two alternatives therefore range between multiple realities (multiple ontologies: Alberti 2016) and a 'flat' ontology in which, while things certainly vary in terms of their forms and their qualities, those assemblages that matter archaeologically do so without any priority granted to them by the human presence, or indeed without privileging any particular substance over any other (Harman 2018, 54; Olsen et al. 2012; Jervis 2019).

While others have reviewed these various ontological moves (Ribeiro 2018a), my concern in this book is to argue that the realities open to archaeological investigation were once known as the means of bringing other forms of humanness into existence. This extends well beyond the conventional assumption in which surviving material residues are understood as the representations of the actions of the same kinds of humans as ourselves. It also extends well beyond the study of things devoid of a human presence. My aim is therefore to establish how different forms of life once brought themselves into existence by performing their own interpretations of the conditions amongst which they grew and developed (cf. Graeber 2015). The resulting diversities of life developed as the products of a biocultural perception.

In an attempt to think about this issue, I will claim that archaeology has not adequately investigated how humanity has brought itself into being, a 'becoming' that comprises various forms of humanness. This emergence of humanity did not happen once, as the result of biological evolution several thousands of years ago, but has been, and remains, an ongoing historical process. The making (or the becoming) of the human is the result of what I will term *biocultural mechanisms*, and it is these mechanisms that have given rise to the considerable diversity that has characterised the practices of the various forms of humanness. It is the histories of the ways that humanness has created itself that, I argue, should be the object of archaeological investigation.

What is life? Systems of biological development

It is nearly eighty years since the three lectures given by Erwin Schrödinger at Trinity College, Dublin were published (Schrödinger 1944). The title that Schrödinger chose for those lectures, and which he maintained in their publication, was: 'What is Life?' It's a simple enough question, and others have since responded, or have posed the same question in the titles of their own works (e.g., Murphy & O'Neill 1995; Margulis & Sagan 1995; Pross 2012; cf. Lazcano 2008). While it has proven possible to list the attributes that many are prepared to accept as being present amongst all living things, it seems that a single, agreed, answer to the question by which life might be defined has remained elusive (Tirard et al. 2010; Kauffman 2019). Nonetheless, all living systems must share a common level of organisation 'which makes a living system a whole, autonomous unity' and where 'reproduction and evolution *are not* constitutive features of the living organization' (Varela et al. 1974, 187, my emphasis). The exclusion of reproduction and evolution from the possible definition of life is because a living organism needs to develop to maturity before it is capable of reproducing, and thus before it can contribute to the possible trajectory of an evolutionary sequence. Living things therefore exist and develop before they can reproduce, and in these terms, they can be identified as autopoietic systems (self-producing or self-developing systems) comprising a network of the components that maintain the further production of those same components (by their growth and repair). It is by these processes of self-production that the organism grows to maturity.

The individual human originates as a single fertilised cell (a zygote) in the womb of the mother before that cell then starts to divide to produce the cells that build the organs of the foetus, the child, and then the adult. The biological process of this self-production is common to any complex organism, and it is one in which the components of that organism continue to produce and repair themselves throughout the organism's lifetime. With the important exception of the foetus's initial development being dependent upon the mother's body, this development and ageing proceeds without the work of an external agency (Rosen 1991). By this I mean that the organism has no external designer or labourer, and it is this that distinguishes its making and remaking from the making and repairing of a machine. Biological systems, the simplest example of which is the cellular stage of development, originate by building an enclosing membrane or skin (Hoffmeyer 2008, 17–38), and this forms the boundary condition that constrains the operation of the organism's internal mechanisms (Montévil & Massio 2015). It is across the semi-permeable boundary of this skin that the necessary flows of energy occur which facilitate the internal work of self-production. Starting from the premise that systems of living matter 'are not adequately described simply as a matter of complex configurations of physical or biochemical processes' (El-Hani et al. 2009, 5), we must understand that all forms of life are biological systems that can only exist as processes of self-production when entwined within various environmental conditions.

If we hope to understand the origins of life, then it is the origins of these systems of self-producing order that we need to understand and the ways that they metabolise energy (Kauffman 1993), rather than the origins of life originating with the means of biological transmission (reproduction) along with its subsequent evolution. It is from this non-evolutionary perspective that the idea of the gene must also be understood, namely in terms of the way that it functions within the cellular process, rather than from the perspective of its supposed role in the transmission of inherited traits (Schrödinger 1944; Dawkins 1978 [1976]). It has been by emphasising the processes of transmission that the function of the gene's role in carrying units of information from one generation to the next has been brought to the fore, with the result that the gene has been treated as if the information that it supposedly carried determines the formation of the cell, and thus of the organism as a whole. However, the question that we need to ask is not 'what does the gene do *for* the cell?', but 'what does the cell do *with* the gene?' (cf. El-Hani et al. 2009).

The definition of what we might mean by the concept of a gene is certainly complex, even to the point that its physical existence has been questioned (Falk 1986; Fogle 1990). Instead of regarding the gene as a unit of information (Maynard Smith 2000), or indeed as being physically manifest in a particular stretch of DNA, it would be more accurate to treat the gene as the outcome of a *process* that resulted from the operation of the elements within the cell, and it is this *process* that gives rise to the cell's function. The problem then becomes how we should conceive of the processes that are involved in cellular replication and the subsequent growth of the organism. In addressing this problem, I follow the current work on biosemiotics (Hoffmeyer 2008; Kull et al. 2009) with its commitment to the Peircean theory of the sign (cf. Hoopes 1991).

The Peircean sign has three elements: (1) the sign vehicle that stands for or indicates (2) some object or value as it is recognised by (3) an interpretant. If the organism is conceived of as an emergent state of becoming that arises from the cellular mechanisms that operate as interpretants, then these interpretive processes employ the chemistry of DNA as a sign vehicle, and they result in the production of proteins. It is these proteins that determine the work that the cell will undertake (its function). This cellular work-cycle is a process sustained by catalysing the energy that can be imported across the cell's membrane from an environmental substrate. Genes are thus only known to us by the ways that certain sections of the DNA code are expressed, and the idea of the gene satisfies our need to identify the agency that causes the formation of proteins. Consequently, we should accept that genes are the objectification of a process by which the sign vehicle of DNA is interpreted in the building and replication of a cell. DNA is matter, and it is the agency of its interpretation that gets us from that matter to its mattering (cf. Kauffman 2019), a 'mattering' which we now characterise by reference to genetics. It follows that the making of life is an interpretive process and the organism's development is a more complex process than the one implied by the traditional claim that the genes provide a 'blueprint' that determines the design of an organism (Moss 2003; Pigliucci 2010).

Given that organisms are built by the accretion of cells, then complex cells (that is eukaryotic cells with a nucleus and with divisions within the surrounding cytoplasm) are, as Lynn Margulis demonstrated, constructed by a process of symbiosis that involves the merger of different simple (prokaryotic) cells. Prokaryotic cells lack a nucleus and are represented today by bacteria and by the biological family of *Archaea*:

> [m]olecular biological, genetic, and high-powered microscopic studies . . . confirm the once radical nineteenth-century idea that the cells of plants and of our animal bodies, as well as those of fungi and all other organisms

> composed of cells with nuclei, originated though mergers of different types
> of bacteria in a specific sequence. (Margulis 1998, 30)

The implication of Margulis's work was radical. Whilst 'the origin of life was concurrent with bacteria', and given that 'bacteria do not have species at all', then speciation is 'a property only of nucleated organisms' that originated 'long after bacteria had evolved nearly all the important metabolic traits displayed by life on earth' (Margulis & Sagan 2002, 55). The origin of life is not, therefore, the origin of speciation.

An organism is a form of life that is therefore a 'far from equilibrium' system, which grows to maturity by the internal agencies of interpretation that are themselves dependent upon the extraction and metabolism of energy from that organism's environment. The reliable development of complex organisms, as given by their long-lived lineages, occurs 'because of reliable interactions between the developing organism and its environment' (Griffiths & Gray 1994, 280). If the reliability of these interactions within an ecology is the process that secures the long-term stability witnessed by the lineage of a form of life, then this counts against the Darwinian assumption that evolutionary change within a species should occur gradually, through the step-by-step modification in the reproduction of individuals, extending over several generations (Darwin 2009 [1859], 278–305). Indeed, the fossil record has failed to reveal these gradual changes (Gould 2002, 840–850; *contra* Dennett 1996, 282–299), and the fossil record confirms the long-term stability in the phenotypic form of a species (Eldredge 1995, 64–78). This stability is then interspersed by horizons of rapid change with the appearance of new species occurring alongside horizons of extinction. It was in light of empirical evidence such as this that Niles Eldredge and Stephen J. Gould proposed that a model of punctuated equilibria was the better description for the shape of evolutionary change than a model of gradual change (Gould & Eldredge 1977). The important point here is that rapid horizons of 'phase change' are to be expected in the history of complex systems (Kauffman 1995, 116–118), meaning that the empirical observations drawn from the fossil record support an approach which looks to the evolution of complex ecosystems, rather than the evolution of relatively autonomous species, or the natural selection of single, mutating, genetic lineages.

It is this complex process of ecosystemic development that evolves, a process of 'downward causation' (Dupré 2010) in which the developing organism is situated within the relations upon which it depends, and it is able to build itself within the changing components of its ecosystem. The relationships of life comprise the flows of materials, energy, and information that are identified from beyond the skin of the organism, and are employed in its development. These ecosystems evolve over time (Oyama 2000), and the description of this form of biocultural evolution could be simply treated as if it were the description of 'all of history' (Margulis 1998, 24).

If archaeology is concerned to understand the ways that forms of humanness have emerged, rather than being an attempt to explain the reasons for the changing patterns of material residue, then such an archaeology will have to treat those residues as part of the conditions of possibility from which a kind of humanness might have constructed itself. Archaeological materials are the residues of those environments within which forms of life, including forms of humanness, have found it possible to live. Humanness was the agency that interpreted those environments; as Stuart Kauffman puts it, '[a]gency introduces meaning into the world! Agency is fundamental to life' (Kauffman 2019, 91).

Why history is not a matter of Darwinian evolution but of biocultural development

The trace of an evolutionary process is marked by the selective transmission of traits over time, and in its recent form, biological evolution has been treated as if the process was governed by the principles of neo-Darwinism (Dawkins 1999; Dennett 1996). These principles focus upon the claim that evolution is the transmission, under natural selection, of genetic material. The further claim is that it is the totality of this material, the genotype, that determines the form of the phenotype. Archaeology, on the other hand, when it is treated as if its purpose is to produce an evolutionary narrative, must concern itself with the ways that various forms of life, in particular the various forms of human life, have been able to develop, and the ways that those processes of development might have changed across both time and space. It is from this latter perspective that archaeology should be treated as the study of the historical conditions within which forms of humanness have developed. It is important to clarify the distinction between neo-Darwinism as it has been applied within biology, and the archaeology of the changing conditions by which forms of life have been able to develop. The direction of neo-Darwinian evolution is determined by natural selection acting on the random inheritance of trait mutations within a population (Mayr 1976, 26–29). By way of contrast, the direction of historical development, which I am arguing for here, is determined by the organism's ability to orientate its own development as the interpretant of the ecosystem of which it is a part.

Given this contrast, I would argue that archaeology's priority cannot be one of tracing the transmission of traits of behaviour, social organisations, or styles of material culture, across the generations, as if these represented the presence and operations of an inherited human trait, but rather to understand the ways communities of humanness once orientated their particular developments with reference to the material and cultural conditions within which those developments took place. And if the neo-Darwinian paradigm, with its emphasis upon the natural selection of random mutations, has indeed died, as many would now claim, having been 'brought down by the weight of its own internal contradictions' (Ingold 2013, 1), then we need to understand why it was ever adopted in the first place, and to be aware of the ideas that have died along with it.

Darwin (2009 [1859]) provided an argument for how biological reproduction could result in species diversity, and consequently he questioned the idea that species diversity was the unchanging product of a momentarily executed design.

In the Darwinian argument it is the reproduction of life that generates the possibilities that are selected for. The following three things should be noted.

First, Darwin did not know what mechanism carried heritable traits from one generation to the next. In 1900 the experimental results that had been achieved nearly fifty years earlier by Gregor Mendel were rediscovered (Jablonka & Lamb 2005, 16–38). These experiments involved controlling the cross-pollination of plants of the pea family, and they demonstrated the particulate and statistically predictable inheritance of individual traits from one generation to the next. The implication appeared to be that such traits were carried by some singular, determinate factor: a unit of inheritance that the Danish botanist Wilhelm Johannsen named the gene, and from whence he defined the 'genotype' as the totality of inherited genetic information that gave rise to the 'phenotype' as a functioning assemblage of traits (Roll-Hansen 2009). The general synthesis of Mendelian inheritance with Darwinian evolution resulted in a distinction being drawn between the phenotype, which is the physical form of the organism upon which, in this model, natural selection acts, and the genotype, being the inherited material, the long-term survival of which is consequential upon natural selection. At the end of the nineteenth century, the biologist August Wiseman had rejected claims that acquired characteristics could be inherited by their being included within the biological material contained in the germ line (i.e. the sperm or ovum cells in sexual reproduction) (Dawkins 1999, 113). In the early 1950s the chemical structure for the gene was accepted as having been identified by Francis Crick and James Watson who, drawing upon the images of X-ray crystallography that had been prepared by Rosalind Franklin, established the famous image of the DNA molecule that is defined by two intertwined polymer strands, weakly bound together by paired bonds formed between four different kinds of nucleobases. DNA thus came to be identified with the basic chemical structure that carried genetic information inherited from one generation to the next (Maynard Smith 2000; Jablonka 2002).

Second, the Darwinian paradigm requires that natural selection must work upon inherited diversity, although diversity within a reproducing population would seem to be reduced over time as a consequence of the operation of natural selection. This apparent contradiction lies at the heart of the Darwinian model of evolution, and it must be overcome by the necessary injection of genetic diversity into the lineages of reproduction. This injection of diversity is supposedly achieved either by mutations that occur during the transfer of genetic information across the generations, or by the drift of new genetic material into a gene pool via the migration of new members into the breeding population (Godfrey-Smith 2009, 53–67). Neither of these suggested solutions appears to be particularly straightforward in sustaining the required diversity of inherited information. Inherited mutations certainly occur although they are guarded against by various biological 'editing' procedures, and when they do occur, they are often catastrophic for the success of the reproductive process (cf. Margulis & Sagan 2002, 29). Genetic drift is also certainly a possibility (Godfrey-Smith 2009, 27–31), although the migration of new genetic material into a population does not account for the evolution of those populations that have become isolated geographically and environmentally, as appears to be required by the model of allopatric speciation.

Third, in 1866 Alfred Wallace wrote to Darwin recommending that he adopt Herbert Spencer's term 'survival of the fittest' as a way of clarifying what he meant by the process of 'natural selection' (www.darwinproject.ac.uk/letter/DCP-LETT-5140.xml#back-mark-5140.f5). Unfortunately, Darwin readily concurred (Dawkins 1999, 179–194), and this has helped to secure the image of evolution as a process of competition between individual organisms. The claim that 'natural selection' implies competition between individuals was initially opposed by the observations and the arguments developed by the anarchist Peter Kropotkin (1902 & 1971, 498–499), although these were ignored at that time and have been ignored since. Writing from a gene-centred perspective on the process of natural selection Richard Dawkins complains that 'fitness' has become a 'verbal trick, . . . contrived to make it possible to talk in terms of individuals, as opposed to true replicators' (i.e. genes in Dawkins's model) (Dawkins 1999, 179). The confusion, as far as Dawkins is concerned, is the focus that the phrase 'survival and the fittest' places upon the reproductive success of the organism when 'that reproductive success is a measure of success in passing on genes' (Dawkins 1999, 185). If this emphasis upon an individual organism's success were indeed warranted, then it would render the occurrence of altruism between organisms a problematic characteristic of behaviour. Why, where individuals were supposedly competing for reproductive success against other conspecifics, would some individuals sacrifice that success on behalf of the success of others and thus also leave the way open for free-loaders and cheats to benefit from their generosity (Trivers 1971)? Considerable effort has gone into building the arguments that have counteracted these concerns from a 'genes point of view'. These arguments have continued to emphasise that natural selection is a matter of genetic survival, and they are based upon William Hamilton's model of inclusive fitness (Hamilton 1964a & 1964b). Inclusive fitness concerns the effects that a pattern of behaviours will have upon the successful reproduction of organisms that are genetically related (Dawkins 1999). Inclusive fitness is a relative, and not an absolute, measure. Hamilton's argument, which strongly influenced the work of Dawkins, was that selection operates on organisms in ways that tend to sustain the behaviours that best secure the reproduction of a particular suite of genes. Inclusive fitness demands altruistic behaviour from individual organisms as a way to ensure the successful reproduction of some proportion of a shared genetic inheritance.

While Darwin had challenged the immutable status of the species as if it were a product of a deistic creation, neo-Darwinian modelling of biological reproduction has meant that natural selection, acting upon the reproduction of organisms with their relatively brief lifespans, appears to result in the ongoing, and cross-generational, survival of the successful lineages that define a species. The 'genes'-eye' view of neo-Darwinian evolution has been well expressed by Richard Dawkins who attributed to organisms the relatively passive role of 'vehicles' that were built, carried, and whose place in various classifications of the natural world was determined by, the more active existence of genetic 'replicators' (Dawkins 1978 [1976]). From this perspective it seemed reasonable to characterise genes as 'selfish' because they only exist to be replicated. The evolution of altruism could then be explained, as we have implied, by the process of 'inclusive fitness', where the altruistic sacrifice of an organism's reproductive potential was taken to increase the survival chances of some proportion of the genetic replicators which that organism shared with its kin.

The claim that the natural selection of a genotypic determinant had designed all forms of life was the basis of the argument offered by E.O. Wilson in his *Sociobiology: The New Synthesis* (Wilson 1975). Arguments such as this have meant that any attempt to introduce a biological reasoning into an understanding of human history has been met with widespread suspicion. My intention here is indeed to utilise current biological ideas in seeking to understand human history, although the basis for doing this is quite different from that which was evoked by sociobiology. In the case of the latter approach, a neo-Darwinian form of biological inheritance is treated as if it were determining human behaviour. It is this approach that has been rejected by those working in the social sciences, as well as by some biologists (e.g. Sahlins 1977; Barlow & Silverberg 1980). The reactions against sociobiology have been partly sustained by the continuing desire to distinguish the processes of human history, as an expression of human intentions and arising from a human consciousness, from those of biological evolution that are supposedly genetically determined and directed by the processes of natural selection.

Resistance to various arguments for a biological determinacy driving human behaviour has depended in part upon distinguishing between human expressions of cultural value as the motivations for human actions, and processes of 'natural' or instinctive behaviour occurring generally across the animal kingdom. The culture:nature dichotomy continues to pose the problem of explaining how human conscious behaviour evolved from the natural selection of the random mutations that supposedly drove biological reproduction. For many commentators this does not seem to be a problem. Indeed, it has even been claimed that the Darwinian principle of the natural selection of inherited variability is applicable beyond the biological case of genetic/species evolution. Dennett, for example, writes that '[i]n a single stroke, the idea of evolution by natural selection unifies the realm of life, meaning, and purpose with the realm of space and time, cause and effect, mechanism and physical law' (Dennett 1996, 21).

If this were indeed the case then all of history could presumably be treated as if it had resulted from the natural selection of transmittable variables, where those variables were 'blindly' generated by what is, in Dennett's view, some form of algorithm. The more general application of Darwinian principles, alongside the neo-Darwinian emphasis upon the selective transmission of genes, was attempted by Dawkins who, by treating Darwinism as 'too big a theory to be confined to the narrow context of the gene' (Dawkins 1978 [1976], 205), raised the possibility that human life is structured by the inheritance of both biological genes and cultural 'memes' (Dawkins 1978 [1976], 203–215). Memes have been treated as the transmittable units of cultural information (Blackmore 1999; Aunger 2002), and these two lines of biological and cultural transmission provide the basis for an assumed process of dual inheritance (Boyd & Richerson 1985; Richerson & Boyd 2005). If cultural inheritance is governed by the teaching and copying of units of behaviour and thought, where variability results from randomised innovation along with the rapid drift of ideas and their mutation, and where selection may arise as the result of various social demands, whilst being otherwise biologically neutral, then the Darwinian principle of descent with modification appears to remain applicable to cultural systems of inheritance (O'Brien 1996; Shennan 2002). But how does cultural behaviour emerge from the evolutionary process: how do cultural values emerge from those of nature?

The distinction between the processes of a human cultural world and those of natural evolution is not, I suggest, to be dissolved by treating the former as if it were simply determined by a reductionist view of the latter (Wilson 1999). Instead I seek, as an alternative, the view that life is responsive, must thus be accepted as being conscious (Thompson 2007), in which agency is fundamental to the making of life (Kauffman 2019), and where both consciousness and agency ensure that life expresses an intentionality towards the things that matter to it.

> We humans, then, are not the only ones who interpret the world. 'Aboutness' – representation, intention, and purpose in their most basic forms – is an intrinsic structuring feature of living dynamics in the biological world. Life is inherently semiotic. (Kohn 2013, 74)

Primarily, the things that matter to life are the foods that provide it with the necessary energy to grow and develop, but in this process humanness, as a form of life, has developed an intentionality towards things that also have a cultural value. As far as I can see this view of intentionality conforms with Dennett's view 'that a particular thing is an Intentional system only in relation to the strategies of someone who is trying to explain and predict its behavior' (Dennett 1971, 87).

Post-Darwinism

The long-term continuity of genetic inheritance is now being questioned (Morange 2006), partly because the preservation of the inherited structure of DNA from one generation to the next is doubted (Charney 2012), and partly because the evidence for the horizontal transfer of genetic material between bacteria (Chan & Bhattacharya 2013; Skippington & Ragan 2011), organisms (Dunning et al. 2019), and from viruses to host organisms can be both demonstrated experimentally and, as we all know only too well, experienced practically. In other words, the replication of lengths of DNA material (a.k.a. genes) does not appear to preserve the stability of that material as was once thought and from this perspective the security of species continuity appears to be vulnerable. The fact that long-term species stability is witnessed in palaeontology might therefore reflect more on the continuity with which genetic material is edited and interpreted than on the continuity of that material itself. If we allow that biological evolution is witnessed by changes in the composition of the reproducing population, given that populations are themselves characterised by the growth, development, and death of their individual members, then it follows that continuity lies in the inherited processes of development of the individuals that make up those populations, and that this depends more upon the continuities in the larger ecosystem than it does upon genetic continuity alone. This is a topic to which we must return in the next two chapters.

The emphasis placed upon genetics as the carrier of inherited information, as if this information alone operated as a set of instructions that determined the form of the organism, treats the form and behaviour of the organism (i.e., the phenotype) as if it was predetermined by the inherited units of genetic information. If, on the other hand, we treat the organism as an ongoing process of growth and development (Oyama 2000; Oyama et al. 2001), then the niche context towards which that organism's life is orientated is the context that secured the continuity of the developmental process. Ingold and Palsson (2013), along with their colleagues, have characterised the organism whose form is determined by its inheritance as concerning the state of the 'being' of a particular life-form, and they have contrasted this with life as a process of 'becoming'. In other words, forms of life are not predetermined and given, instead they are processes of 'becoming', they are developing and growing. The point of departure for Oyama, Ingold, Palsson, and others then becomes the move away from the neo-Darwinian programme at the point at which we might treat evolution *not* as the path followed by the transmission, under the control of natural selection, of the determinate units of genetic information, but as the changing processes by which particular forms of life have been able to develop and so bring themselves into existence by their use of the resources that are available to them (Godfrey-Smith 2009). As Ingold has argued, evolution:

> does not lie in the mutation, recombination, replication and selection of transmissible traits. It is rather a life process. And at the heart of this process is ontogenesis. The failure to account for the ontogenetic emergence of phenotypic form is the Achilles heel of the entire neo-Darwinian paradigm. For it has proceeded as if the form were already there, prefigured in the virtual space of the genotype or its cultural equivalent. (Ingold 2013, 6)

The developmental processes that affect the growth of individual organisms and organic systems are more than the result of a genetic blueprint directing an individual's development, given that genes (or for that matter memes, if either were to actually exist) do not actually do anything. The many developmental resources inherited by an individual, and which extend well beyond the DNA molecule, include the contexts that enable inherited information to be acted upon. Recent moves towards a 'post-Darwinian' model of evolution (Kull 1999) are therefore based upon the need to understand the evolution of the organism's developmental processes that are directed towards its growth within particular niche ecologies (Oyama 2000).

From the perspective of evolutionary development (sometimes referred to as 'EvoDevo') the content or meaning of an information source, such as the DNA within a cell, or the food and resources of security beyond the organism, is not contained in the material itself but it is assembled by the processes enacted by the agency of a developing interpretant. It is an approach that is understood from the perspective of Peirce's theory of semiotics (El-Hani et al. 2009). Peirce established semiosis as the processes in which an interpretant, having identified a sign as standing for some object or quality, responds to that identification. In biological terms the living cell contains facilities for which segments of DNA specify some mode of reaction by the interpretant, and where the interpretant should be seen as the process that traces the cell's development.

The treatment of life as a semiotic process (Hoffmeyer 2008; Emmeche & Kull 2011; Kull et al. 2009) therefore questions any distinction that is drawn between a biological determinism, as applied to the agencies of the so-called natural or living world, and a cultural indeterminism, as it is applied to a human enculturated agency. By overcoming the nature:culture dichotomy in our understanding of the making of life, the process of semiosis means that we can understand the development of life in general as a process of self-definition and self-making (Maturana & Varela 1980). This self-making process is only possible because biological systems identify and interpret available sources of information and exploit the available sources of energy (metabolism) that together sustain a particular niche of adaptation (Odling-Smee et al. 2003). Understanding this process sustains the claim that life is, in general, conscious at various levels. This means that life recognises the conditions that sustain its development (Thompson 2007), and it therefore acts with intentionality (that is, it acts towards the object of material conditions that sustain it). If this argument is accepted then the discipline of biology is situated between what would today be regarded as the natural sciences and those regarded as the humanities.

Much has therefore changed, or is at least changing, to move us away from the gene-centred view of life that once so annoyed Gould (1980). It was Gould who commented on the emphasis upon genetics as 'a theory developed entirely from understanding the nature of constituent matter in its smallest pieces', a reductionist theory that has dominated the biological and 'popular science' literature in the third quarter of the last century (Huneman & Walsh 2017a). Today it is possible to chart our understanding of life's diversity as shifting from a perception of that diversity as the result of the selective transmission of lineages of genetic information, towards a perception of life concerning the development of organisms as part of a wider ecology. Darwin chose to close his 1859 volume (along with all of its subsequent editions) with a contemplation upon 'an entangled bank, clothed with many plants of many kinds, with birds singing on the bushes, with various insects flitting about, and with worms crawling through the damp earth' (Darwin 2009 [1859], 426).

It was by this means that he invited reflection upon the processes that had constructed each of these diverse forms of life. We can now recognise this entangled bank as an ecology that cannot be characterised simply as if it were a mechanistic assemblage of separate genetic lineages; rather, it is a complex system of development where each part of the system is integrated within the whole, and where the whole displays emergent qualities that cannot be calculated as if the sum of the parts made up the whole. It is in this light that Capra and Luisi have noted that the:

> outstanding property of all life is the tendency to form multileveled structures of systems within systems . . . cells combine to form tissues, tissues to form organs, and organs to form organisms. These in turn exist within social systems and ecosystems. . . . The properties of the parts are not intrinsic properties, but can be understood only within the context of the larger whole. (Capra & Luisi 2014, 64–66)

Conclusion

The critique of the neo-Darwinian synthesis rejects the idea that 'the component processes of evolution – inheritance, development, innovation and adaptive population change – are discrete and quasi-autonomous' (Huneman & Walsh 2017b, 2). We might also question the category of *species* that has achieved the status of describing the different kinds of life as if they were the relatively static building blocks making up an ecology and operating as the mutable vehicles of Darwinian evolution. Perhaps we need to move beyond ideas of multispecies interaction (cf. Birch 2018) and find a language that better treats ecologies as complex systems (cf. Bak 1996), with the important implications for an archaeology that recognises forms of humanness as emergent within particular historical ecologies. Humanity has evolved, and continues to evolve, by its practices under the guise of these different forms of humanness. This kind of human history/evolution is generated by the processes of development which were made possible by means of the various networks through which materials, energy, and information had flowed. The methodological challenge for archaeology is therefore to understand the dynamic processes of becoming which had once occupied those material contexts whose residues are collected archaeologically.

7

THE MAKING OF POPULATIONS

Living with things

Many problems flow from the simple prejudice that there is a quality that is essential to the definition of 'us' humans. This commonly held quality is often perceived to be a kind of ill-defined 'human nature' (Hull 1986; cf. Kronfeldner 2018; Hannon & Lewens 2018), and it is the one thing that is often believed to be fundamental in defining 'what it is to be human'. From a western perspective it is a quality that apparently lies within our physical existence and it belongs to us individually. Despite the realisation that humanity has evolved as part of the natural world, it is this essentially 'human quality' that is often treated as if it separates us from the rest of the animal kingdom (Kronfeldner 2018). It is therefore unlikely that we would regard members of the animal kingdom in the same light in which we regard ourselves: we are often happy to give credence to claims about our own 'inner being', whilst regarding talk of the inner blackbird or the inner dormouse as ridiculous. In a similar vein, Ingold notes the ease with which we refer to ourselves as 'human beings' but, he asks: 'why we do not also speak of "elephant beings" and "mouse beings". Are not elephants just elephants and mice just mice?' (Ingold 2013, 7). The claim we make to the special nature of our own kind of embodied selfhood would seem to signal our desire to cling to the idea of an inner self, whilst at the same time expressing what for many is a profound scepticism towards the existence of the human soul. Given that the widespread commitment to an inner being is no longer to be founded, at least for many people in the western world, upon a form of spirituality, but is founded instead upon the presence of our physical bodies alone, then the potential challenge of locating the innate quality of humanity appears to be addressed by relocating it from the spiritual soul to the mind. The mind is treated as originating with the activity of the biological brain, from whence our hopes and desires supposedly originate. If we appear no longer to have souls then we do at least have minds courtesy of our brains, and many elements of outward behaviour are treated as if they were the expressions of some inner mental condition. This would imply that the physical products of human behaviour are the symbolic representations of a prior cognitive state (our 'ideas'), but our brains must grow, develop, and ultimately decay as part of our bodies, and it is our bodies that act, and that act with a purpose.

John Searle, in discussing the background upon which social norms might become possible, has argued that '[t]he Background . . . is simply a set of skills, stances, preintentional assumptions and presuppositions, practices and habits. All of these, as far as we know, are realised in human brains and bodies' (Searle 1983, 154). Why does Searle refer to 'human brains and bodies'? Human brains are, after all, parts of human bodies, and bodies do not live and develop without brains any more than brains function without living bodies. We can certainly allow that specific organs, such as the stomach, have particular roles in sustaining the functioning of our bodies, but it would be odd indeed to discuss a human behaviour, such as eating and digesting, as if it were the product of 'human stomachs and bodies'. So why would Searle refer to 'human brains and bodies'?

The treatment of biologically modern humans as the thinking species (*homo sapiens*) that is a user of symbols, and therefore capable of abstract thought, has resulted in the consequent emphasis upon tracing the forward evolution of the brain towards a primate with these capabilities, including the use of language (Deacon 1997). This has resulted in archaeologists claiming that the first evidence of 'symbolic' expression in the production of material culture must also signify the first appearance of biologically modern humans onto the stage of history (Hopkinson 2013; cf. Mellars et al. 2007). Perhaps it is time to reconsider the value that we place upon our cognitive abilities when we seek to define ourselves (cf. Tallis 2011)?

In the last chapter the case was made that different forms of humanness have been created as humans have grown, with a developing ability, to participate proficiently in differently structured worlds. The aim of this argument has been to shift the emphasis away from claims that the cultural order of things was imposed cognitively upon the world, and to claim that it was by performance amongst things that bodies became familiar with the shape of the particular world that they inhabited. From this perspective 'human nature' identifies the comfort that people feel in their familiarity with the world as they know it, and in the embodied confidence that comes with knowing how to act aright in that world. The aim of this chapter will be to consider briefly how those performances might have changed as the result of the different ways that human relations with plants and animals emerged during the periods that marked the beginning of agricultural systems in south-western Asia and in Europe.

Lambros Malafouris (2013) has produced a full-length study of 'material engagement theory', which is an archaeological attempt to override the distinction drawn between an inner cognitive state and its supposed external expression. He builds upon earlier arguments in favour of treating the human mind as an 'extended' or 'distributed' condition that exploits the possibilities offered by the processes of memory storage that operate outside the brain, via such mechanisms as note-taking (Clark 2008). Malafouris then offers us the idea of the mind as a system that integrates an engagement between bodies and things. It is in the nature of many things that actions and emotions, expressed by the body, are directed towards them (cf. Barrett 2013).

The argument that embodied performance expresses the value of things in ways that are signalled to others, poses a particular challenge to archaeology. Renfrew has commented, for example, that '[t]he mistake made by commentators who focus exclusively upon the "mind" is that they emphasize the potential for rich symbolic behaviour without indicating that the ultimate criterion is the praxis in the material world' (Renfrew 2001, 129). I take 'praxis in the material world' to refer to an interpretive performance that was directed towards some material condition. Whilst agreeing with this assessment I am also aware that such performances need leave little by way of an archaeological trace. This allows us to reject the idea of a 'sapient paradox', by which the lack of material expression for much of the earliest history of a human cognitive existence has been characterised as contradicting certain archaeological expectations (Renfrew 1996). Cognitively modern human communities might well have emerged some 150kya, by performing (and by this I would also include speaking), and thus by communicating their interpretations of their landscapes. This might certainly have resulted in a dynamic and eventful history of shared and developing understandings, alongside the processes of colonisation (Gamble 1993), but during such a time, at least to the archaeological observer, nothing much appears to have happened before the end of the Pleistocene.

Abandoning the 'brain-centric' definition of what it is to be human (Tallis 2011 & 2020) requires us to accept that the emergence of humanity, expressed in its various forms of humanness, was simply embodied and performed like any other form of life. All forms of life develop through their responses to the conditions in which they find themselves, and they trace a path moving from growth and development to death. As we have already noted (Chapter 6), and as John Dupré (2012) has argued, human life cannot therefore be characterised as if it was represented by a static form of being, but instead it has always been a process of development. This developmental, or process, perspective on the developing practices of life means that we should recognise, among many other things, the vulnerability that accompanies the birth and immature development of the human infant (Taylor 2010). Timothy Taylor has emphasised that the development in the embodied skills of becoming a certain kind of human (a form of humanness) is achieved by one who learns how to inhabit a particular environment of material things. Things are therefore technologies of becoming. These material contexts are developed and extended throughout an individual's lifetime, and their long-term, technical histories have facilitated the various strands of human evolution. The implication of this argument is that the development and growth of individual bodies is not simply a matter of biology. Instead the development of embodied skills is achieved by virtue of the sensory familiarity gained from living within a landscape of things and in the company of others. This process affirms the self's growing understanding of its own existence. This perspective means that our understanding of the historical processes of *becoming* returns us to the Peircean concept of the *interpretant* (Short 2004; see page 79). This concept matters to us because the sign is the material context of an interpretant's development, and something of this context has survived as the residues that are recovered archaeologically. Human agency cannot therefore be treated as if it emerged as the author who had engraved some meaning upon the material world, and the challenge of archaeology is not to seek to interpret the residue as if it were the representation either of human actions or the representation of the cognitive motivations resulting in those actions. The alternative is to accept that the material conditions of life were the things to which the human agent had responded as an interpretant, and that it was through these responses that the agent made themselves. The interpretant's development grew from the realisation that certain things had a significance for it, and the validity of the actions executed in response towards those things could be seen and evaluated by others. It is from this that co-operation between the participants could emerge (Adami & Hintze 2018). The material therefore made particular kinds of social 'becomings' possible.

This results in the important conclusion that the replication of a population comprising a kind of humanness is not the same thing as the replication of a biological population because the former is the product of biocultural replication, while the latter is supposedly the product of biological replication alone. The distinction (which will be important in the consideration of DNA analysis, below) might entice us towards using it to distinguish the worlds of humanness from the world of 'nature'. This is a line of reasoning that I would be unhappy to follow because I am unconvinced that humanity is the only form of life that learns from, and develops strategically, its embodied practices. It is certainly the case, for example, that forms of humanness are not the only forms of life that develop the embodied mechanisms of social recognition and strategic development (Wilson 2012).

In the previous chapter I already commented upon the widely held assumption that a form of life is prefigured by its genetic line of inheritance. If that were indeed the case then that form of life might well be genetically maladapted to the material conditions within which it develops, given that those conditions might have changed since the reproduction of previous generations that had submitted for selection. It might also be maladapted to any new environments that were open for colonisation (Ward 2018, 50). Development that requires the continuity of a form of life therefore depends upon life's inherent plasticity. It is the ability to recognise, and to adapt to, changing conditions, rather than a dependency upon the adaptive success of previous generations, that is the requirement for an emergent form of life to be reproductively successful. As John Dupré puts it: 'the best way to persist is not always determinable in advance; it will often be adaptive, to have the capacity to respond flexibly to environmental contingencies' (Dupré 2018, 96).

He goes on to suggest that:

> distinctive modes of flexibility characterize the major different modes of organization of life. For microbes, plasticity is chemical or metabolic. Microbes appear to be able to extract energy from almost any chemical substance from which this is in principle possible. . . . These chemical capacities of microbes are exploited by . . . most multicellular eukaryotic organisms, most obviously . . . in digestion. (Dupré 2018, 96)

Neo-Darwinian modelling of the process of natural selection acting upon populations of genetic variability therefore offers a deceptively simple model for far more complex evolutionary and historical processes. By referring to the evolution of developmental systems, the complexity of the evolutionary process becomes clearer. Individual organisms and populations develop as 'far from equilibrium' systems because of their abilities to seek out and appropriate the energy necessary to stay alive, to grow, and thus to develop. Various forms of life, from the simple cells of bacteria and archaea, to plants and animals, and on to whole populations, sustain their reproductive capability by various degrees of behavioural flexibility. In the case of humans, as Taylor (2010) has argued, evolving technologies do not so much represent the environments to which those humans had adapted throughout their histories, rather they operated as part of the 'exoskeleton' that sustained an evolving humanness. Humans in this form have always diversified as cyborgs (Clark 2003), and archaeology should be able to provide some understanding of these different human-cyborg histories.

A developing ecology of organisms, such as those imagined by Darwin living in his 'entangled bank' (page 102), is able to sustain the order reproduced across the generations by the exchange of energy. This is a process that starts with the conversion of energy from the sun into glucose by plant photosynthesis, where the plants have themselves responded to soils, drainage, and climate (Nealon 2016). We need to understand how the different components of each ecology had arranged themselves to map a gradient in the flows of energy. Ecologies, to which humans have added a range of material technologies, degrade the input of a highly structured source of solar energy, such that the entire 'ecosystem must be viewed as an active element with processes and structure, configuring itself to capture and degrade as much energy as possible' (Schneider & Sagan 2005, 226). In this way the ecological system has determined the living trajectories of its component organisms, and it is thus in this way that the ecologies to which others once belonged might be best understood, as a series of processes and flows of energy, information, and materials (Harvey 1996).

Consciousness

Among forms of life, consciousness is practised in ways that range from being conscious of the presence of food, the differences between the fertile and the inhospitable, between light and dark, heat and cold, danger and security, and on to the presence of others and the interpreted qualities of things (Thompson 2007; cf. Godfrey-Smith 2017). This obviously extends the definition of consciousness by accepting that different forms of life are selective of the things to which they respond. Human consciousness appears to be special simply because it can name those things, and it can select its responses to some things by endowing them with certain cultural values. The various levels of consciousness with which life operates therefore display three common characteristics. The first is the expression of an intentionality, in the technical meaning of the term. Consciousness in other words is orientated towards things: consciousness can only exist by being conscious *of something*. Secondly it is situated, by which I mean that consciousness is orientated by means of a particular embodied facility, and it is practised from a particular perspective. Thirdly, consciousness develops along with the biologically embodied conditions within which it grows. These three features amount to treating consciousness as relational. In other words, life is not conscious *per se*, but it becomes conscious of something by means of its own situated and embodied development. This is important because it means that the kind of consciousness that marked different forms of humanness occurred as ways of recognising value in a set of material conditions. Artur Ribeiro has developed this point, and drawing in part upon the work of Vincent Descombes (Ribeiro 2018a & 2018b; Descombes 1986 & 2001), Ribeiro emphasises that 'action is always an intention towards the external world' (Ribeiro 2018b, 29). Therefore, in understanding the actions of others:

> we cannot rely on causal processes or something that is internal to humans. Wanting to attend the World Cup depends on the existence of the World Cup as an object that is external to cause-effect conjunctions and external to humans, . . . This means that a link can be established between teleological and historical explanations, . . ., if the object of an intention is external, . . . it would mean that understanding intentions requires understanding the external object – *an object that is specific to a historical period*. (Ribeiro 2018b, 52, original emphasis omitted, my emphasis added)

This hints at how an archaeology of consciousness might work. Not as speculation upon what human agents might have 'meant' in the traces that resulted from their actions, but as an understanding as to the material foci towards which those actions were directed (Chapter 8).

Forms of life grow and develop by means of their access to the resources necessary for their sustenance and protection. This is the practical recognition of the qualities of things relative to a particular interpretant. Different manifestations of the qualities of things became recognisable to populations of practitioners, as they moved and negotiated the networks of things, spaces, and people. Eloise Govier (2019) has argued that archaeologists, in considering the relationship between humans and things, should start by questioning the assumption that these are relationships in which causes necessarily lead to effects. She bases her case on the work of Karan Barad, commenting on Barad's statement that '"causes" and "effects" emerge through intra-actions' (Barad 2007, 214). This implies, Govier argues, 'that causes and effects emerge in phenomena rather than through "unilateral" movements from causes to effects' (Govier 2019, 51). The argument might be put most simply by considering the archaeological treatment of the human:thing relationship. In today's archaeology this is widely conceived as a relationship in which human motivations caused things to become the kinds of things that they are for us today. Alternatively the human:thing relationship is conceived, by Govier, as one that was articulated by bodily movement, and by the attention of a particular kind of embodied humanness that directed itself towards, and was in effect caused by, its growing recognition of the qualities that existed in things. It was therefore those things that made particular kinds of humanness, and not the humanness that made those things. In selecting the work of Malafouris to exemplify her argument she notes that he 'focuses on the hylonoetic ("thinking through and with matter"), and presents the concept as an alternative to hylomorphism' (Govier 2019, 52). The latter model is one in which a process is often conceived in a way that the object is formed in the internal mind and then is projected onto the material.

Life as a construct

It is important to reiterate some of the principles that I have sought to establish up to this point. First, I regard the growth and development of individuals, and of their populations, to have resulted from the development of individual human interpretants driven by the desire to be recognised by others. This was achieved by utilising the available biocultural resources and it resulted in the development of socialised communities. The individual being, and the population to which those individuals belonged, therefore described, in the case of humanity, a form of humanness. This can be regarded as a biocultural form of becoming, and this can be investigated archaeologically by considering the material values that were its intentional focus (Chapter 8). Second, we can distinguish between individuals, populations of individuals, and ecologies. The latter are held together by flows of energy, materials, and information and they contain different populations, architectures, and technologies. We need not assume that all humans have always perceived themselves as comprising individual entities, but we should assume that life emerges as an interpretive process of construction. It is the histories of 'life as it was constructed' that are the object of archaeological investigation.

Constructing populations

Kristian Kristiansen (2014) suggests that the recovery of ancient DNA (aDNA) from human skeletal and soft-tissue material (Reich 2018) heralds the beginning of a third scientific revolution in archaeology. He compares the impact of this recent analytical development with the impacts on archaeology that resulted from two previous developments in science. The first of these, he argues, occurred in the late nineteenth century and claimed the antiquity of, and the non-deistic origins for, humanity. The second occurred with the scientific procedures of analysis that arose after 1950, including radiocarbon dating, and that established the methodological and intellectual basis for the New Archaeology. Kristiansen's third scientific revolution is the one marked by the recovery of aDNA data. This has included the mapping of haplogroup distributions across Eurasia. Haplogroups are sections of DNA (alleles) that function and are inherited together, and are therefore indicative of a line of biological descent. This does not deny that the full range of biocultural inherited material is employed in ways that sustain the plasticity of an interpreted response in the reproduction of a particular population (Chapter 6).

Kristiansen has argued that aDNA analysis has enabled archaeology to define 'population changes and bottlenecks which can then be compared to other forms of archaeological and historical evidence' (Kristiansen 2014, 13). It is important to note that Kristiansen is referring here to the ideal of a biological population. The excitement generated by the newly available genetic data cannot be doubted. The recovery of these data, along with the new funding opportunities available to some individuals and institutions, the computational ability to handle large data sets, and the theoretical developments that have accompanied these changes, lead Kristiansen to herald the beginnings of a new kind of archaeology (cf. Kintigh et al. 2014). He suggests, for example, that a new European prehistory can now be written, allowing 'for much more [human, plant and animal] mobility than ever imagined just ten years ago' (Kristiansen 2014, 14 insertion mine).

Any attempt to explain the history of a human population as if it were consequential upon the selective reproduction of a single biological entity alone is clearly beset with difficulties. As I have argued, a population is reproduced by individuals whose development shares access to a wider set of biocultural resources than are mapped by aDNA alone. These include language, place, biological and material inheritance, as well as the traditions of energy extraction that are necessary to sustain life, and the plasticity of responses to changing conditions. An ecology contains portions of a number of populations that interact, and ecologies have the overall function of degrading an energy gradient. Treating the definition of a population in purely biological terms would seem to enable the identification of biologically migrant groups within an ecology, although this is clearly fraught with ethical and moral implications (Frieman & Hofmann 2019). Indeed, the definition of a population, on the basis of its inheritance of a particular set of biological traits, is often a strategy that is politically driven by the desire to identify those that appear to derive from 'outsiders'. These 'outsiders' are those who supposedly also lack the necessary biological roots that define an indigenous population, and where biological inheritance is falsely equated with cultural inheritance. However, if we treat a human population not as a thing with a history, but as a process that makes its own history, then we should accept that human identities and systems of value were routinely remade amongst the members of a biocultural population. A single ecology therefore contains a number of such populations, including forms of humanness, and it is within these various populations that there will be those who reach maturity and who reproduce (Mayr 1976, 26–29 & 53–63). If we focus upon the processes of identity formation to characterise the ways that human populations were made over time, then we will see that these populations cannot be reduced to a simple lineage of biological inheritance. If what matters is the ways that various forms of biocultural inheritances were employed in the processes of a population's development, then the distribution of haplogroups recovered from ancient human bodies cannot by themselves map the distribution of a population. In the pre-state conditions of European prehistory, it is hardly surprising that populations emerged that had resulted from the complex mix of human movement, cultural influences, and biological interbreeding.

One further point now needs to be made against the recent tendency to treat living things (treated here as interpretants) and non-living things as if they had the same ontological status (Olsen & Witmore 2015, 189). The ontological difference between the two states of existence is one that defines the ways that each emerges via a different process of becoming. Living things emerge by building and developing an order that is sustained by their recognition of the conditions that enable their intake of energy (Schrödinger 1944, 71, characterised this as the process of 'negative entropy'), whilst non-living things emerge by migrating to the lowest possible level of energy, and thus towards a state of disorder (entropy). My argument is therefore that the biocultural being emerges as an interpretant whose motivation is its own development through seeking to increase and to sustain the order in its body. It achieves this by identifying sources of free energy within certain given material conditions. This is very different from the non-living interpretant (if such a thing might be taken to exist) that seeks a path towards its lowest possible state of order. This is why rivers flow downhill and not uphill.

Neolithic populations

Archaeology has claimed that the major change in the prehistory of south-western Asia and continental Europe occurred with the move from hunter-gatherer economies to those of agriculturalists. This change is taken to have involved the first cultivation of crops and the management of newly domesticated animals. It must have included all the ancillary changes that we might presume sustained new procedures of land, plant, and animal management (see Chapter 8). These included changes in the organisation and obligations of human labour and new techniques for the production of a wide range of cultural materials. Amongst the latter were the location and timing of the technologies that were employed in the preparation of food and its service. In other words, this was a fundamental change simply because it meant that new forms of life had come into existence (cf. Henry 2019).

The subtle implication of the archaeological language used to characterise these changes is important. By referring to the adoption of agriculture as the adoption of 'new methods of food production', rather than as a complex change in the relationships operating between the reproduction of plants, humans, and animals, the adoption appears to have been one that was instigated by humanity. This conforms with the traditional assumption that it is humanity, rather than animals or plants, that can be endowed with the role of a 'producer'. This, in turn, has maintained the dominant place of humanity in the 'adoption of agriculture', resulting in archaeologists questioning 'why human societies initially established and subsequently sustained relationships of domestication with some species' (Smith 2007, 188). A very different perception is gained if we were to allow that 'domestication' marks a long-term process in which human reproduction responded to the ongoing evolutionary changes occurring in the plants and animals that had shared the landscape with them (Fuller et al. 2012). Domestication, from this perspective, was not something that humans 'did' to certain grasses and animals, but rather it was a condition that emerged within the evolving practices of the entire ecology that extended across south-western Asia (cf. Rindos 1984, 141). Agriculturalists therefore emerged from within an ecology of evolving domestication. My point in what follows is not therefore to deny that other kinds of entity, a world of all things, emerged alongside particular kinds of humanness (cf. Crellin & Harris 2020, 45), but it is an attempt to understand what it took for a new kind of humanity (the agriculturalist) to have emerged between south-western Asia and Europe during the Holocene.

Stephen Shennan has sought to describe the establishment of the developing agricultural practices across the continent of Europe as the result of an evolutionary process guided by natural selection (Shennan 2018). Shennan utilises a Darwinian model of evolution in discussing the possible historical development of biocultural systems of replication, and this will cause us some confusion in the way we might handle his work. By adopting a perspective that necessitates distinguishing between an evolving biological population that had randomly generated mutations in the process of its reproduction, and the natural process that selected for the reproductive potential of some of those mutations, Shennan pitches the status of the developing human biological population against that of an environmental base of plants and animals. It was this base, Shennan argues, that had selected for the variable reproductive success of the human population. He suggests that this approach prompts the need to understand the processes by which the biological reproduction of farmers had out-competed those of hunter-gatherers in Europe. Shennan proposes that 'life history theory' enables him to assess this process by reference to the allocations of energy that the members of a human population might have made to take the best advantage of the resources that were available to them. In this model the exploitation of additional sources of energy, for a human population's development, should have resulted in increased levels of fitness expressed by that population's reproductive success. If the shift to agriculture marked an optimum allocation of energy in a beneficial trade-off between the output resulting from the labour required by food production against the labour input required for the reproductive success of that population, then this would seem to explain the demographic growth that accompanied the transition to farming (Bocquet-Appel 2002 & 2011).

In this model, the seemingly unplanned but beneficial contrast of cultivation over foraging might be expressed in terms such that the positive balance achieved between the input of energy required for the procurement of food, and the energy that was then made available to be dissipated by the consumption of that food, was greater in the case of cultivation compared with that of foraging. This contrast therefore provided for increased reserves of energy that could be appropriated, and then invested, in child rearing and in the elaboration of material culture production. However, it was on the reproduction of the evolved ecology as a whole that the development of each form of life had depended, given that these were ecologies of co-dependencies, rather than each being a niche constructed by, and for, a human population. It was in this light that David Rindos, in discussing the role of plants in this period, made the following observation:

> [t]oo little consideration has been given to the important role plants have played in establishing and maintaining the dynamics of agricultural systems. Plants have contributed as much to the evolution of the agroecology as have humans, for it was plants that created the situation in which certain types of human behaviours became selectively advantageous. (Rindos 1984, 142; see also Nealon 2016)

In his discussion of the evolution of agricultural origins in Asia, Rindos distinguished between the processes of domestication and those of agricultural management (Rindos 1980, 752, & 1984, 138–189). Domestication occurred in Asia as the result of an evolving symbiotic relationship between humans and certain plant taxa. An increasingly domesticated population of plants and animals thus emerged through their morphological and behavioural divergence from their progenitor communities, along with their increasing reliance upon the human control of land for their existence. The time taken for this divergence to have occurred amongst plants is likely to have been longer than Rindos allowed (Shennan 2018, 35–36), but his perspective upon processes of co-evolution reiterates the point also made by Shennan (2018, 36): the reproduction of these proto-domesticated plants did not imply any kind of 'invention' of agriculture by humanity. The transference of agricultural practices into Europe meant, by way of contrast, that they were carried by a system of land management, a very different process from the co-evolution of crops, human and animal behaviour in Asia. Amy Bogaard's analysis demonstrating that central European agriculture was practised as an intensive garden-plot cultivation where plots could be maintained for a number of seasons by manuring, rather than as the shifting 'slash and burn' agricultural systems as was once thought (Childe 1929, 45ff.), means that the rapidity of the colonisation of the loessic soils of central Europe in the sixth millennium BCE is now more difficult to understand (Bogaard 2004a, 161), and must depend in part upon a relatively rapid growth of agricultural populations.

The resources of domesticated grasses, cattle, goats, and sheep that were eventually introduced for human use across most of Europe therefore originated amongst the plants, animals, and people whose breeding patterns had evolved in south-western Asia. If population growth does help us to explain the success and expansion of these agricultural populations, then it must indicate the effectiveness with which the fertility of the land was being released, stored, and allocated through the growth of the colonising and domesticated animal bodies, and in the annual harvested product that was derived from domesticated grasses (Barrett 2014b). The symbiotic relationship that had evolved between the emerging categories of humanness, along with those of plants and animals throughout the period of the Epi-Palaeolithic of south-western Asia (Zeder 2008; Asouti & Fuller 2012) meant that it was the evolution of plants and animals in Asia that had made humans into farmers.

The development of the isolated reproduction of a domesticated subset amongst the wider populations of plants and animals of south-western Asia was presumably facilitated by the emergent practices of land management on behalf of the human population which had encouraged changes in the morphology of the plants collected and the animals culled (but for animal populations see Zeder 2008). This allows us to begin to recognise the broadly contemporary nature (*contra* Bar-Yosef & Meadow 1995) of the phase change that had occurred as a region-wide process of niche formation within the complex ecologies of Asia (Smith 2007; Zeder 2011 & 2015). The Neolithic therefore emerged as an integrated form of life, meaning that an assemblage of different practices was performed by practitioners whose work expressed the understanding of a commonly recognised logic. This conforms with the argument recently made by Despina Catapoti and Maria Relaki (Catapoti & Relaki 2020), who have argued that the Neolithic cannot be represented by a particular list of attributes. Instead they assert that the Neolithic emerged as a single and more general form of engagement with the material world. Their treatment of archaeological residues therefore requires that they abandon attempts to ground the archaeological record of a 'Neolithic' upon the possession of certain finished articles that might represent the individual workings of, for example, the processes of sedentism, agriculture, and pottery manufacture. Instead they characterise the key elements of a distinctly Neolithic assemblage as being those that were created by working within a common structure or *chaîne opératoire*. They argue that this commonality of making, or becoming (they use the term *poesis*), resulted from the general application of a 'dough-based technology':

> we use *bread* as a shorthand for the variety of flour-and-water foodstuffs deriving from cereal processing; *pottery*, to indicate one of the main artefacts emerging out of working clay (which includes a broad range of other items, such as figurines, clay sickles, house models, etc.); and *mudbricks* to represent the huge variety of earthen architecture characterizing the Neolithic (e.g. mud walls, wattle and daub, plasters, floors, storage pits, etc. . . .). (Catapoti & Relaki 2020, 3, original emphasis)

There was therefore a commonality in the performances that underpinned all these 'operational sequences' that were involved in the making of things. It was a commonality that helps to define assemblages of *Neolithic* material culture. It is in this way, they argue, that we can recognise that the Neolithic, as a whole, was a mode of practice (a form of life). This way of 'knowing how to act' emerged in history by means of its own evolved suite of practices, and the *chaîne opératoire* that operated across technologies was not only a process that ordered techniques, but one that also ordered 'at the same time *gestures* and tools' (Leroi-Gourhan 1993, 114, my emphasis). It is Leroi-Gourhan's reference to gestures that reminds us that it was through the sequential making of things that bodies were also made. They were made by teaching, learning, and adopting a common routine of performance, an obligation of how to behave in a way that was recognisable to others. Neolithic bodies were therefore made through their relationships with things, land, animals, plants, and others: a commonality of understandings by which others could be recognised as being similar to the self (see page 85). And, as Catapoti and Relaki suggest, this means that while we can prioritise that which was shared (a similar *technics*) over that which was distinct (diverse material outcomes), we must also prioritise the *becoming* of life over its *being*.

The origins of an agricultural *commonality of practice* was the product of a lengthy ecological evolution that occurred in south-western Asia and that charted the direction of plant, animal, and human development (Boyd 2018). It was this tradition that brought forms of life into existence and that spread westwards, perhaps driven by a complex, systemic interaction between an increasing population size amongst humans and the greater risks posed to the entire system given its investment in a limited set of increasingly localised food resources (Rindos 1984, 271–285). It is a version of this system of agricultural management that eventually reached the west coasts of temperate Europe, arriving in Britain and Ireland around 6,000 years ago.

The European continent sustained existing populations of hunter-gatherers throughout the period of its colonisation by agricultural practices, although the density of these earlier populations will have varied considerably in their distribution across the continent. A geographical frontier was therefore likely to have existed, periodically, between the two modes of existence (Dennell 1985). Radiocarbon chronologies and distribution patterns support this expectation, along with evidence for a 'leap-frog' colonisation of domesticates into areas of forager exploitation (Bogucki 2003, 267–268). The overall speed of the dispersal of 'domestic' ecologies across Europe seems to have been rapid, although there also appear to have been lengthy periods of stabilisation along some of its various frontiers (Bogucki 2000, Fig. 8.1). Indeed, the patterns of initial colonisation by the new forms of life, accompanying systems of agricultural management, are more likely to have been represented by a patchwork of occurrences (e.g. Hofmann et al. 2013) than by a broad frontier wave of advance across the continent as a whole (Ammerman & Cavalli-Sforza 1979). It was across the patchwork of frontier zones that Marek Zvelebil and Peter Rowley-Conwy had originally envisaged the slow adoption of agricultural resources by the existing hunter-gatherer populations (Zvelebil & Rowley-Conwy 1984). Their 'availability model' proposed that a long-term 'substitution phase' of exchanged materials existed between the two systems, resulting in the eventual adoption of farming by foraging communities (Zvelebil & Lillie 2000, 59; Zvelebil & Dulokhanov 1991). The behavioural changes that supposedly drove this adoption of farming by the indigenous communities in continental Europe have been variously explained as being prompted by the depletion of traditional resources (e.g., Rowley-Conwy 1984), or by the pressures of social competition (e.g., Bender 1978). In other words, these models assumed that agriculture was adopted as a strategic initiative by the indigenous populations of hunter-gatherers. It was this general model that Rowley-Conwy came to reject, a rejection that was based in part upon his recognition that no such substitution phase could be identified in northern Europe (Rowley-Conwy 2004, 97). There are other problems associated with the suggested uptake of agricultural practices by hunter-gatherers, not least the so-called 'scheduling crisis' in which autumn sowing (Bogaard 2004a, 50–59) would coincide with the maximum availability of wild plant foods and hunted fauna. Bogaard concludes that while these activities are not necessarily mutually exclusive:

> [t]he decision to sow cereals in the autumn rather than in the spring implies that cereal cultivation displaced these other activities to some extent. The implication is that the indigenous adoption of agriculture would have entailed a rapid commitment to a new farming way of life. (Bogaard 2004a, 162)

The model of an indigenous adoption of agricultural practices is now further questioned by the recent mitochondrial and aDNA analysis (Bramanti et al. 2009; Lipson et al. 2017; Mathieson et al. 2018). This more recent work implies that agriculture was established across Europe from the tenth millennium BCE onwards not only as the result of Europe's colonisation by populations of domesticated plants and animals, but also as the result of the colonisation of the European human DNA lineages by haplogroups, all of which had derived ultimately from southwestern Asia. It is important to repeat that while we should accept the plasticity that has always been involved in the construction of human communities (as argued in Chapter 6), DNA haplogroups are themselves currently understood to have been spread by interbreeding. The DNA evidence is therefore taken to indicate that the colonisation of Europe by cultivated plants and domesticated animal stock was also accompanied by an incoming human population.

The idea that farming resources could be adopted by hunter-gatherers would seem to maintain the claim for a human exceptionalism because it assumes that humans stood in opposition to, and acted on, the environments that they occupied. This is to treat foraging and farming as two alternative technologies for extracting energy from the environment, a view that treats humanness not as something created through its practices with things, but as a constant and inherent capability (humanity) that acted on things simply by changing the organisation of its behaviour and the technologies that it had employed, once the more effective technology of farming had been demonstrated to it.

The archaeological indicators for the adoption of farming in Europe have long been assumed to have been accompanied by other technological developments that include such things as the early use of ceramics, new forms of lithic working, and the creation of complex domestic and monumental architecture. Andrew Jones and Emilie Sibbesson (2013) have argued, with reference to the British sequences of material, that the grouping of all these changes, along with the adoption of domesticates, into a single chronological horizon of change that is equated with the beginning of the Neolithic, expresses nothing more than an archaeological expectation that a dramatic horizon of change must have existed at this time, an expectation that has resulted from archaeology's failure to explore the possibility that the material changes arose from a long-term and diverse set of behavioural changes. Jones and Sibbesson's argument aligns with that of Julian Thomas who has characterised the European Neolithic as having emerged as 'heterogeneous assemblages of persons, animals, structures, and artefacts' resulting from 'new relationships between people and material things' (Thomas in Robb 2013, 678). But the new assemblages of things must have sustained a new assemblage of practices within which a new kind of humanness will have emerged (cf. Henry 2019; Hofmann 2013, 156ff.). Thomas has argued that in Britain and Ireland these heterogeneous relationships arose as the result of the, presumably *ad hoc*, adoption of new technologies, including the management of domesticated plants and animals, by members of the indigenous population (Thomas 2013), although this argument, as we have indicated, can be questioned. My own point would be that the emergent European biocultural populations associated with agriculture were no more an indigenous population of hunter-gatherers who had become farmers than they were colonists who had travelled from south-western Asia.

The human DNA haplogroups that are currently associated with the spread of agriculture were the consequence of long-term processes in the biological mixing and migration of DNA lineages that, by the fifth millennium BCE, had left their trace on the human bodies recovered from the burials that are distributed across large parts of the European continent (e.g. Hofmann 2015). Given the increasingly detailed archaeological resolution that is now available from all other cultural and biological data for early farming communities at this time (cf. Bickle & Whittle 2014), along with the uncertain attempts to generalise about the migratory dynamics of entire populations based upon current aDNA data (cf. Mathieson et al. 2018), the uneven sampling of the limited assemblage of Epi-Palaeolithic skeletal material from Europe (although see Hofmann 2015, 458), and our recognition of the complexity of the subsequent analytical processes (Reich 2018, 99–114), it is tempting to hesitate in any attempt to draw too firm a picture of human population dynamics for this period. Nonetheless, the link between the dynamics of human population growth, its resulting expansion westwards, and the colonisation of Europe with agricultural practices is one that is by now widely accepted (Shennan 2018). The link between the factors of biological, cultural, and economic reproduction implies that whilst hunter-gatherer populations were likely to have been subsumed within the reproduction of the new agricultural populations, the spread of farming in Europe was not the result of the adoption of the available domesticates of plants and animals by the indigenous populations (e.g. Brace et al. 2018; González-Fortes et al. 2017; Olalde et al. 2018). Alongside any attempt to model the complexities of the processes of colonisation, we also need to understand why hunter-gatherer populations on the European continent did not achieve their own transformation by adopting the practices of agriculture that had become available to them across the boundary conditions to which Dennell and Zvelebil drew attention. In this regard it is important to recognise the very considerable input of energy that is initially required if systems of agricultural management are to realise their potential in terms of food production (Nelson pers.comm.). This, and the possible seasonal conflicts in scheduling labour-intensive activities involving the practices of both hunter-gathering and farming, would certainly count against the kind of *ad hoc* adoption of agriculture by hunter-gatherers.

The reproductive isolation of areas of plant growth, of animal grazing, and the human interpretation of food and drink preparation and service, were the mutually reinforcing components of the kind of energy system that contained the means by which a 'humanness of domestication' could develop (cf. Goody 1976 & 1982). Each form of life maintained, in its different ways, the flows of energy and information which sustained the different kinds of ecology that were the fields of security and growth inhabited by certain kinds of plants, animals, and human practices. If, as Deacon has argued (1997, 72–73), all humans had, long before the adoption of agriculture, evolved the additional potential to develop a symbolic reading of these various ecological relationships, then it was the relationships between plants, animals, and people that were experienced as the reproduction of the values that brought forth the different categories of people that were further mediated by the preparation and service of foodstuffs. It was thus different kinds of humanity that were mapped onto the land over which those different communities held rights, along with the kinds of work that they did, and the food and the drink that they were served and that they consumed, and who occupied the spaces provided by the increasingly complex forms of architecture that were constructed by early agriculturalists (cf. Watkins 2010; see also Chapter 8).

Agricultural practices were thus a kind of behavioural grammar and syntax, as Catapoti and Relaki have argued. This grammar had evolved in south-western Asia, as a human intentionality that evolved alongside the plants and animals of Asia, directing itself by such means as the production, preparation, service, and consumption of food and drink (cf. Braidwood et al. 1953). Archaeologists have created distinctive domains separating out the processes of subsistence, adaptation, cultural production, and social evolution, and readings of the surviving patterns of different material residues might indeed signify such things, but they would have been meaningless from the perspective of those who engaged with materials in ways that embodied their own forms of life. The complex process of bread production recently attested at Shubayqa 1 in north-eastern Jordan at around 14.6k–11.6k cal. BP, a production that was occurring before the development of systems of agricultural management in that region (Arranz-Otaegui et al. 2018), was as much a semiotic process as it was the product of subsistence practices. The same realisation must also accompany the interpretation of the cult site of Göbekli Tepe in south-eastern Turkey with its monumental architecture dating to around 10k cal. BP. This site appears to have witnessed the production of beer and the consumption of meat, presumably in feasting ceremonies (Dietrich et al. 2012). The gods were not born along with these origins of agriculture as Jacques Cauvin suggests (2000), for the simple reason that their presence could always have been recognised indexically in the ways that they had created the form of the landscape and of the cosmos. What was new was that with the symbolic representation of sacred cosmologies in the sculpted form as in the stones at Göbekli Tepe, it had become possible to experience the presence of that cosmos under the controlled conditions of the more localised and restricted space of a building.

The hunter-gatherers of continental Europe could not have become a halfway stage on a path towards the Neolithic by the exchange and adoption of some elements of the neighbouring 'farming strategies', as Marek Zvelebil once suggested (Zvelebil 1986). The demands of agricultural production are simply too onerous. Hunting will still have occurred amongst early agriculturalists, but the demands of resource management and production would surely have meant that agriculture and foraging were mutually exclusive regimes. Each population of foragers and of agriculturalists will therefore have maintained their own, quite different, ways of becoming human by the processes of interpreting the land, plants, animals, and cosmos of their different ecologies. It was within these ecologies that they extracted the food requirements that had sustained them. The argument that different forms of life are embedded in different ecologies goes some way to explain why a clear distinction exists between the archaeological residues resulting from the indigenous lives of hunter-gatherers and those resulting from the lives of the agriculturalists that spread across the European continent (Rowley-Conwy 2004 & 2011).

Conclusion

If we were to restrict our understanding of the newly won aDNA data to signifying various population dynamics, as if these populations were defined simply by their biological inheritance, and if we then employed those dynamics to explain such things as the origins of European agriculture, we would not understand the ways that the lives of those populations were lived. The means by which we claim to know the past must include both our readings of the signs of the past that we see around us, as well as our interpretation of the ways that others might once have experienced and interpreted those same material signs. Symmetrical analysis was introduced by David Bloor who showed that all forms of knowledge must be understood 'symmetrically', as the different ways of becoming part of the world (Bloor 1991). The present does not explain the past, but if we were to recognise the dissonance between our own perceptions of the residual materials, and that of the forms of life that brought themselves into existence with reference to those materials, then we might begin to engage more effectively with the lives that archaeology enables us to study.

8

THE CULTURES OF LIFE

A cultural systemics

Modern archaeological procedures are designed to identify, and to describe, a material residue with the further aim of establishing the historical causes resulting in its formation. These causes prioritise human activity, and they concern the ways in which that activity was organised. In the first half of the twentieth century the similarities that were observed in the ordering of the residues were taken to represent the common practices of production that were socially, or ethnically, determined:

> [s]imilar assemblages of archaeological types are found repeatedly associated together because they were made, used or performed by the same people at the same time. Different assemblages of associated types occur at the same time because they were made by different peoples. Cultures are assemblages of types that are associated because they are made by the same people. (Childe 1956, 111–112)

Archaeological cultures were therefore equated with material variability and this was assumed to represent the actions of a particular 'people', and it was as a result of these culturally designed actions of production that different kinds of 'people' could be identified archaeologically.

'Culture' has been one of the most difficult, and potentially misleading, terms employed in archaeology. One assumption that has enabled its use by archaeologists, and which was expressed by Gordon Childe (above), was that a culture was the cognitive and inherited awareness of people as to how their activities should be executed, leading to the view that socially sustained cultural beliefs were represented archaeologically by the form of their material products. More recently, the use of the term 'culture' has been widely critiqued within anthropology, and these critiques have now also had an impact upon archaeological thinking. The central question has been whether the same material reality that we all share (the one ontological condition) might have been perceived and worked from diverse cultural perspectives, or whether the expressions of a cultural diversity actually imply the existence of different realities existing for different peoples (see page 90; Venkatesan 2010). My aim is to avoid the traditional archaeological convention that treats culture as if it was a set of behavioural rules that are represented by an output of material regularities. Instead my aim is to treat cultural behaviour as the various ways in which different kinds of humanness, and their various solidarities, have grown by exploring their various understandings of things that they encountered in the company of others (cf. Graeber 2015). Cultural life was lived as a way of coping with the world as it was occupied, and through various forms of behaviour to bring that particular reality into view. This definition of culture, as a negotiated set of practices occurring within a particular material ecology, accepts that various forms of life have grown and have developed by learning to live in ways that became culturally meaningful, and thus recognisable to those around them. In practice this means that different realities have existed to sustain different perceptions, and that our own understanding of reality is no different in this regard than any other.

Childe had employed archaeological procedures to track the paths of cultural influences that had supposedly crossed from one region to another. It was the New Archaeology that identified the intellectual weakness at the heart of this reasoning. That weakness was deemed to have arisen because Cultural Archaeology could only ever describe material change in terms of trait changes, and it could only ever explain those trait changes as the result of externally derived cultural influences. This kind of reasoning had been questioned in the United States of America since the 1950s (e.g. Willey & Phillips 1958, 51–52) and, as Binford noted, because assemblages of artefacts were treated, not as the products of cultural *systems*, but as assemblages of individual traits, as a result any change in an individual trait was treated as if it had resulted from '"blending," "directional influences," and "stimulation" between and among "historical traditions"' (Binford 1962, 217). In his later examination of the archaeological analysis of mortuary residues Binford argued that whilst archaeology had assumed that 'ideas or beliefs were the relevant variables to be used in understanding cultural or behavioural differences and similarities' (Binford 1971, 7), he was of the opinion that, in the analysis of material variability:

> differences in ideas and knowledge . . . are never sufficient causes for . . . changes or differentiations. . . . It is only after we understand the organizational properties of cultural systems that we can meaningfully make comparisons among them in terms of cultural content. (Binford 1971, 25)

Cultural explanations for change were slowly abandoned in Europe as the radiocarbon chronology was increasingly accepted as having broken many of the previously assumed lines of cultural influence (Renfrew 1973c).

The demand of the New Archaeology, to explain the ways that human behaviour had contributed to material change, required that the *functionality* of that behaviour be established. As Binford argued, functionality could only be understood in systemic terms, simply because the function of any behavioural component was given by how that component had operated in relation to the other components in the same system – either to sustain the system's stability or to bring about its change. Material change was therefore analysed as if it was an attempt to correct for systemic maladjustments. All the examples of a non-diffusionist archaeology that have been discussed in the earlier chapters of this book treated the assemblages of material residues as if they represented systems of one sort or another, whether these were systems of economic and social organisation, or systems of belief and signification.

The 'cultural system', whose operation was determined by its organisational properties, provided the New Archaeology with the basis upon which to explain the changes that were observed in the material (cf. Willey & Phillips 1958). Despite earlier assumptions that the organisation of these systems could be described in social terms (e.g. papers in Binford & Binford 1968), it was not until Renfrew in 1973 (Renfrew 1973d), and then Redman and his colleagues some five years later (Redman et al. 1978), that the workings of cultural systems were explicitly recast as arising from 'social' processes. This change in perception meant that because categories of behaviour could be described in social terms, they must also have had social functions, implying that categories of behaviour functioned according to the social values that had been recognised by the participants of the system. This was likely to mean that each social system was open to internal conflict and to challenges between those belonging to different categories of social status, an argument that was denied by Renfrew (1972, 487) who saw social systems as being inherently stable. However, others argued that each social system was necessarily structured in ways that ensured the preservation of a dominant, if contested, political and moral legitimacy (Miller & Tilley 1984).

New Archaeology's demand that archaeology should establish the causal explanations for systemic change was met by operating as if such explanations would identify processes that had driven different kinds of systemic change. These processes were therefore assumed to have been generally applicable to numerous historical situations. The implication was that, whatever their cultural differences, archaeological systems were structured by the same processes that were attested in anthropological accounts of similarly organised populations. This meant that analogies could be drawn between archaeological cases and anthropological accounts (cf. Fahlander 2004; see page 78). But why should the systemic causes that had resulted in archaeological residues find comparable analogies amongst recent anthropological accounts? Anthropology in particular, and social theory in general, had developed from the seventeenth century CE onwards in a European context. This was a time when some Europeans had begun to reflect upon their own industrial and imperial histories, and when European domination, conversion, and enslavement of indigenous non-European peoples had already occurred.

Anthropology therefore emerged as a European way of 'seeing' others. Given this context, it might be supposed that most social and anthropological reasoning is inherently modernist and Eurocentric in its origins (cf. Viveiros de Castro 2017 [2009]). As such, the use of anthropological and sociological analogies in archaeology is now seen as problematic, if not entirely inappropriate for use in our study of the distant past.

The debate as to whether change in the systemic organisation of cultural behaviours was driven by either the adaptive demands resulting from environmental changes, or by the internal contradictions that gave rise to strategies of control and resistance, has resulted in replacing the archaeology of the large-scale regularities identified by Cultural Archaeology (e.g. Childe 1957) with analyses of the more localised scales of systemic integration. Such a change in the scale of analysis was advocated by both Binford and Renfrew (e.g. Renfrew 1969a & 1977). It was also implicit in many studies within the tradition of an Interpretive Archaeology. However, if we are to treat archaeology as an examination of materials that were used to build an earlier form of life, then another scale of analysis might be called for.

Rather than attempting to explain how material conditions might have originated as the result of localised systemics, perhaps we should consider the possibility that the forms of life that archaeology seeks to understand had extended, by means of their interpretive strategies, well beyond the reach of the individual social and political system (Arnason 1988, 88). If this possibility is accepted then we might well need to revisit the earlier, and long since abandoned, study of large-scale material-cultural regularities. Indeed, we might question whether the criticisms of diffusionist reasoning were robust enough to have resulted in the abandonment of this larger scale of analysis (cf. Roberts & Vander Linden 2011a). If the spatial extent of a form of life was indeed extensive, and if we need to consider the mechanisms that had sustained those forms of life, then the more localised structures of social and political organisation must have emerged from within these larger-scale traditions of life.

In their review of the traditional concept of an archaeological culture, Benjamin Roberts and Marc Vander Linden (2011b) have recognised the anachronism whereby, having been rejected as the means to explain change, the concept of culture has nevertheless remained the short-hand, if somewhat inaccurate, label to describe the large-scale material coherencies. Stephen Shennan (2000, 812) has noted that the past was likely to have been inhabited by organisational units that were geographically smaller than the extensive patterns of cultural regularity that are recorded archaeologically. He has concluded that these larger cultural patterns must be explained as resulting from processes other than those which had governed the more local systems of social and political organisation. In taking this argument forward Shennan has sought to avoid the traditional assumption that the patterns of material cultural uniformity were simply the products of 'human group traditions', whereby cultural change could be treated as the product of population displacement, or as the spread of a dominant cultural tradition. The alternative, Shennan proposes, is to treat archaeological cultural regularities as mapping the transmission of information and skills. It was the *transmission* of cultural traditions and information that occurred within the fluctuating histories of a population's reproduction that needed to be understood in Shennan's view. He has maintained that the transmission of cultural information was governed by the principle of 'descent with modification' (Shennan 2000, 824–826), and he later emphasised (Shennan 2018, 3–6, and above pages 117–118) that the reproduction of a population should be regarded as 'the single most important factor in understanding culture change', a process that was guided by natural selection.

It is important to notice that Shennan seems to believe that a single point of origin must have existed for any tradition of cultural uniformity. This is rather like the Darwinian assumption that life had itself spread out from a single point of origin (Darwin 2009 [1859], 112–113). We should however allow that the ways people might have understood their world could well have originated 'rhizomatically' from amongst a broader set of backgrounds and origins, rather than diffusing out from a single point of origin.

Cultural histories

If cultural practices can be defined as the ways people performed an increasing, and practical, understanding of their material universe by orientating themselves towards that material in ways that expressed their knowledge of how they should behave, then these were the practices that made particular kinds of humanness. It was people's discovery of how to cope by living amongst things in the company of others, that endowed those things with their particular significance. The patterning of the things recovered archaeologically did not therefore result simply from the transmission of a tradition of production. It was also part of the context through which people had once been able to recognise their own agency. A cultural history is therefore given by more than a sequence of things; it is the history of the embodied dispositions by which a biocultural population developed by making itself into a form of humanness.

Artur Ribeiro has noted how archaeologists have failed to make the case for the importance of the philosophy of history in their various attempts to formulate a conception of the human past (Ribeiro 2018b). As a result, archaeologists appear unaware of the implications that arise from the historical understandings that are necessary for all archaeological interpretations. The historical interpretations envisaged by Ribeiro are not narratives that describe a sequence of materials, nor do they describe how such a sequence was created. Instead, historical narratives trace what was possible in the building of a common level of understanding amongst people, and the ways that the resources utilised in those understandings (including things, memories, and beliefs) could provide the means by which local solidarities and political structures had emerged.

The belief that the history of cultural systems could occur under conditions of systemic autonomy (Renfrew 1969a & 1977; Renfrew & Cherry 1986) was initially challenged by the application of World Systems Theory to the operation of the ancient world (see page 68; cf. Kristiansen 1998). The application of this theory to pre-capitalist worlds has not been without its critics (Schneider 1977; Ratnagar 2001; Harding 2013). The criticism does not however negate the argument that relationships between ancient political and social systems must have been interactive and porous, leading us to doubt claims for the systemic isolation and autonomy of the processes' political and material development (Smith 2005). It was surely the degree of systemic openness that had sustained the flows of goods, peoples, plants, animals, and beliefs, all of which are indicated archaeologically by certain extensive material distributions, as well as by the current isotopic and DNA evidence for human and animal mobility (Kristiansen 2014, 13).

Archaeologists have long claimed to be able to recognise the prior existence of different systems of social organisation, and they have also modelled the movement of materials as indicative of the exchanges occurring between systems (Renfrew 1975). The problem, however, is to establish the mechanisms that had sustained these flows of people, information, and resources. This raises the suspicion that archaeology requires another kind of spatial interpretation, beyond recognising of the extent of political organisations, and the mapping of exchanged materials. Such a third scale of analysis would force a return to consider the continental and trans-continental patterning of different areas of material coherency. This patterning might indicate the ground for a particular order to the world that provided legitimacy for the more local social and political practices. Indeed, we might be tempted to treat such an order as ideological, being the generative matrix that regulated 'the relationship between visible and non-visible, between imaginable and non-imaginable' (Žižek 1994, 1).

Michael Rowlands and Johan Ling have referred to the contradiction represented by European Bronze Age archaeology which claims to see the evidence for mobility occurring alongside the evidence for long-term regional identities. As a response, and by assuming that these two kinds of evidence resulted from the operation of a single set of processes, Rowlands and Ling have sought to understand the evidence in terms of hybrid, creole, and cosmopolitan practices which ensured the existence of a general identity across communities, whilst also facilitating the strategies of resistance that constructed local, political obligations (Rowlands & Ling 2013, 517; cf. Rowlands 2010).

Archaeology has previously sought to represent many exchanges extending across regions and between social groups as the exchange of 'prestige' items between elites that had accompanied acts of diplomacy and the negotiation of marriage alliances. On the other hand, the function of the bulk exchange of raw materials has been assumed to satisfy the deficiency of local raw material availability, such as the need for copper, lead, and tin to satisfy the needs of bronze production in the lowland regions of Europe (cf. Sherratt 1976). However, the bulk movement of raw materials is difficult to understand outside the contexts of either diplomacy, or commercial trade operating within some kind of monetary economy (cf. Barrett & Boyd 2019, 57). What we can assume is that numerous forms of exchange must have operated on the basis of authority, power, and trust between most of the participants. The actions of participants in any voluntary exchange relationship must have been recognisable, interpretable, and indeed predictable, to each participant (cf. Cronk & Leech 2013). Trust itself can only exist between people when they hold in common some understanding, however schematic, of the forces that govern their lives. Such an understanding would have been expressed through the practices of 'institutions, techniques, myths, or other practices and products', in ways that were 'constant across languages and political societies', and whose 'institutions and organisations . . . spread spatially over time' to an extent that was 'bigger than political society' (Feuchtwang & Rowlands 2019, 7–8).

Trust is the recognition of a degree of shared humanness, manifest in the way that co-respondents behaved in relation to the world of things. In sustaining relations of trust two things must follow, each of which is archaeologically significant. In one, people shared a common disposition towards things and towards events which was expressed in ways that extended widely across geographical regions. In the second, institutions of solidarity, and the obligations of political authority, will have arisen within these worlds by the construction of relationships and values that arose locally (Komter 2005). The latter systems would have arisen, for example, when some individuals claimed, by their actions, the attributes of a cultural purity that others might have accepted or have been unable to resist. The claims of purity, and the status that it endowed upon some, might then have been inherited along the lines of a particular genealogy. By recognising that human identities were performed relative to cultural materials, we find ourselves developing a definition of civilisational practices that differs from that which is more commonly employed in archaeology.

The current archaeological presumption is to treat civilisation as a level of achievement on a polity's path of development. This achievement is often assumed to have moved that polity onto a higher level of organisational complexity, along with increased degrees of social differentiation and display. This current view of civilisation was the one that was employed by Childe (Childe 1950) and pursued by Renfrew who wrote that the growth of civilisation marked the creation of 'a larger and more complex environment, not only in the natural field through increasing exploitation of a wider range of resources of the ecosystem, but also in the social and spiritual fields' (Renfrew 1972, 11). From this perspective civilisation might represent a particularly elaborate form of a material insulation that cocooned an elite from the 'natural' brutalities of barbarism. However, if we were to pursue a different concept of civilisation (cf. Feuchtwang & Rowlands 2019), then it must be based upon the following two observations.

First, all forms of life, as I have repeatedly argued, have been constructed out of the ways that lives were lived as understandings of the worlds inhabited. While an increasing corpus of material culture certainly created the possibility for a materially embellished environment, it did not necessarily determine that environment's interpretation. The important point, and the one that distinguishes the approach followed here from earlier attempts to trace 'cultural influences', is that the solidarities of 'life as it was lived' need not have conformed with the geographical distribution of individual traits. Instead the solidarities of trust, authority, and understanding arose through the degrees to which forms of behaviour were able to recognise comparable worlds. The implication for archaeology is that the extent of a common cultural existence cannot be simply 'read off' from a uniform pattern of material traits. Instead the merits of each case have to be argued for.

Second, if we avoid the racist assumption that only some people possess the innate ability to become 'civilised', then growth in the idea of a common form of humanness has only ever been possible by virtue of its ability to express, to broadcast, and to experience, mutual understandings between the members of that particular kind of humanity. It is hardly surprising therefore that an elite might create itself by both expressing, and thus by broadcasting, its own understandings of the world and of its own origins by its access to, and its interpretation of, restricted media such as writing, or the esoteric reading of forms of artistic representation (e.g. Clark 1969), or by spiritual revelation.

Obviously, we need to establish archaeological procedures that can identify the difference between the local pragmatics of living, the structures of political cohesion, and the more general and more widely applicable principles by which larger patterns of cultural coherency could be recognised. Martin Furholt (2019) has recently distinguished between the intention of a practice (such as the intention to mark an individual's death by means of a single grave burial ritual), and the things that were employed by those practices (such as the choice of either corded ware vessels or beakers to be included amongst the grave furniture). The distinctions drawn by Furholt allow us to define three different levels of practice. These are: (1) the function of the practice (to bury the dead); (2) the acknowledgment of a generally accepted order of things (the becoming into being of the individual, the group, and of sexualised lives, and their ultimate death); (3) the local mechanisms that needed to be employed to construct the acceptance of that order (corpse orientation and artefact assemblage). This is similar to the structuralist distinctions which recognise that a functional need (1), is satisfied by a grammar that structures a way of life (2), by employing the practices of speaking and behaving by which that structure is lived (3). My argument is that the structural grammar (2), was widely shared (as implied by Furholt's identification of single grave rituals), and was the product of localised practices by which the structure was lived (3), and it was out of the latter that political obligations were built.

If these distinctions are accepted then they mean that the examination of archaeological residues should enable us to recognise the ways lives were lived by reference to two axes: one was the localised ways that structural conditions were experienced, and these generated the second axis which was the widely accepted structural conditions that had governed life. Local forms of political authority will have drawn upon these two dimensions to carve out systems of control. Politics becomes a process by which reference to the widely understood structural conditions is used to legitimate the control of local resources. As an example of how this analysis might work, and the problems that it raises, I will consider the contrasts that existed between the early Neolithic of central Europe and the Neolithic established along Europe's northern and western margins.

The early Neolithic in Europe

The early Neolithic of central and north-western Europe provides two contrasting ways in which the lives of these early farmers were structured. The practices by which the biological realities of life were addressed, that is the ways that people fed themselves and dealt with death, reveal marked differences in the establishment of agriculture between the two regions.

Between the sixth and the fourth millennia BCE a substantial migration of new forms of life appeared in the western part of the Eurasian landmass (see page 117), marking a significant dislocation in the long-term history of the biocultural composition of the human, plant, and animal populations found in the region (Shennan 2018). The Linearbandkeramik (LBK) cultural assemblage of material marks the earliest occurrence of this change and is believed to have originated from the northern extension of the Starčevo-Körös-Criş culture complex of the Balkan Neolithic (Shennan 2018, 86–101). Initially, the LBK was assumed to represent a widespread cultural uniformity arising from the rapid colonisation of the loess soils of central Europe. The agricultural practices that Gordon Childe, along with others, had asserted accompanied this colonisation were ones in which:

> [t]hey cultivated a plot till it would bear no more, and then another, and so on until they had used up all the land round the hamlet; thereupon they shifted bag and baggage to a new site on fresh virgin soil. (Childe 1957, 106)

This short-term, high-yield, cultivation was the model for a spreading colonisation driven by the land-use strategy and a growing population. The LBK material is now known to have been both earlier in the period it covers and longer in its making than writers such as Childe had allowed, and the practices involved are now also known to have expressed a greater degree of regional diversity than had once been suggested (Modderman 1988; Hofmann & Bickle 2011; Bickle & Whittle 2013a & 2013b). The model of LBK cultivation has changed significantly since Childe wrote, mainly as the result of work by Amy Bogaard (2004a).

Bogaard's argument is based on her analysis of crop residues (Bogaard 2004a & 2004b) and it argues that LBK settlement was associated with long-lived and intensively utilised small-plot agriculture, with the fertility of those plots being enhanced by their grazing and deliberate manuring (cf. Halstead 1989). These were agricultural systems in which households seemingly maintained, across the generations, their use-rights over particular areas of cultivated land (Bogaard 2004b, 51–53; Bogaard et al. 2011, 397), and isotopic evidence recovered from animal remains supports the existence of local grazing and the gathering of locally sourced fodder (Bogaard et al. 2016, 30–36). Consequently, Bogaard characterises the LBK agricultural system as one that utilised small 'garden plots' of intensive cultivation that were also associated with intensive livestock husbandry (Bogaard 2004a & 2004b).

Current archaeological analyses of LBK settlements and cemeteries have yielded a substantial reportage on various categories of deposits, finds, and structures, along with their comparanda. The aim of this work appears to be designed to accumulate a corpus of these assemblages upon which to base generalisations concerning their various formation processes. In other words, the material is taken to represent the processes of its formation, and it is these processes that are assumed to make the history of the period. However, let us start from the premise that history was made instead by those people who found ways of living amongst the material conditions that archaeology recovers. We are unlikely to establish the conceptualised schemes by which people had understood their world (cf. Hodder 1990), but we can propose how the things that once existed might have guided the embodied practices that made the history of the LBK possible.

The extent to which we can understand the principles that structured the lives of the LBK populations is obviously constrained by the survival of the archaeological data, as well as by our own lack of imagination (cf. Tringham 1991). The archaeology of the occupied landscapes of the LBK is currently dominated by the structural remains of timber longhouses (Claßen 2009; Hofmann & Bickle 2009; Hofmann & Smyth 2013), and the practices of living within the LBK world do seem to have been dominated by the references made towards the house, and thus, presumably, towards the household, its land, and its produce. Settlement clusters of these houses are known (Kuper et al. 1977), and these imply the formation of alliances between households, although the extent to which these alliances were indicative of emergent forms of settlement-wide political domination over individual households is unclear. A significant analytical problem resides with the fact that our understanding of the ways that the longhouses were used, and the length of their occupation, is inhibited by the eroded state of most of the ground plans (Hofmann 2013, 159–161), and the lack of a detailed radiocarbon chronology for the structures on any one settlement site. The case has been made that, in their 'developed' form, houses were composed of three structural units, some examples of which might have resulted from the extension and elaboration of an earlier building (Waterbolk & Modderman 1958/59; Rück 2009, 160 & Fig. 4). The elaboration and scale of these structures would presumably have emphasised the identity of their households, although the plans do not indicate the existence of complex entrances, which might have been expected, demarcating the formal boundary between the interior of the house and the outside world (Hofmann pers.comm.). Nonetheless entrance porches might well have existed at many of the south-eastern or southern gable-ends of these structures (Rück 2009, 166–168). Some foundation deposits are associated with some houses, although no obvious pattern in these exists, and with no particular emphasis upon deposits associated with possible house entrances (Hofmann pers.comm.). Households, whose day-to-day identities might have been signified by the house, might also have been perceived as deriving historically from one or more regional 'clans'. The existence of such clans has been claimed, based upon recognisable similarities in the traditions of craft production, in particular the regional distribution of different styles of pottery decoration (Strein 2011), and it was membership of such clans that might have facilitated access to clay sources and stone quarries. If the biocultural identity of a population was therefore dominated by an individual's membership of a household, signified by the house itself, and if that household had maintained widespread clan identities through its earlier patterns of recruitment, then we might seek to equate LBK societies with the 'house societies' that were discussed in the anthropology of Lévi-Strauss (1982, 174) and have been drawn into the archaeology of the early settlements of south-eastern Europe by Dušan Borić (2008).

The archaeological plans of LBK settlements are assumed to include the plans of some abandoned houses (e.g. Kuper et al. 1977), some of which appear to have been burnt (Hofmann pers.com.). Once again, the lack of surviving floors along with radiocarbon dating means that the problem of calculating the length of each building's occupancy remains unresolved (Modderman 1970; Rück 2009, 177–180; Midgley 2005, 130; Hofmann 2013, 161), and population estimates for each settlement cluster also remain contentious. Any suggested short-lived occupancy of these buildings (cf. Bradley 1998, 44) and thus the short-lived continuity of the household as a basic unit of production and consumption within the larger biocultural population is problematic, given the continuity of land-use that is indicated by Amy Bogaard's analysis of crop residues.

In her recent discussion of the human remains that have been recovered from the tell and settlement sites belonging to the Starčevo-Körös-Criş cultures of the Balkan Neolithic, Alexandra Ion has suggested that the 'archaeology of death' reveals that becoming dead was a far longer temporal process than the one that was marked by the moment of a biological death. The process of becoming dead in these cases had entailed a lengthy and staged involvement of the deceased's body with members of the living community during which time the 'becoming dead' seems to have remained a member of the living community (Ion 2020). The ability to keep the dead as part of the community through a ritualised involvement with their bodies might also have existed amongst the LBK communities. Many of the dead were certainly deposited on or near to the settlements and this might imply that the continuity of the household community might also have been extended to include the dead. Mortuary rituals that were located within or close to the settlements could therefore have entangled the living and the dead within a single community, and if this was indeed the case then it was likely to have made the abandonment of these locations traumatic for those who were involved. It does seem that the mortuary rituals were structured by recognising a political status that failed to reach much beyond that of a particular household, while the corpse itself carried isotopically the history of that person's movement that was determined by rules of kinship and residence (Brandt et al. 2014, 107).

All the factors would seem to indicate that the LBK occupation was structured by the continuity and reproductive success of households, and that this was signified by the houses themselves (Hachem & Hamon 2014), rather than being structured by the colonisation of new lands. Nonetheless, the longevity of activity on the settlement, the numbers of buildings, and the density of settlement across central Europe, imply the substantial and perhaps rapid growth in the overall size of the population (cf. Shennan 2018). There is therefore the need to recognise that the distinction between the processes of colonisation and expansion, and those of settlement growth and the infilling of the landscape, were likely to have been driven by different strategies of biocultural reproduction. Indeed, the archaeology of central European colonisation by domesticates might itself be difficult to identify, being overlain as it is likely to have been by the archaeology of later LBK consolidation and development.

The congregation of houses on early LBK settlements implies that if, as Modderman (1988) had argued (cf. Claßen 2009), the household was the basic social unit of the LBK, then the politics of settlement nucleation entails a process of development that presumably involved the pooling of labour that was directed towards the management of the domesticated populations of plants and animals, as well as the working of the cultivated and grazing lands. The enlargement of the settlement, and thus the increase in the available forces of production, might have been instigated by the need to extend the technologies of cultivation, including perhaps the maintenance of plough teams (Goody 1976). Household politics itself seems to have developed through the sexual and age divisions of labour (Brandt et al. 2014), and these labour divisions were also engendered, in part, by the biographies of mobility and residence (Bentley et al. 2012; Szécsényi-Nagi et al. 2014; for a more subtle reading of these data see Bickle 2020). The rituals and formal practices that had bound together the members of these household alliances have yet to be examined in any detail, although these were likely to have included feasting practices dominated by performances involving animal slaughter and meat sharing.

The tensions that could work against the alliances between households may have arisen, at least in part, because it was the house, and not the larger settlement, that had structured the patterns of behaviour, physical, relationships and material resources by providing the spatial configuration of the houses within which people grew and within which many things must have gained their familiarity. The formation of wider alliances between households might have been further disrupted by a rivalry based upon each household's reproductive success. It was therefore in the household that we might expect to locate the theatre in which many of the socio-political demands, structured by age and by gender, were performed (cf. Bourdieu 1990, 271–283). It was therefore the house, its land, and its produce that might have structured the ways that individuals behaved towards others, things, and places (Hofmann 2013). There may well have been times when these

localised systems of solidarity became so dominant that they resulted in the abandonment of any moral commitment towards those who might have challenged
or have lain outside these identities, and this might be witnessed by the rising
evidence for violence in the later LBK, violence that might have involved the mas-
sacre of entire households (Schulting & Fibiger 2014; Meyer et al. 2014).

The importance of the recent excavations of the LBK settlement at Vaihingen an der Enz (Bogaard et al. 2016) is not only determined by the very high
resolution of the data that have been collected, but by the ways that the site's
sequence illustrates how some of the tensions involved in the processes of settlement nucleation were played out. The forty or so houses belonging to the early
phase of Vaihingen settlement, the early and short-lived enclosure ditch, and the
identification, by Hans-Christoph Strien (in Bogaard 2012; Bogaard et al. 2016),
of the regional clan groupings to which clusters of houses on this settlement
appear to have been aligned (Bogaard et al. 2016, Fig. 6), might all imply that the
entire early sequence at Vaihingen was a failed attempt to subsume local clan and
household identities within an overriding identity manifest in a nucleated settlement. On the basis of the weed flora recovered from amongst the surviving grain,
and which indicate the kinds of cultivable soils from which the crops, and thus
the weeds, were gathered, different households had maintained, and presumably
inherited, access to different portions of cultivable land, some close to and some
further way from the settlement itself. The size of the settlement had fluctuated
over time, and the degree of settlement nucleation fragmented at the end of its
earliest phase of its history. There is no evidence that ecological 'crises' prompted
these fluctuations, instead it seems that agriculturally disadvantaged households
had moved away from this nucleation of houses: the centre in this case simply
could not hold. This fragmentation of the settlement community might also have
been accompanied by a change in feasting practices that is implied by the shift
away from an earlier dominance of cattle bone towards that of pig (Bogaard et al.
2016, 15–17), thus resulting in a lowering in the quantities of meat provided by
the individual act of slaughter.

> The Vaihingen situation suggests that LBK communities could break down
> when certain households were disadvantaged in the location of their ara-
> ble plots, prompting them to found new settlements or to join pre-existing
> communities elsewhere. An emerging hypothesis is thus that the need for
> households to be advantageously embedded in communities and local set-
> tings, allowing good access to proximate arable land that could be intensively
> managed, was at least one motivation for the spread of the LBK. (Outram &
> Bogaard 2019, 161)

The drawing of households into a single nucleated settlement had attempted
to override the centrifugal forces provided by the dispersed nature of each household's traditional lands, along with the traditions of production and resource
allocations that might have mapped widespread kinship relations amongst the

regional 'clans' (Bogaard et al. 2016, Fig. 6). These pressures may have made the mechanisms driving settlement nucleation vulnerable to fragmentation, and while the processes of settlement nucleation can be observed amongst other early agri-culturalists of south-eastern Europe (e.g. Gaydarska et al. 2019), it appears that the LBK system of population congregation ultimately failed. The recent and detailed analysis of the radiocarbon chronology for the Neolithic sequence in the middle Rhine valley has revealed a 'yawning gap' of some two centuries in the settle-ment sequence between the end of the LBK and the earliest middle Neolithic settlements that are defined by their use of Hinkelstein ceramics (Denaire et al. 2017, 1130). It appears that such a gap in the settlement sequence is also attested elsewhere along the Rhine valley (Denaire et al. 2017, 1136), indicating a cata-strophic depopulation of central Europe at the end of the sixth and the beginning of the fifth millennia BCE. While this break in the settlement sequence prompts the archaeological desire to explain it by reference to a single cause, we must allow for a diversity of reasons, including those that we cannot 'see' (cf. Shennan 2018, 101–105). These various factors might include the ways that the density of the populations would render them vulnerable to the spread of infection and to plague (Rascovan et al. 2019), or the ways that climatic variations would impact negatively on a nucleated settlement system already weakened by other kinds of social tensions (Gronenborne et al. 2014). The problem of attempting to iden-tify causal factors that might 'explain' material change has already been noted (see page 17), and future work might simply seek instead to identify some of the vulnerabilities within the reproduction of these biocultural systems that could have been contributing factors in the failure of these early agricultural settlements (cf. Bocquet-Appel et al. 2014).

The early Neolithic on the Atlantic margins of Europe stands in contrast with that of the central European LBK. The agricultural settlement of Atlantic Europe was established from the fifth and fourth millennia onwards. It marked the end of the process of biological colonisation that had brought agriculture into Europe along two main routes. One was through south-eastern and central Europe, attested for in central Europe in the sixth millennium BCE by the LBK, and which, in the fifth millennium, had extended to the north and west beyond the Paris basin into Belgium, and into Britain and Ireland by the beginning of the fourth millennium (Whittle & Cummings 2007; Whittle et al. 2011). The second route was around the coastal lands of the northern Mediterranean shores (Zeder 2008; de Vareilles et al. 2020), and this brought agriculture into southern France and then into south-western France and the Iberian Peninsula (Scarre 2002; Arias 2007). The Neolithic of Atlantic Europe was therefore colonised by an extension of the agricultural systems of central Europe, a colonisation that had occurred and had emerged during the post-LBK settlement of Europe. The regions that this agricultural colonisation entered were ones that had supported a substantial hunter-gatherer population, a biocultural population that presumably participated in its own extinction.

The archaeological remains of the earliest agricultural settlement of Atlantic Europe are not dominated by substantial longhouses and settlement clusters (e.g. Smyth 2014), although some more substantial domestic buildings are known (Thomas 2013, 285–313). Instead archaeological reference for early Neolithic structures tends to be made to mounds and more substantial enclosures whose attachment to patterns of long-lived settlement locations have yet to be adequately demonstrated (Thomas 2013, 315–353). Many, but not all, of the mounds had either contained, or had been built over, mortuary deposits (Midgley 2005), and these include the monuments that have been categorised as megalithic tombs (Laporte & Scarre 2016; Schulz Paulsson 2017). It was these structures that were once treated as testimony to the complex diffusion of cultural influences that might even have been expressions of a religious conversion disseminated by sea-borne contacts from the Mediterranean (Daniel 1963), and they have long been taken as indicative of complex rituals involving collective burial. It was these so-called 'megalithic tombs' that Renfrew argued could be understood from a non-diffusionist perspective (Renfrew 1976; see page 45).

Chronological uncertainties certainly accompany our understanding of the sequences of Neolithic materials around the Atlantic and Baltic margins of Europe (cf. Vander Linden 2011, 299; but see Whittle et al. 2011). It is therefore difficult to recognise a period of agricultural colonisation that predates the first stages of monument building, although this horizon of settlement might well have existed (cf. Case 1969). It is with these uncertainties in mind that we might accept the claim that the stone and earthen mounds originated at about the same time that Neolithic agriculture was established (cf. Scarre 2002, 24). Whatever the case, the mounds must have been a necessary and integral component that enabled the successful process of colonisation.

A number of commentators have sought to examine whether it was in the new soil regimes, the existing population densities of hunter-gatherers, or the coastal environment of the region as a whole, that the factors prompting these developments might lie (e.g. Hodder 1990, 178ff., & 1982b; Thomas 2013). Andrew Sherratt suggested that the contrast between the material of the central European Neolithic of the sixth millennium BCE, and that of north-west Europe, which had originated from the fifth millennium onwards, was one that risked being over-drawn:

> [i]t would be a mistake, . . ., to draw too sharp a line between early constructions in earth and stone and the substantial timber buildings of contemporary Neolithic groups in central Europe; or to see the effort devoted to 'religious' structures as fundamentally different in character from that devoted to 'domestic' structures elsewhere. (Sherratt 1990, 147)

Sherratt's desire to downplay the contrast between these building traditions has been repeated by Martin Furholt and Johannes Müller who suggest that models emphasising differences between the Neolithic of north-west Europe and that of the *contemporary* late and post-LBK developments in central Europe 'overlook the parallelism of developments in many key processes of these regions' (Furholt & Müller 2011, 26). The parallelism that Furholt and Müller believe they see is one in which different categories of monument (enclosures in west-central Europe and mounds in north-western Europe) can both represent the similar functions that were satisfied by the building of these non-settlement monuments. This claimed equivalence implies that the motivation to construct these different types of monument was to satisfy a similar functional requirement.

The reliance upon explaining monument construction through an equivalence of their undefined functions certainly reduces the contrast between the regions. It is important therefore to understand why such an argument misses the point. Let us begin by considering Furholt and Müller's discussion of monuments as representing a particular category of building. Monuments, they tell us, are not defined by their 'colossality' alone; instead, '[w]e normally think of a monument as something that is not entirely to be explained by any functional need but shows a distinct quality that could be called a *surplus of meaning*'. Upon this basis, they go on to define the 'surplus of meaning' of monuments in the following way: 'a *surplus of meaning* is realised by iconic signs or written text, or by a non-functional colossality. It might be achieved through a unique form, a distinguished, pre-eminent position in the landscape, and/or an outstanding elaboration . . .' (Furholt & Müller 2011, 16, my emphasis).

This so-called 'surplus of meaning' is therefore recognised by Furholt and Müller as being the indigenous meaning that is 'surplus' to, or that goes beyond the understanding of, the modern archaeologist. It was the Neolithic population who, according to Furholt and Müller, saw the mounds and enclosures as 'iconic', implying that they represented some mentally derived value to the contemporary population but where that value is now beyond the comprehension of any archaeological understanding. The two regions are therefore treated as being comparable simply because they both contained populations of agriculturalists who happened to represent, by monument building, beliefs that are now incomprehensible to us.

But way of an alternative we might see these differently designed monuments as being the technologies that could reveal different kinds of cultural order (i.e. meanings) to those who had lived and farmed these landscapes. That cultural order was not represented by the mounds in north-western Europe, any more than it was represented by the longhouses belonging to an earlier LBK. Instead it could only have emerged though the interaction between the ways that human bodies had moved across and had farmed these landscapes, and in these ways had engaged with these structures. Lesley McFadyen has repeatedly emphasised the way that the variable nature of the deposits, the stratigraphic sequences (including breaks in construction), and the complexities of the mounds' stability, had all resulted from the repetitive, developing, complex, and embodied performances that had occurred at these locations (McFadyen 2006 & 2007). A form of humanness was therefore created by uniting the embodied performances demanded by agricultural production with those that were involved in caring for and extending these mounds. Agriculturalists did not make each mound so it might represent some abstraction (the ancestral presence), or its function (a tomb), or what for us amounts to some mystery (a surplus of meaning). Instead they worked by building and by depositing things as a way of understanding where they fitted into the world by bringing into view that world from a particular perspective, and from which these mounds, and the behaviours that they demanded, made sense (Tilley 1996, 213–214; Barrett & Ko 2009). This was the construction of a meaningful assemblage comprising things and bodily practices. I take it that this is what McFadyen means when she refers to 'building as a practice in itself' (in Benson & Whittle 2007, 348), given that the details of the structural sequences that are recorded archaeologically trace the movement and efforts of human bodies in making the mound at that particular place. These practices were quite unlike those that were involved in digging and constructing an enclosure ditch, let alone the work involved in the construction and inhabitation of a timber longhouse.

Andrew Sherratt noted that the differences between the early Neolithic of central Europe and the early Neolithic of north-western Europe amounted to:

> a fundamental difference in the structure of settlement. Whereas the village was the basic settlement unit and primary community of Neolithic central Europe (whether in the form of a Balkan tell or a looser aggregation of substantial timber longhouses in the loess zone), early Neolithic settlement in western Europe was insubstantial and dispersed. The element of permanence seems to have been provided not by the settlements themselves, but by monumental tombs and enclosures. (Sherratt 1990, 149)

This is surely the point. That whilst the lives that were lived as part of the central European LBK might have been committed to a world view that was confirmed by the reproduction of the household, that focus was different in north-western Europe because here it included not only places of agricultural production but also places in the landscape that were marked by lengthy and complex acts of mound building, depositional practices, and mortuary rituals. These were different forms of life that were achieved by bringing into focus different understandings of the landscape and different perceptions of the places of biocultural existences within those landscapes. Thus, while the products of agrarian practices in these different regions might well have resulted in comparable organic residues (Bogaard & Jones 2007), and while settlements in the LBK might, from our perspective, have been functionally equivalent to the mounds constructed around the northern and western margins of Europe, inasmuch as both appear to have represented an order that had structured these worlds in such a way as to bring together communities who converged upon particular locations, the two regions remained examples of two very different kinds of Neolithic humanness simply because the populations of those regions had, through their routine actions, constructed different understandings of their place in the processes that were involved in the reproduction of their own lives.

Conclusion

The above argument returns to the main theme of this book, which is against the common assumption that archaeological materials should be treated as if they represented (or recorded) human actions, the function of those actions, or their cultural, social, or economic motivations. The materials might do all these things but, as the archaeology of the twentieth century has demonstrated, this reasoning does not get us very far, and it certainly does not result in explaining why certain things were done. It would surely be better to treat archaeological materials as the surviving residues of the things that people had once lived amongst, and where the task of archaeology is one of understanding something of the ways that different forms of life became possible by living amongst those things. This might awaken us to the ways that all forms of life have sought to understand the worlds that they have occupied, rather than the futility of humanity attempting to impose some prior notion of order upon that world.

EPILOGUE

The error of twentieth-century archaeology was to assume that the history of human behaviour was structured by some form of ultimate reality. Once the nature of that reality was established, so it was assumed, then the patterns of human behaviour would be explained. It was this assumption that resulted in archaeology attempting to build, by a combination of observation, analogy, and theory, the mechanisms to establish the reality that had supposedly determined the past actions of humans. These past actions had supposedly resulted in the formation of an archaeological record, with the result that archaeologists, studying the record, have sought the reality behind the actions they thought they could observe.

The New Archaeology claimed that the ultimate reality of causation comprised the environments, to which human communities had to adapt by employing the technologies available to them. Social Archaeology then extended this approach by claiming that the adaptive procedures had also to satisfy the demands of various forms of social organisation, and Interpretive Archaeology proposed that all human practices had utilised a semiotic logic that made sense to those social beings who were involved. Much of the debate concerning these options took place in a discourse that theorised the ways these various determinates could have operated. What appears to have been missing from these various historical narratives was an understanding of how such ultimate determinants might have arisen in the first place.

In their critical review of the work of Lynn Meskell and Robert Preucel (2004), Timothy Webmoor and Christopher Witmore (2008, 57) draw attention to the claim that 'in constructing objects *society* also constructs people' (Meskell & Preucel 2004, 14, my emphasis). This endows society with a primacy in the role of determining the construction of both people and objects. The previous chapters have attempted to offer one answer to the question that is posed, but is seemingly never answered, by Webmoor and Witmore, namely '[w]hat is this "social stuff" that supposedly designates something more real than materials'? (2008, 58).

In attempting to answer this question I have accepted that a real distinction separates living from non-living things. Living things exist in the ways that non-living things do not simply because living things are able to identify those aspects of the world around them that are necessary for them to grow and to develop (cf. Kohn 2013; Kull et al. 2009, 168). This means that the identification of any living thing should also include the assemblage of all those things within which its existence is entangled, in other words it would be the definition of the process of being alive, or one of becoming, within a wider ecology. Any attempt to define the living thing in itself, a process of objectification, would only be possible by stripping out all those other things within which its growth was entangled, a process that Bruno Latour has described as one of 'purification' (Latour 1993, 10–12). It follows that humanity appears to be an unstable category because various forms of humanness have developed within different assemblages of things. The processes of growing and developing as a person have always involved the interpretation of some aspects of the assemblages within which that person lives. This has always been a way to discover the values that have sustained different forms of humanness. It is the latter, the interpretation of the material conditions of life through praxis, that constitutes the 'really real' for any form of humanness, rather than the 'really real' simply being a world of concrete things. Bluntly, this means that forms of human life have not all inhabited the same world. Differences between kinds of humanness are constituted as the forms of life that have inhabited, or have been forced to inhabit, worlds that have always been worlds beyond their choosing. These cannot be treated as if they were cultural differences, that is as if they were the imposition of a cultural veneer upon a common material base (Venkatesan 2010). Thus, if we accept with Marx that the 'first premise of all human history is, of course, the existence of living human individuals' which are 'the real individuals, their activity and the material conditions under which they live' (Marx 1845/6), then the social is made by the convergence of individual lives upon a common understanding of their world.

> It is thus the laws of life within the individual, the laws that 'make him or her act', that determine the structure of a society. And thus all social activity, which apparently takes place outside of us, following seemingly objective rules, in reality finds its prefiguration and laws in ourselves and in our living subjectivity. (Henry 2019, 45)

Archaeology matters because its investigations should remind us of the ways that all of us live depending upon the ways that we can gain an understanding of, and engagement with, our worlds. We are not justified to impose an understanding upon others by supressing, destroying, or otherwise enslaving those lives, nor are we justified in attempting to deny access to that world in ways that include its destruction, and in so doing deny the ways in which it can be seen and experienced by others.

BIBLIOGRAPHY

Abramiuk, M.A. 2012, *The Foundations of a Cognitive Archaeology*, Cambridge MA: The MIT Press.

Adami, C. & A. Hintze 2018, Thermodynamics of evolutionary games, *Physical Review E*, 97(062136), 1–8, DOI: 10.1103/PhysRevE.97.062136.

Adkins-Regan, E., T.J. DeVoogd & J.M. Moore 2010, Social behaviour and bird song from a neural and endocrine perspective, in T. Székely, A.J. Moore, & J. Komdeur (eds.) *Social Behaviour: Genes, Ecology and Evolution*, Cambridge: Cambridge University Press, 59–84.

Alberti, B. 2016, Archaeologies of ontology, *Annual Review of Anthropology*, 45, 163–179, DOI: 10.1146/annurev-anthro-102215-095858.

Alberti, B., S. Fowles, M. Holbraad, Y. Marshall, & C. Witmore 2011, 'Worlds otherwise': archaeology, anthropology, and ontological difference, *Current Anthropology*, 52(6), 896–912, DOI: 10.1086/662027.

Alberti, B., A.M. Jones, & J. Pollard (eds.) 2013, *Archaeology After Interpretation: Returning Materials to Archaeological Interpretation*, Walnut Creek: Left Coast Press.

Ammerman, A.J. & L.L. Cavalli-Sforza 1979, The wave advance model for the spread of agriculture in Europe, in C. Renfrew & K.L. Cooke (eds.) *Transformations: Mathematical Approaches to Culture Change*, London: Elsevier, 275–293.

Anderson, J.R., P. Pettitt, & D. Biro (eds.) 2018, Evolutionary thanatology: impacts of the dead on the living in humans and other animals, *Philosophical Transactions of the Royal Society B*, 373(1754).

Ardrey, R. 1976, *The Hunting Hypothesis: A Personal Conclusion Concerning the Evolutionary Nature of Man*, Glasgow: William Collins.

Arias, P. 2007, Neighbours but diverse: social change in north-west Iberia during the transition from the Mesolithic to the Neolithic (5500–4000 cal BC), in A. Whittle & V. Cummings (eds.) *Going Over: The Mesolithic-Neolithic Transition in North-west Europe* (Proceedings of the British Academy 144), Oxford: Oxford University Press, 53–71.

Arnason, J.P. 1988, Social theory and the concept of civilisation, *Thesis Eleven*, 20, 87–105.

Arranz-Otaegui, A., L.G. Carretero, M.N. Ramsey, D.Q. Fuller, & T. Richter 2018, Archaeobotanical evidence reveals the origins of bread 14,400 years ago in northeastern

Jordan, *Proceedings of the National Academy of Sciences of the United States of America*, 115(31), 7925–7930.

Arrington, R.L. 2001, Following a rule, in H-J. Glock (ed.) *Wittgenstein: A Critical Reader*, Oxford: Blackwell, 119–137.

Asouti, E. & D.Q. Fuller 2012, From foraging to farming in the southern Levant: the development of Epipalaeolithic and Pre-pottery Neolithic plant management strategies, *Vegetation History and Archaeobotany*, 21(2), 149–162.

Aunger, R. 2002, *The Electric Meme: A New Theory of How We Think*, New York: The Free Press.

Bak, P. 1996, *How Nature Works: The Science of Self-organized Criticality*, New York: Springer-Verlag.

Barad, K. 2007, *Meeting the Universe Halfway: Quantum Physics and the Entanglement of Matter and Meaning*, Durham NC: Duke University Press.

Barker, G. 1995, *A Mediterranean Valley: Landscape Archaeology and the Annales History of the Biferno Valley*, Leicester: Leicester University Press.

Barker, G. 2006, *The Agricultural Revolution in Prehistory: Why Did Foragers Become Farmers?* Oxford: Oxford University Press.

Barker, P. 1982, *Techniques of Archaeological Excavation* (3rd edition), London: Batsford.

Barlow, G.W. & J. Silverberg (eds.) 1980, *Sociobiology: Beyond Nature/Nurture? Reports, Definitions and Debate* (AAAS Selected Symposium 35), Boulder: Westview Press.

Barrett, J.C. 1994, *Fragments from Antiquity: An Archaeology of Social Life in Britain, 2900–1200 BC*, Oxford: Blackwell.

Barrett, J.C. 2011, The Neolithic Revolution: an ecological perspective, in A. Hadjikoumis, E. Robinson, & S. Viner (eds.) *Dynamics of Neolithisation in Europe: Studies in Honour of Andrew Sherratt*, Oxford: Oxbow Books, 66–89.

Barrett, J.C. 2012, Are models of prestige goods economies and conspicuous consumption applicable to the archaeology of the Bronze to Iron transition in Britain? In A.M. Jones, J. Pollard, M.J. Allen, & J. Gardiner (eds.) *Image, Memory and Monumentality: Archaeological Engagements with the Material World* (Prehistoric Society Research Paper 5), Oxford: Oxbow Books, 6–17.

Barrett, J.C. 2013, The archaeology of mind: it's not what you think, *Cambridge Archaeological Journal*, 23(1), 1–17.

Barrett, J.C. 2014a, The material constitution of humanness, *Archaeological Dialogues*, 21(1), 65–74.

Barrett, J.C. 2014b, Some possible conditions necessary for the colonisation of Europe by domesticates, in A. Whittle & P. Bickle (eds.) *Early Farmers: The View from Archaeology and Science* (Proceedings of the British Academy 198), Oxford: Oxford University Press, 39–51.

Barrett, J.C. 2016, The new antiquarianism? *Antiquity*, 90, 1681–1686.

Barrett, J.C. & M.J. Boyd 2019, *From Stonehenge to Mycenae*, London: Bloomsbury.

Barrett, J.C. & I. Ko 2009, A phenomenology of landscape: a crisis in British landscape archaeology? *Journal of Social Archaeology*, 9(3), 275–294.

Bar-Yosef, O. & R.H. Meadow 1995, The origins of agriculture in the Near East, in T. Douglas Price & A. Birgitte-Gebauer (eds.) *Last Hunters, First Farmers: New Perspectives on the Prehistoric Transition to Agriculture*, Santa Fe: School of American Research Press, 39–94.

Bender, B. 1978, Gatherer-hunter to farmer: a social perspective, *World Archaeology*, 10(2), 204–222.

Bennett, J. 2010, *Vibrant Matter: A Political Ecology of Things*, Durham NC: Duke University Press.

Benson, D. & A. Whittle (eds.) 2007, *Building Memories: The Neolithic Cotswold Long Barrow at Ascott-Under-Wychwood, Oxfordshire*, Oxford: Oxbow Books.

Bentley, A.R., P. Bickle, L. Fibiger, G.M. Nowell, C.W. Dale, R.E.M. Hedges, J. Hamilton, J. Wahl, M. Francken, G. Grupe, E. Lenneis, M. Teschler-Nicola, R-M. Arbogast, D. Hofmann, & A. Whittle 2012, Community differentiation and kinship among Europe's first farmers, *Proceedings of the National Academy of Sciences*, 109, 9326–9330.

Bhaskar, R. 1997, *A Realist Theory of Science* (2nd edition), London: Verso.

Bickle, P. 2020, Thinking gender differently: new approaches to identity difference in the central European Neolithic, *Cambridge Archaeological Journal*, 39(2), 201–218.

Bickle, P. & A. Whittle (eds.) 2013a, *The First Farmers of Central Europe: Diversity in LBK Lifeways*, Oxford: Oxbow Books.

Bickle, P. & A. Whittle (eds.) 2013b, LBK lifeways: a search for difference, in P. Bickle & A. Whittle (eds.) *The First Farmers of Central Europe: Diversity in LBK Lifeways*, Oxford: Oxbow Books, 1–27.

Bickle, P. & A. Whittle 2014, Introduction: integrated and multi-scalar approaches to early farmers in Europe, in A. Whittle & P. Bickle (eds.) *Early Farmers: The View from Archaeology and Science* (Proceedings of the British Academy 198), Oxford: Oxford University Press, 1–19.

Binford, L.R. 1962, Archaeology as anthropology, *American Antiquity*, 28(2), 217–225.

Binford, L.R. 1967, Smudge pits and hide smoking: the use of analogy in archaeological reasoning, *American Antiquity*, 32(1), 1–12.

Binford, L.R. 1968, Post-Pleistocene adaptations, in S.R. Binford & L.R. Binford (eds.) *New Perspectives in Archaeology*, Chicago: Aldine Press, 313–341.

Binford, L.R. 1971, Mortuary practices: their study and potential, in J.A. Brown (ed.) *Approaches to the Social Dimensions of Mortuary Practices*, Washington DC: Memoirs of the Society for American Archaeology No. 25, 6–29.

Binford, L.R. 1972, *An Archaeological Perspective*, New York: Seminar Press.

Binford, L.R. 1973, Interassemblage variability – the Mousterian and the 'functional' argument, in C. Renfrew (ed.) *The Explanation of Culture Change: Models in Prehistory*, London: Duckworth, 227–254.

Binford, L.R. 1981a, *Bones: Ancient Men and Modern Myths*, London: Academic Press.

Binford, L.R. 1981b, Behavioral archaeology and the 'Pompeii Premise', *Journal of Anthropological Research*, 37(3), 195–208.

Binford, L.R. 1982, Objectivity-explanation-archaeology 1981, in C. Renfrew, M.J. Rowlands, & B.A. Segraves (eds.) *Theory and Explanation in Archaeology: The Southampton Conference*, London: Academic Press, 125–138.

Binford, L.R. 1983, *In Pursuit of the Past: Decoding the Archaeological Record*, London: Thames and Hudson.

Binford, L.R. 1985, 'Brand X' versus the recommended product, *American Antiquity*, 50, 580–590.

Binford, L.R. 1987, Data, relativism and archaeological science, *Man*, 22, 391–404.

Binford, L.R. 2001, *Constructing Frames of Reference: An Analytical Method for Archaeological Theory Building Using Ethnographic and Environmental Data*, Berkeley: University of California Press.

Binford, S.R. & L.R. Binford (eds.) 1968, *New Perspectives in Archaeology*, Chicago: Aldine Publishing Company.

Bintliff, J. 2011, The death of archaeological theory? In J. Bintliff & M. Pearce (eds.) *The Death of Archaeological Theory?* Oxford: Oxbow Books, 7–22.

Birch, S.E.P. 2018, Introduction, in S.E.P. Birch (ed.) *Multispecies Archaeology*, Abingdon: Routledge, 1–17.

Bird-David, N. 1990, The giving environment: another perspective on the economic systems of hunter-gatherers, *Current Anthropology*, 31, 189–206.

Blackmore, S. 1999, *The Meme Machine*, Oxford: Oxford University Press.

Bloch, M. 1971, *Placing the Dead*, London: Seminar Press.

Bloor, D. 1991, *Knowledge and Social Imagery* (2nd Edition), Chicago: University of Chicago Press.

Bloor, D. 2002 [1997], *Wittgenstein, Rules and Institutions*, London: Routledge.

Boast, R. 1997, A small company of actors: a critique of style, *Journal of Material Culture*, 2(2), 173–198.

Bocquet-Appel, J-P. 2002, Paleoanthroplogical traces of a Neolithic demographic transition, *Current Anthropology*, 43(4), 637–650.

Bocquet-Appel, J-P. 2011, When the world's population took off: the springboard of the Neolithic demographic transition, *Science*, 333(6042), 560–561.

Bocquet-Appel, J-P., J. Dubouloz, R. Moussa, J-F. Berger, A. Tresset, E. Ortu, J-D. Vigne, R. Bendrey, S. Bréhard, D. Schwartz, A. Salavert, M.F. Sanchez-Goñi, D. Ertlen, Y. Gauvry, G. Davtian, M. Vander Linden, E. Lenneis, L. Noiret, A. Guillaumont, & M. O'Connor 2014, Multi-agent modelling of the trajectory of the LBK Neolithic, in A. Whittle & P. Bickle (eds.) *Early Farmers: The View from Archaeology and Science* (Proceedings of the British Academy 198), Oxford: Oxford University Press, 53–69.

Bogaard, A. 2004a, *Neolithic Farming in Central Europe: An Archaeological Study of Crop Husbandry Practices*, London: Routledge.

Bogaard, A. 2004b, The nature of early farming in central and south-east Europe, *Documenta Praehistorica*, 31, 49–58.

Bogaard, A. 2012, *Plant Use and Crop Husbandry in an Early Neolithic Village: Vaihingen an der Enz, Baden-Wurttemberg*, Bonn: GmbH.

Bogaard, A. 2014, Framing farming: a multi-stranded approach to early agricultural practice in Europe, in A. Whittle & P. Bickle (eds.) *Early Farmers: The View from Archaeology and Science* (Proceedings of the British Academy 198), Oxford: Oxford University Press, 181–196.

Bogaard, A. & G. Jones 2007, Neolithic farming in Britain and central Europe: contrast or continuity, in A. Whittle & V. Cummings (eds.) *Going Over: The Mesolithic–Neolithic Transition in North-west Europe* (Proceedings of the British Academy 144), Oxford: Oxford University Press, 357–375.

Bogaard, A., R. Krause, & H-C. Strien 2011, Towards a social geography of plant use in an early farming community: Vaihingen an der Enz, south-west Germany, *Antiquity*, 89, 395–416.

Bogaard, A., R-M. Arbogast, R. Ebersbach, R.A. Fraser, C. Knipper, C. Krahn, M. Schafer, M. Styring, & R. Krause 2016, The Bandkeramik settlement of Vaihingen an der Enz, Kreis Ludwigsburg (Baden-Württemberg): an integrated perspective on land use, economy and diet, *Germania*, 94, 1–60.

Bogucki, P. 2000, How agriculture came to north-central Europe, in T.D. Price (ed.) *Europe's First Farmers*, Cambridge: Cambridge University Press, 197–218.

Bogucki, P. 2003, Neolithic dispersals in riverine interior central Europe, in A.J. Ammerman & P. Biagi (eds.) *The Widening Harvest: The Neolithic Transition in Europe – Looking Back, Looking Forward*, Boston MA: Archaeological Institute of America, 249–272.

Borić, D. 2008, First households and 'house societies' in European prehistory, in A. Jones (ed.) *Prehistoric Europe: Theory and Practice*, Oxford: Wiley-Blackwell, 109–142.

Botterill, G. 2010, Two kinds of causal explanation, *Theoria*, 76, 287–313, DOI:10.1111/j.1755-2567.2010.01079.x.

Bourdieu, P. 1977, *Outline of a Theory of Practice* (translated by R. Nice), Cambridge: Cambridge University Press.

Bourdieu, P. 1990, *The Logic of Practice* (translated by R. Nice), Cambridge: Polity Press.

Boyd, B. 2018, An archaeological telling of multispecies co-inhabitation: comments on the origins of agriculture and domestication narrative in Southwest Asia, in S.P. Birch (ed.) Multispecies Archaeology, London: Routledge, 251–270.

Boyd, R. & P.J. Richerson 1985, *Culture and the Evolutionary Process*, Chicago: University of Chicago Press.

Brace, S., Y. Diekmann, T.J. Booth, Z. Faltyskova, N. Rohland, S. Mallick, M. Ferry, M. Michel, J. Oppenheimer, N. Broomandkhoshbacht, K. Stewardson, S. Walsh, M. Kayser, R. Schulting, O.E. Craig, A. Sheridan, M. Parker Pearson, C. Stringer, D. Reich, M.G. Thomas, & I. Barnes 2018, Population replacement in Early Neolithic Britain, bioRxiv reprint Feb. 18, 2018, DOI.org/10.1101/267443.

Bradley, R. 1978, *The Prehistoric Settlement of Britain*, London: Routledge and Kegan Paul.

Bradley, R. 1991, The pattern of change in British prehistory, in T. Earle (ed.) *Chiefdoms: Power, Economy and Ideology*, Cambridge: Cambridge University Press, 44–70.

Bradley, R. 1997, 'To see is to have seen': craft traditions in British field archaeology, in B.L. Molyneaux (ed.) *The Cultural Life of Images*, London: Routledge, 62–72.

Bradley, R. 1998, *The Significance of Monuments: On the Shaping of Human Experience in Neolithic and Bronze Age Europe*, London: Routledge.

Braidotti, R. 2019a, *Posthuman Knowledge*, Cambridge: Polity Press.

Braidotti, R. 2019b, A theoretical framework for the critical posthumanities, *Theory, Culture and Society*, 36(6), 31–61.

Braidwood, R.J. 1958, Vere Gordon Childe, 1892–1957, *American Anthropologist*, 60(4), 733–736.

Braidwood, R.J., J.D. Sauer, H. Helbaek, P.D. Mangelsdorf, H.C. Cutler, C.S. Coon, R. Linton, J. Steward, & A.L. Oppenheim 1953, Symposium: did man once live by beer alone? *American Anthropologist*, 55(4), 515–526, DOI: 10.1525/aa.1953.55.4.02a00050.

Brain, C.K. 1981, *The Hunters or the Hunted: An Introduction to African Cave Taphonomy*, Chicago: University of Chicago Press.

Braithwaite, R.B. 1964, *Scientific Explanation: A Study of the Function of Theory, Probability and Law in Science*, Cambridge: Cambridge University Press.

Bramanti, B., M.G. Thomas, W. Haak, M. Unterlaender, P. Jores, K. Tambets, I. Antanaitis-Jacobs, M.N. Haidle, R. Jankauskas, C-J. Kind, F. Lueth, T. Terberger, J. Hiller, S. Matsumura, P. Forster, J. Burger 2009, Genetic discontinuity between local hunter-gatherers and central Europe's first farmers, *Science*, 327(5949), 127–140, DOI: 10.1126/science.1176869.

Brandt, G., C. Knipper, N. Nicklisch, R. Ganslmeier, M. Klamm, & K.W. Alt 2014, Settlement burials at the Karsdorf LBK site, Saxony-Anhalt, Germany: biological ties and residential mobility, in A. Whittle & P. Bickle (eds.) *Early Farmers: The View from Archaeology and Science* (Proceedings of the British Academy 198), Oxford: Oxford University Press, 95–114.

Buchli, V.A. 1995, Interpreting material culture: the trouble with text, in I. Hodder, M. Shanks, A. Alexandri, V. Buchli, J. Carman, J. Last, & G. Lucas (eds.) *Interpreting Archaeology: Finding Meaning in the Past*, London: Routledge, 181–193.

Capra, F. & P.L. Luisi 2014, *The Systems View of Life: A Unifying Vision*, Cambridge: Cambridge University Press.

Carver, M. 2009, *Archaeological Investigation*, London: Routledge.

Case, H.J. 1969, Neolithic explanations, *Antiquity*, 43(171), 176–186.

Catapoti, D. & M. Relaki 2020, Why the Neolithic is (r)evolutionary, *Journal of Material Culture*, 25, 1–20.

Cauvin, J. 2000, *The Birth of the Gods and the Origins of Agriculture* (translated by T. Watkins), Cambridge: Cambridge University Press.

Chan, C.X. & D. Bhattacharya 2013, Analysis of horizontal genetic transfer in red algae in the post-genomics age, *Mobile Genetic Elements*, 3(6), e27669, DOI:10.4161/mge.27669.

Chapman, R. 1981, The emergence of formal disposal areas and the 'problem' of megalithic tombs in prehistoric Europe, in R. Chapman, I. Kinnes, & K. Randsborg (eds.) *The Archaeology of Death*, Cambridge: Cambridge University Press, 71–81.

Chapman, R. 2003, *Archaeologies of Complexity*, London: Routledge.

Chapman, R. & K. Randsborg 1981, Approaches to the archaeology of death, in R. Chapman, I. Kinnes, & K. Randsborg (eds.) *The Archaeology of Death*, Cambridge: Cambridge University Press, 1–24.

Chapman, R. & A. Wylie 2016, *Evidential Reasoning in Archaeology*, London: Bloomsbury.

Charney, E. 2012, Behavior genetics and postgenomics, *Behavioral and Brain Sciences*, 35, 331–410, DOI:10.1017/S0140525X11002226.

Childe, V.G. 1929, *The Danube in Prehistory*, Oxford: Clarendon Press.

Childe, V.G. 1939, The Orient and Europe, *American Journal of Archaeology*, 43(1), 10–26.

Childe, V.G. 1940, *Prehistoric Communities of the British Isles*, London: Chambers.

Childe, V.G. 1950, The urban revolution, *The Town Planning Review*, 21, 3–17.

Childe, V.G. 1956, *Piecing Together the Past*, London: Routledge & Kegan Paul.

Childe, V.G. 1957, *The Dawn of European Civilization* (6th edition), London: Routledge & Kegan Paul.

Childe, V.G. 1958, *The Prehistory of European Society*, London: Penguin Books.

Childe, V.G. 1965, *Man Makes Himself* (4th edition), London: Fontana.

Cipolla, C.N. 2018, Earth flows and lively stone: what differences does 'vibrant' matter make? *Archaeological Dialogues*, 25(1), 49–70.

Clark, A. 2003, *Natural Born Cyborgs: Minds, Technologies, and the Future of Human Intelligence*, Oxford: Oxford University Press.

Clark, A. 2008, *Supersizing the Mind: Embodiment, Action, and Cognitive Extension*, Oxford: Oxford University Press.

Clark, J.G.D. 1952, *Prehistoric Europe: The Economic Basis*, London: Methuen.

Clark, J.G.D. 1954, *Excavations at Star Carr: An Early Mesolithic Site at Seamer near Scarborough, Yorkshire*, Cambridge: Cambridge University Press.

Clark, J.G.D. 1957, *Archaeology and Society: Reconstructing the Prehistoric Past* (3rd edition), London: Methuen.

Clark, K. 1969, *Civilisation: A Personal View*, London: John Murray.

Clarke, D.L. 1968, *Analytical Archaeology*, London: Methuen.

Clarke, D.L. 1972a, Models and paradigms in contemporary archaeology, in D.L. Clarke (ed.) *Models in Archaeology*, London: Methuen, 1–60.

Clarke, D.L. 1972b, A provisional model of an Iron Age society and its settlement system, in D.L. Clarke (ed.) *Models in Archaeology*, London: Methuen, 801–869.

Claßen, E. 2009, Settlement history, land use and social networks of early Neolithic communities in western Germany, in D. Hofmann & P. Bickle (eds.) *Creating Communities: New Advances in Central European Neolithic Research*, Oxford: Oxbow Books, 95–110.

Cohen, N. 1977, *The Food Crisis in Prehistory: Overpopulation and the Origins of Agriculture*, New Haven: Yale University Press.

Collingwood, R.G. 1994, *The Idea of History* (Revised edition), Oxford: Oxford University Press.

Crellin, R.J. & O.T. Harris 2020, Beyond binaries: interrogating ancient DNA, *Archaeological Dialogues*, 27, 37–56, DOI:10.1017/S1380203820000082.

Cronk, L. & B.L. Leech 2013, *Meeting at Grand Central: Understanding the Social and Evolutionary Roots of Co-operation*, Princeton: Princeton University Press.

Crossland, Z. 2014, *Ancestral Encounters in Highland Madagascar: Material Signs and Traces of the Dead*, Cambridge: Cambridge University Press.

Currie, A. 2018, *Rock, Bone and Ruin: An Optimist's Guide to the Historical Sciences*, Cambridge MA: The MIT Press.

Daniel, G.E. 1950a, *A Hundred Years of Archaeology*, London: Duckworth.

Daniel, G.E. 1950b, *The Prehistoric Chamber Tombs of England and Wales*, Cambridge: Cambridge University Press.

Daniel, G.E. 1960, *The Prehistoric Chamber Tombs of France: A Geographical, Morphological and Chronological Survey*, London: Thames and Hudson.

Daniel, G.E. 1963, *The Megalith Builders of Western Europe* (2nd edition), London: Penguin Books.

Daniel, G. 1964, *The Idea of Prehistory*, London: Penguin Books.

Dart, R.A. 1949, The predatory implemental techniques of Australopithecus, *American Journal of Physical Anthropology*, 7(1), 1–38.

Darwin, C. 2009 [1859], *On the Origin of Species by Means of Natural Selection or The Preservation of Favoured Races in the Struggle for Life* (ed. W. Bynum), London: Penguin Books.

Dawkins, R. 1978 [1976], *The Selfish Gene*, London: Granada Publishing.

Dawkins, R. 1999, *The Extended Phenotype: The Long Reach of the Gene* (Revised edition), Oxford: Oxford University Press.

Deacon, T. 1997, *The Symbolic Species: The Co-evolution of Language and the Human Brain*, London: Allen Lane The Penguin Press.

DeLanda, M. 2016, *Assemblage Theory*, Edinburgh: Edinburgh University Press.

Denaire, A., L. Philippe, J. Wahl, C.B. Ramsey, E. Dunbar, T. Goslar, A. Bayliss, N. Beavan, P. Bickle, & A. Whittle 2017, The cultural project: formal chronological modelling of the Early and Middle Neolithic sequence in Lower Alsace, *Journal of Archaeological Method Theory*, 24, 1072–1149.

Dennell, R. 1985, The hunter-gatherer/agricultural frontier in prehistoric Europe, in S.W. Green & S.M Perlman (eds.) *The Archaeology of Frontiers and Boundaries*, London: Academic Press, 113–139.

Dennett, D.C. 1971, Intentional systems, *The Journal of Philosophy*, 68(4), 87–106.

Dennett, D.C. 1996, *Darwin's Dangerous Idea: Evolution and the Meaning of Life*, London: Penguin Books.

Descombes, V. 1986, *Objects of All Sorts: A Philosophical Grammar*, Oxford: Oxford University Press.

Descombes, V. 2001, *The Mind's Provisions: A Critique of Cognitivism*, Oxford: Oxford University Press.

De Vareilles, A., L. Bouby, A. Jesus, L. Martin, M. Rottoli, M. Vander Linden, & F. Antolín 2020, One sea but many routes to sail: the early maritime dispersal of Neolithic crops from the Aegean to the western Mediterranean, *Journal of Archaeological Science: Reports*, 29, 102140, DOI.org/10.1016/j.jasrep.2019.102140.

De Waal, F. 2016, *Are We Smart Enough to Know How Smart Animals Are?* London: Granta Books.

Dietrich, O., M. Heun, J. Notroff, K. Schmidt, & M. Zarnkow 2012, The role of cult and feasting in the emergence of Neolithic communities: new evidence from Göbekli Tepe, south-eastern Turkey, *Antiquity*, 86, 674–695.

Dray, W. 1957, *Laws and Explanation in History*, Oxford: Oxford University Press.

Dray, W. 1959, 'Explaining what' in history, in P. Gardiner (ed.) *Theories of History*, Glencoe IL: The Free Press, 403–408.

Drennan, R.D., T. Earle, G.M. Fienman, R. Fletcher, M.J. Kolb, P. Peregrine, C.E. Paterson, C. Sinopoli, M.E. Smith, M.L. Smith, B.L. Stark, & M.T. Stark 2012, Comparative Archaeology: a commitment to understanding variation, in M.E. Smith (ed.) *The Comparative Archaeology of Complex Societies*, Cambridge: Cambridge University Press, 1–3.

Dunnell, R.C. 1978, Style and function: a fundamental dichotomy, *American Antiquity*, 43(2), 192–202.

Dunning L.T., J. K. Olofsson, C. Parisod, R.R. Choudhury, J.J. Moreno-Villena, Y. Yang, J. Dionora, W.P. Quick, M. Park, J.L. Bennetzen, G. Besnard, P. Nosil, C.P. Osborn, & P-A. Christin 2019, Lateral transfers of large DNA fragments spread functional genes among grasses, *Proceedings of the National Academy of Sciences of the United States of America*, 116(10), 4416–4425.

Dupré, J. 2010, It is not possible to reduce biological explanations to explanations in chemistry and/or physics, in F.J. Ayala & R. Arp (eds.) *Contemporary Debates in Philosophy of Biology*, Chichester: Willey-Blackwell, 32–47.

Dupré, J. 2012, *Processes of Life: Essays in the Philosophy of Biology*, Oxford: Oxford University Press.

Dupré, J. 2018, Human nature: a process perspective, in E. Hannon & T. Lewins (eds.) *Why We Disagree About Human Nature*, Oxford: Oxford University Press, 92–107.

Earle, T.K. 1977, A reappraisal of redistribution: complex Hawaiian chiefdoms, in T.K. Earle and J.E. Ericson (eds.) *Exchange Systems in Prehistory*, New York: Academic Press, 213–229.

Earle, T. 1991, *Chiefdoms: Power, Economy, and Ideology*, Cambridge: Cambridge University Press.

Earle, T.K. & R.W. Preucel 1987, Processual archaeology and the radical critique (with comments), *Current Anthropology*, 28(4), 501–538.

Edgeworth, M. 2016, Grounded objects: archaeology and speculative realism, *Archaeological Dialogues*, 23(1), 93–113, DOI:10.1017/S138020381600012X.

Ekholm, K. 1977, External exchange and the transformation of central African social systems, in J. Friedman & M.J. Rowlands (eds.) *The Evolution of Social Systems*, London: Duckworth, 115–136.

Ekholm, K. 1980, On the limitations of civilization: the structure and dynamics of global systems, *Dialectical Anthropology*, 5(2), 155–166.

Eldredge, N. 1995, *Reinventing Darwin: The Great Evolutionary Debate*, London: Weidenfeld & Nicolson.

El-Hani, C.N., J. Queiroz, & C. Emmeche 2009, *Genes, Information, and Semiosis*, Tartu: Tartu University Press.

Emmeche, C. & K. Kull 2011, *Towards a Semiotic Biology: Life Is the Action of Signs*, London: Imperial College Press.

Evans, J. 1956, *A History of The Society of Antiquaries*, London: Society of Antiquaries.

Fagan, B. 2001, *Graham Clark: An Intellectual Biography of an Archaeologist*, Boulder: Westview Press.

Fahlander, F. 2004, Archaeology and anthropology: brothers in arms? On analogies in 21st century archaeology, in F. Fahlander & T. Oestigaard (eds.) *Material Culture and other Things – Post-disciplinary Studies in the 21st Century*, Gothenburg: University of Gothenburg, 157–180.

Falk, R. 1986, What is a gene? *Studies in the History and Philosophy of Science*, 17, 133–173.

Feuchtwang, S. & M. Rowlands 2019, *Civilisation Recast: Theoretical and Historical Perspectives*, Cambridge: Cambridge University Press.

Flannery, K.V. 1967, Review article. Culture history versus cultural process: a debate in American archaeology, *Scientific American*, 217(2), 119–122.

Flannery, K.V. 1968, Archaeological systems theory and Early Mesoamerica, in B.J. Meggers (ed.) *Anthropological Archaeology in the Americas*, Washington DC: The Anthropological Society of Washington, 67–87.

Flannery, K.V. 1972, The cultural evolution of civilisations, *Annual Review of Ecology and Systematics*, 3, 399–426.

Flannery, K.V. 1973, The origins of agriculture, *Annual Review of Anthropology*, 2, 271–310.

Flannery, K.V. (ed.) 1976, *The Early Mesoamerican Village*, New York: Academic Press.

Flannery, K.V. & M.C. Winter 1976, Analyzing household activities, in K.V. Flannery (ed.) *The Early Mesoamerican Village*, New York: Academic Press, 34–47.

Flannery, K. & J. Marcus, 2012, *The Creation of Inequality: How Our Prehistoric Ancestors Set the Stage for Monarchy, Slavery and Empire*, Cambridge MA: Harvard University Press.

Fogle, T. 1990, Are genes units of inheritance? *Biology and Philosophy*, 5, 349–371.

Foucault, M. 1972, *The Archaeology of Knowledge* (translated by A.M. Sheridan Smith), London: Tavistock.

Frankenstein, S. & M.J. Rowlands 1978, The internal structure and regional context of early Iron Age society in southwest Germany, *Bulletin of the Institute of Archaeology of London*, 15, 73–112.

Frere, J. 1800, Account of flint weapons discovered at *Hoxne* in *Suffolk*, *Archaeologia*, 13, 204–205.

Fried, M.H. 1967, *The Evolution of Political Society: An Essay in Political Society*, New York: Random House.

Friedman, J. 1994, *Cultural Identity and Global Process*, London: Sage.

Friedman, J. & M.J. Rowlands (eds.) 1977, *The Evolution of Social Systems*, London: Duckworth.

Frieman, C.J. & D. Hofmann 2019, Present pasts in the archaeology of genetics, identity, and migration in Europe: a critical essay, *World Archaeology*, DOI:10.1080/00438243.2019.1627907.

Fritz, J.M. 1973, Relevance, archaeology and subsistence theory, in C.L. Redman (ed.) *Research and Theory in Current Archaeology*, New York: John Wiley & Sons, 59–82.

Fritz, J.M. & F.T. Plog 1970, The nature of archaeological explanation, *American Antiquity*, 35, 405–412.

Fuller, D.Q., G. Willcox, & R.G. Allaby 2012, Early agricultural pathways: moving outside the 'core area' hypothesis in Southwest Asia, *Journal of Experimental Botany*, 63(2), 617–633 DOI:10.1093/jxb/err307.

Furholt, M. 2019, Re-integrating archaeology: a contribution to aDNA studies and the migration discourse on the 3rd millennium BC in Europe, *Proceedings of the Prehistoric Society*, 85, 115–129.

Furholt, M. & J. Müller 2011, The earliest monuments in Europe – architecture and social structure (5000–3000 cal BC), in M. Furholt, F. Luth, & J. Muller (eds.) *Megaliths and Identities: Early Monuments in Neolithic Societies from the Atlantic to the Baltic*, Bonn: GmbH, 15–32.

Gamble, C. 1993, *Timewalkers: The Prehistory of Global Colonisation*, Stroud: Alan Sutton.

Gamble, C. 2007, *Origins and Revolutions: Human Identity in Earliest Prehistory*, Cambridge: Cambridge University Press.

Gamble, C. 2014, The anthropology of deep history, *Journal of the Royal Anthropological Institute* (new series), 21, 147–164.

Gaydarska, B., M. Nebbia, & J. Chapman 2019, Trypillia megasites in context: independent urban development in chalcolithic Eastern Europe, *Cambridge Archaeological Journal*, 30(1), 97–121.

Gellner, E. 1982, What is structuralisme? in C. Renfrew, M.J. Rowlands, & B.A. Segraves (eds.) *Theory and Explanation in Archaeology: The Southampton Conference*, London: Academic Press, 97–123.

Giddens, A. 1979, *Central Problems in Social Theory: Action, Structure and Contradiction in Social Analysis*, London: The Macmillan Press.

Giddens, A. 1981, *A Contemporary Critique of Historical Materialism: Vol. 1, Power, Property and the State*, London: The Macmillan Press.

Giddens, A. 1984, The *Constitution of Society: Outline of the Theory of Structuration*, Cambridge: Polity Press.

Gilman, A. 1991, Trajectories towards social complexity in the later prehistory of the Mediterranean, in T. Earle (ed.) *Chiefdoms: Power, Economy, and Ideology*, Cambridge: Cambridge University Press, 146–168.

Giot, P.R. 1963, *Les Civilisations Atlantiques du Néolithique à l'Âge du Fer*, Rennes: Laboratoire d'Anthropologie.

Godelier, M. 1977a, Economy and religion: an evolutionary optical illusion, in J. Friedman & M.J. Rowlands (eds.) *The Evolution of Social Systems*, London: Duckworth, 3–11.

Godelier, M. 1977b, Politics as 'infrastructure': an anthropologist's thoughts on the example of classical Greece and the notions of relations of production and economic determinism, in J. Friedman & M.J. Rowlands (eds.) *The Evolution of Social Systems*, London: Duckworth, 13–28.

Godfrey-Smith, P. 2009, *Darwinian Populations and Natural Selection*, Oxford: Oxford University Press.

Godfrey-Smith, P. 2017, *Other Minds: The Octopus and the Evolution of Intelligent Life*, London: William Collins.

González-Fortes, G., E.R. Jones, E. Lightfoot, C. Bonsall, C. Lazar, A. Grandal-d'Anglade, M.D. Garralda, L. Drak, V. Siska, A. Simalcsik, A. Boroneant, J.R.V. Romaní, M.V. Rodríguez, P. Arias, R. Pinhasi, A. Manica, & M. Hofreiter 2017, Paleogenomic Evidence for multi-generational mixing between Neolithic farmers and Mesolithic hunter-gatherers in the Lower Danube Basin, *Cell Biology*, 27(12), 1801–1810.

Gonzáles-Ruibal, A. 2018, Ethics of archaeology, *Annual Review of Anthropology*, 47, 345–60, DOI.org/10.1146/annurev-anthro-102317-045825.

Goody, J. 1976, *Production and Reproduction: A Comparative Study of the Domestic Domain*, Cambridge: Cambridge University Press.

Goody, J. 1982, *Cooking, Cuisine and Class: A Study in Comparative Sociology*, Cambridge: Cambridge University Press.

Gould, S.J. 1980, Sociobiology and the Theory of Natural Selection, in G.W. Barlow & J. Silverberg (eds.) *Sociobiology Beyond Nature/Nurture? Reports, Definitions and Debate*, Boulder: Westview Press, 257–269.

Gould, S.J. 2002, *The Structure of Evolutionary Theory*, Cambridge MA: The Belknap Press, University of Harvard.

Gould, S.J. & N. Eldredge 1977, Punctuated equilibria: the tempo and mode of evolution reconsidered, *Paleobiology*, 3, 115–151.

Govier, E. 2019, Do you follow? Rethinking causality in archaeology, *Archaeological Dialogues*, 26, 51–55.

Graeber, D. 2015, Radical alterity is just another way of saying 'reality': a reply to Eduardo Viveiros de Castro, *Hau: Journal of Ethnographic Theory*, 5(2), 1–41.

Griffiths, P.E. & R.D. Gray 1994, Developmental systems and evolutionary explanation, *The Journal of Philosophy*, 91(6), 277–304.

Gronenborne, D., H-C. Strien, S. Dietrich, & F. Sirocko 2014, 'Adaptive cycles' and climate fluctuations: a case study from Linear Pottery Culture in western Central Europe, *Journal of Archaeological Science*, 51, 73–83.

Gunnell, J.G. 2014, *Social Enquiry After Wittgenstein and Kuhn: Leaving Everything as It Is*, New York: Columbia University Press.

Hachem, L. & C. Hamon 2014, Linear pottery culture household organisation: an economic model, in A. Whittle & P. Bickle (eds.) *Early Farmers: The View from Archaeology and Science* (Proceedings of the British Academy 198), Oxford: Oxford University Press, 159–180.

Halstead, P. 1989, Like rising damp? An ecological approach to the spread of farming in south-east and central Europe, in A. Milles, D. Williams, & N. Gardner (eds.) *The Beginnings of Agriculture*, Oxford: British Archaeological Reports, 23–53.

Halstead, P. 2004, Life after Mediterranean polyculture: the subsistence subsystem and the Emergence of Civilisation revisited, in J.C. Barrett & P. Halstead (eds.) *The Emergence of Civilisation Revisited*, Oxford: Oxbow Books, 189–206.

Hamilton, W.D. 1964a, The genetical evolution of social behaviour I, *Journal of Theoretical Biology*, 7, 1–16.

Hamilton, W.D. 1964b, The genetical evolution of social behaviour II, *Journal of Theoretical Biology*, 7, 17–32.

Hannon, E. & T. Lewens (eds.) 2018, *Why We Disagree about Human Nature*, Oxford: Oxford University Press.

Harding, A. 2013, World systems, cores and peripheries in prehistoric Europe, *European Journal of Archaeology*, 16(3), 378–400.

Harman, G. 2018, *Object-Orientated Ontology: A New Theory of Everything*, London: Penguin Random House.

Harris, E.C. 1989, *Principles of Archaeological Stratigraphy* (2nd edition), London: Academic Press.

Harris, O.J.T. & C.N. Cipolla 2017, *Archaeological Theory in the New Millennium: Introducing Current Perspectives*, London: Routledge.

Harvey, D. 1996, *Justice, Nature and the Geography of Difference*, Oxford: Blackwell.

Hawkes, C.F.C. 1954, Archaeology theory and method: some suggestions from the Old World, *American Anthropologist*, 56(2), 155–168.

Hawkes, J. 1968, The proper study of mankind, *Antiquity*, 42(168), 255–262.

Hempel, C.G. 1942, The function of general laws in history, *The Journal of Philosophy*, 39(2), 35–48.

Hempel, C.G. & P. Oppenheim 1948, Studies in the logic of explanation, *Philosophy of Science*, 15(2), 135–175.

Henare, A., M. Holbaard, & S. Wastell 2007, Introduction: thinking through things, in A. Henare, M. Holbraad, & S. Wastell (eds.) *Thinking Through Things: Theorizing Artefacts Ethnographically*, London: Routledge, 1–31.

Henry. M. 2019, *Marx: An Introduction* (translated by K. Justaert), London: Bloomsbury.

Higgs, E.S. & M.R. Jarman 1975, Palaeoeconomy, in E.S. Higgs (ed.) *Palaeoeconomy: Being the Second Volume of Papers in Economic Prehistory by Members and Associates of the British Academy Major Research Project in the Early History of Agriculture*, Cambridge: Cambridge University Press, 1–7.

Hill, J.N. (ed.) 1977, *The Explanation of Prehistoric Change*, Albuquerque: University of New Mexico Press.

Hobbes, T. 2017 [1651], *Leviathan*, London: Penguin Books.

Hodder, I. 1982a, *Symbols in Action: Ethnoarchaeological Studies in Material Culture*, Cambridge: Cambridge University Press.

Hodder, I. (ed.) 1982b, *Symbolic and Structural Archaeology*, Cambridge: Cambridge University Press.

Hodder, I. 1982c, Theoretical archaeology: a reactionary view, in I. Hodder (ed.) *Symbolic and Structural Archaeology*, Cambridge: Cambridge University Press, 1–16.

Hodder, I. 1990, *The Domestication of Europe: Structure and Contingency in Neolithic Societies*, Oxford: Blackwell.

Hodder, I. 2012, *Entangled: An Archaeology of Relationships between Humans and Things*, Oxford: Wiley-Blackwell.

Hodder, I. 2018, Things and the slow Neolithic: the Middle Eastern transformation, *Journal of Archaeological Method and Theory*, 25, 155–177.

Hodder, I., M. Shanks, A. Alexandri, V. Buchli, J. Carman, J. Last, & G. Lucas (eds.) 1995, *Interpreting Archaeology: Finding Meaning in the Past*, London: Routledge.

Hoffmeyer, J. 2008, *Biosemiotics: An Examination into the Signs of Life and the Life of Signs*, Scranton: University of Scranton Press.

Hofmann, D. 2013, Intimate connections: bodies and substances in flux in the early Neolithic of central Europe, in C. Watts (ed.) *Relational Archaeologies: Humans, Animals, Things*, London: Routledge, 154–172.

Hofmann, D. 2015, What have genetics ever done for us? The implications of aDNA data for interpreting identity in early Neolithic central Europe, *European Journal of Archaeology*, 18(3), 454–476, DOI: 10.1179/1461957114Y.0000000083.

Hofmann, D. & P. Bickle (eds.) 2009, *Creating Communities: New Advances in Central European Neolithic Research*, Oxford: Oxbow Books.

Hofmann, D. & P. Bickle 2011, Culture, tradition and settlement burials of the *Linearbandkeramik* (LBK) culture, in B.W. Roberts & M. Vander Linden (eds.) *Investigating Archaeological Cultures: Material Culture, Variability and Transmission*, New York: Springer, 183–200.

Hofmann, D., J. Pechtl, R.A. Bentley, P. Bickle, L. Fibiger, G. Grupe, J. Hamilton, R. Hedges, M. Schultz, & A. Whittle 2013, Southern Bavaria, in P. Bickle & A. Whittle (eds.) *The First Farmers of Central Europe: Diversity in LBK Lifeways*, Oxford: Oxbow Books, 205–248.

Hofmann D. & J. Smyth (eds.) 2013, *Tracking the Neolithic House in Europe: Sedentism, Architecture, and Practice*, New York: Springer.

Holbraad, M. & M.A. Pedersen 2017, *The Ontological Turn: An Anthropological Exposition*, Cambridge: Cambridge University Press.

Hoopes, J. 1991, *Peirce on Signs: Writings on Semiotic by Charles Sanders Peirce*, Chapel Hill: University of North Carolina Press.

Hopkinson, T. 2013, 'Man the symboller': a contemporary origins myth, *Archaeological Dialogues*, 20(2), 215–241, DOI: 10.1017/S138020381300024X.

Hull, D.L. 1986, On human nature, *Proceedings of the Biennial Meeting of the Philosophy of Science Association*, 2, 3–13.

Huneman, P. & D.M. Walsh (eds.) 2017a, *Challenging the Modern Synthesis: Adaptation, Development and Inheritance*, Oxford: Oxford University Press.

Huneman, P. & D.M. Walsh 2017b, Introduction: challenging the modern synthesis, in P. Huneman & D.M. Walsh (eds.) *Challenging the Modern Synthesis: Adaptation, Development and Inheritance*, Oxford: Oxford University Press, 1–33.

Ingold, T. 1994, Introduction to culture, in T. Ingold (ed.) *Companion Encyclopedia of Anthropology*, London: Routledge, 329–349.

Ingold, T. 2000, *The Perception of the Environment: Essays in Livelihood, Dwelling and Skill*, London: Routledge.

Ingold, T. 2013, Prospect, in T. Ingold & G. Palsson (eds.) *Biosocial Becomings: Integrating Social and Biological Anthropology*, Cambridge: Cambridge University Press, 1–21.

Ingold, T. 2016, A naturalist abroad in the museum of ontology: Philippe Descola's *Beyond Nature and Culture*, *Anthropological Forum*, 26(3), 301–320.

Ingold, T. & G. Palsson (eds.) 2013, *Biosocial Becomings: Integrating Social and Biological Anthropology*, Cambridge: Cambridge University Press.

Ion, A. 2020, Why keep the old dead around? Bringing together theory and method in the study of human remains from Balkan (E)Neolithic settlement, *Documenta Praehistorica*, 47, 348–366.

Jablonka, E. 2002, Information: its interpretation, its inheritance, and its sharing, *Philosophy of Science*, 69(4), 578–605.

Jablonka, E. & M.J. Lamb, 2005, *Evolution in Four Dimensions: Genetic, Epigenetic, Behavioral, and Symbolic Variation in the History of Life*, Cambridge MA: The MIT Press.

Jarman, M.R. & D. Webley 1975, Settlement and land use in Capitanata, Italy, in E.S. Higgs (ed.) *Palaeoeconomy: Being the Second Volume of Papers in Economic Prehistory by Members and Associates of the British Academy Major Research Project in the Early History of Agriculture*, Cambridge: Cambridge University Press, 177–224.

Jervis, B. 2019, *Assemblage Thought and Archaeology*, London: Routledge.

Johnson, A.L. 2014, Exploring adaptive variation among hunter-gatherers with Binford's frames of reference, *Journal of Archaeological Research*, 22, 1–42, DOI 10.1007/s10814-013-9068-y.

Johnson, M. 2010, *Archaeological Theory: An Introduction* (2nd edition), Chichester: Wiley-Blackwell.

Jones, A. & E. Sibbesson 2013, Archaeological complexity: materials, multiplicity, and the transition to agriculture in Britain, in B. Alberti, A.M. Jones, & J. Pollard (eds.) *Archaeology After Interpretation: Returning Materials to Archaeological Theory*, Walnut Creek: Left Coast Press, 151–172.

Kant, I. 2007 [1781], *The Critique of Pure Reason* (translated by M.W. Weigelt), London: Penguin Books.

Kauffman, S.A. 1993, *The Origins of Order: Self-organisation and Selection in Evolution*, Oxford: Oxford University Press.

Kauffman, S.A. 1995, *At Home in the Universe: The Search for the Laws of Self-organization and Complexity*, Oxford: Oxford University Press.

Kauffman, S.A. 2019, *A World Beyond Physics: The Emergence and Evolution of Life*, Oxford: Oxford University Press.

Kintigh, K.W. 2006, The promise and challenge of archaeological data integration, *American Antiquity* 71, 567–578.

Kintigh, K.W., J.H. Altschul, M.C. Beaudry, R.D. Drennan, A.P. Kinzig, T.A. Kohler, W.F. Limp, H.D.G. Maschner, T.R. Pauketat, P. Peregrine, J.A. Sabloff, T.J. Wilkinson, H.T. Wright, & M.A. Zedar 2014, Grand challenges for archaeology, *American Antiquity*, 79(1), 5–24.

Kirby, V. 1997, *Telling Flesh: The Substance of the Corporeal*, London: Routledge.

Kohn, E. 2013, *How Forests Think: Toward an Anthropology Beyond the Human*, Berkeley: University of California Press.

Komter, A.E. 2005, *Social Solidarity and the Gift*, Cambridge: Cambridge University Press.

Kristiansen, K. 1978, The consumption of wealth in Bronze Age Denmark, in K. Kristiansen & C. Paludan-Miller (eds.) *New Directions in Scandinavian Archaeology*, Copenhagen: National Museum Press, 158–190.

Kristiansen, K. 1998, *Europe Before History*, Cambridge: Cambridge University Press.

Kristiansen, K. 2014, Towards a new paradigm? The third scientific revolution and its possible consequences in archaeology, *Current Swedish Archaeology*, 22, 11–34.

Kronfeldner, M. 2018, *What's Left of Human Nature? A Post Essentialist, Pluralist, and Interactive Account of a Contested Concept*, Cambridge MA: The MIT Press.

Kropotkin, P. 1902, *Mutual Aid: A Factor of Evolution*, http://dwardmac.pitzer.edu/Anar chist_Archives/kropotkin/mutaidcontents.html Accessed July 2019.

Kropotkin, P. 1971, *Memoirs of a Revolutionist*, London: Dover Publications.

Kuhn, T.S. 1970 [1962], *The Structure of Scientific Revolutions: Second Edition, Enlarged*, Chicago: University of Chicago Press.

Kull, K. 1999, Outlines for a post-Darwinian biology, https://www.researchgate.net/pub lication/237431708 Accessed March 2020.

Kull, K., T. Deacon, C. Emmeche, J. Hoffemeyer, & F. Stjernfelt, 2009, Theses on biosemiotics: prolegomena to a theoretical biology, *Biological Theory*, 4(2), 167–173.

Kuper, A. 1988, *The Invention of Primitive Society: Transformations of an Illusion*, London: Routledge.

Kuper, R., J. Lüning, P. Stehli, & A. Zimmerman, 1977, *Der bandkeramische siedlungsplatz Langweiler 9*, Bonn: Rheinishe Ausgrabungen 18.

Laland, K.N. & M.J. O'Brien 2011, Cultural niche construction: an introduction, *Biological Theory*, 6, 191–202, DOI 10.1007/s13752-012-0026-6.

Laporte, L. & C. Scarre (eds.) 2016, *The Megalithic Architectures of Europe*, Oxford: Oxbow Books.

Laszlo, E. 2002, The new holism: the grand prospect for science and society, *World Futures*, 58(2–3), 137–147. DOI.org/10.1080/02604020210689.

Latour, B. 1993, *We Have Never Been Modern* (translated by C. Porter), New York: Prentice-Hall.

Latour, B. 2005, *Reassembling the Social: An Introduction to Actor-Network Theory*, Oxford: Oxford University Press.

Lazcano, A. 2008, What is life? A brief overview, *Chemistry and Biodiversity*, 5, 1–15.

Leach, E. 1973, Concluding address, in C. Renfrew (ed.) *The Explanation of Culture Change: Models in Prehistory*, London: Duckworth, 761–771.

Lee, R.B & I. DeVore (eds.) 1968, *Man the Hunter*, Chicago: Aldine Publishing Company.

Leroi-Gourhan, A. 1964, *Les religions de la préhistoire*, Paris: Presses Universitaires de France.

Leroi-Gourhan A. 1993, *Gesture and Speech*, Cambridge MA: MIT Press.

Levin, M.E. 1973, On explanation in archaeology: a rebuttal to Fritz and Plog, *American Antiquity*, 38(4), 387–395.

Lévi-Strauss, C. 1982, *The Way of the Masks* (translated by S. Modelski), Washington: University of Washington Press.

Lewis-Williams, D. 2002, *The Mind in the Cave: Consciousness and the Origins of Art*, London: Thames and Hudson.

Lipson, M., A. Szécsényi-Nagy, M. Swapan, A. Pósa, B. Stégmár, V. Keer, N. Rohland, K. Stewardson, M. Ferry, M. Michel, J. Oppenheimer, N. Broomandkhoshbacht, E. Harney, S. Nordenfelt, B. Llamas, B.G. Mende, K. Köhler, K. Oross, M. Bondár, T. Marton, A. Osztás, J. Jakucs, T. Paluch, F. Horváth, P. Csengeri, J. Koós, K. Sebők, A. Anders, P. Raczky, J. Regenye, J.P. Barna, S. Fábián, G. Serlegi, Z. Toldi, E.G. Nagy, J. Dani, E. Molnár, G. Pálfi, L. Márk, B. Melegh, Z. Bánfai, L. Domboróczki, J. Fernández-Eraso, J.A. Mujika-Alustiza, C.A. Fernández, J.J. Echevarría, R. Bollongino, J. Orschiedt, K. Schierhold, H. Meller, A. Cooper, J. Burger, E. Bánffy, K.W. Alt, C. Lalueza-Fox, W. Haak, & D. Reich 2017, Parallel palaeogenomic transects reveal complex genetic history of early European farmers, *Nature*, 551, 368–372.

Lucas, G. 2012, *Understanding the Archaeological Record*, Cambridge: Cambridge University Press.

Lyman, R.L., M.J. O'Brien, & R.C. Dunnell 1997, *The Rise and Fall of Culture History*, New York: Plenum Press.

Malafouris, L. 2013, *How Things Shape the Mind: A Theory of Material Engagement*, Cambridge MA: MIT Press.

Margulis, L. 1998, *The Symbiotic Planet: A New Look at Evolution*, London: Weidenfeld & Nicolson.

Margulis, L. & D. Sagan 1995, *What Is Life?* London: Weidenfeld & Nicolson.

Margulis, L. & D. Sagan 2002, *Acquiring Genomes: A Theory of the Origin of Species*, New York: Basic Books.

Marshall, Y. & B. Alberti 2014, A matter of difference: Karen Barad, ontology and archaeological bodies, *Cambridge Archaeological Journal*, 24(1), 19–36, DOI: 10.1017/S0959774314000067.

Marx, K. 1845/6, *The German Ideology: Critique of Modern German Philosophy According to Its Representatives Feuerbach, B. Bauer and Stirner, and of German Socialism According to Its Various Prophets*, https://www.marxists.org/archive/marx/works/1845/german-ideology/ch01a.htm Accessed March 2020.

Marx, K. 1867, *Capital: A Critique of Political Economy. Volume 1: The Process of Production of Capital*. Moscow: Progress Publishers, https://www.marxists.org/archive/marx/works/download/pdf/Capital-Volume-I.pdf Accessed July 2019.

Mathieson, I., S. Alpaslan-Roodenberg, C. Posth, A. Szécsényi-Nagy, N. Rohland, S. Mallick, I. Olalde, N. Broomandkhoshbacht, F. Candilio, O. Cheronet, D. Fernandes, M. Ferry, B. Gamarra, G.G. Fortes, W. Haak, E. Harney, E. Jones, D. Keating, B. Krause-Kyora, I. Kucukkalipci, M. Michel, A. Mittnik, K. Nägele, M. Novak, J. Oppenheimer, N. Patterson, S. Pfrengle, K. Sirak, K. Stewardson, S. Vai, S. Alexandrov, K.W. Alt, R. Andreescu, D. Antonovic', A. Ash, N. Atanassova, K. Bacvarov, M.B. Gusztáv, H. Bocherens, M. Bolus, A. Boroneant, Y. Boyadzhiev, A. Budnik, J. Burmaz, S. Chohadzhiev, N.J. Conard, R. Cottiaux, M. Čuka, C. Cupillard, D.G. Drucker, N. Elenski, M. Francken, B. Galabova, G. Ganetsovski, B. Gély, T. Hajdu, V. Handzhyiska, K. Harvati, T. Higham, S. Iliev, I, Jankovic', I. Karavanic', D.J. Kennett, D. Komšo, A. Kozak, D. Labuda, M. Lari, C. Lazar, M. Leppek, K. Leshtakov, D. Lo Vetro, D. Los, I. Lozanov, M. Malina, F. Martini, K. McSweeney, H. Meller, M. Menđušic', P. Mirea, V. Moiseyev, V. Petrova, T.D. Price, A. Simalcsik, L. Sineo, M. Šlaus, V. Slavchev, P. Stanev, A. Starovic', T. Szeniczey, S. Talamo, M. Teschler-Nicola, C. Thevenet, I. Valchev, F. Valentin, S. Vasilyev, F. Veljanovska, S. Venelinova, E. Veselovskaya, B. Viola, C. Virag, J. Zaninovic', S. Zäuner, P.W. Stockhammer, G. Catalano, R. Krauß, D. Caramelli, G. Zariŋa, B. Gaydarska, M. Lillie, A.G. Nikitin, I. Potekhina, A. Papathanasiou, D. Boric', C. Bonsall, J. Krause, R. Pinhasi, & D. Reich 2018, The genomic history of southeastern Europe, *Nature*, 555, 197–210, DOI:10.1038/nature25778.

Maturana, H.R. & F.J. Varela 1980, *Autopoiesis and Cognition: The Realization of the Living*, Dordrecht: D. Reidel Publishing Company.

Maynard Smith, J. 2000, The concept of information in biology, *Philosophy of Science*, 67(2), 177–194.

Mayr, E. 1976, *Evolution and the Diversity of Life: Selected Essays*, Cambridge MA: The Belknap Press.

McFadyen, L. 2006, Building technologies, quick and slow architectures and early Neolithic long barrow sites in southern Britain, *Archaeological Review from Cambridge*, 21(1), 117–134.

McFadyen, L. 2007, Neolithic architecture and participation – practices of making in early Neolithic Britain, in J. Last (ed.) *Beyond the Grave: New Perspectives on Barrows*, Oxford: Oxbow Books, 22–29.

McGuire, R.H. 1993, Archaeology and Marxism, *Archaeological Method and Theory*, 5, 101–157.

Meillassoux, C. 1972, From reproduction to production, *Economy and Society*, 1(1), 93–105.

Meillassoux, Q. 2008, *After Finitude: An Essay on the Necessity of Contingency* (translated by R. Brassier), London: Continuum.

Mellars, P., K. Boyle, O. Bar-Yosef, & C. Stringer (eds.) 2007, *Rethinking the Human Revolution: New Behavioural and Biological Perspectives on the Origin and Dispersal of Modern Humans*, Cambridge: McDonald Institute for Archaeological Research.

Mellor, D.H. 1982, Chance and degrees of belief, in R. McLaughlin (ed.) *What? Where? When? Why?* Dordrecht: D. Reidel, 49–68.

Meskell, L. & R.W. Preucel 2004, Knowledges, in L. Meskell & R.W. Preucel (eds.) *A Companion to Social Archaeology*, Oxford: Blackwell, 3–22.

Meyer C., C. Lohr, O. Kürbis, V. Dresely, W. Haak, C.J. Adler, D. Gronenborn, & K.W. Alt 2014, Mass graves of the LBK: patterns and peculiarities, in A. Whittle and P. Bickle (eds.) *Early Farmers: The View from Archaeology and Science* (Proceedings of the British Academy 198), Oxford: Oxford University Press, 307–325.

Midgley, M.S. 2005, *The Monumental Cemeteries of Prehistoric Europe*, Stroud: Tempus.

Miller, D. 1982, Artefacts as products of human categorisation processes, in I. Hodder (ed.) *Symbolic and Structural Archaeology*, Cambridge: Cambridge University Press, 17–25.

Miller, D. & C. Tilley (eds.) 1984, *Ideology, Power and Prehistory*, Cambridge: Cambridge University Press.

Modderman, P.J.R 1970, Linearbandkeramik aus Elsoo und Stein, *Analecta Praehistorica Leidensia*, 3, passim.

Modderman, P.J.R. 1988, The linear pottery culture: diversity in uniformity, *Berichten van de Rijksdienst voor het Oudheidkundig Bodemonderzoek*, 38, 63–139.

Montévil, M. & M. Massio 2015, Biological organisation as closure of constraints, *Journal of Theoretical Biology*, 372, 179–191.

Moore, H.L. 1982, The interpretation of spatial patterning in settlement residues, in I. Hodder (ed.) *Symbolic and Structural Archaeology*, Cambridge: Cambridge University Press, 74–79.

Morange, M. 2006, Post-genomics, between reduction and emergence, *Synthese*, 151, 355–360.

Morgan, C.G. 1973, Archaeology and explanation, *World Archaeology*, 4(3), 259–276.

Moro Abadía, O. 2017, Bridging the gap in archaeological theory: an alternative account of scientific 'progress' in archaeology, *World Archaeology*, 49(2), 271–280.

Moss, L. 2003, *What Genes Can't Do*, Cambridge MA: The MIT Press.

Murphy, M.P. & L.A.J. O'Neill 1995, *What is Life? The Next Fifty Years: Speculations on the Future of Biology*, Cambridge: Cambridge University Press.

Nealon, J.T. 2016, *Plant Theory: Biopower & Vegetable Life*. Stanford: Stanford University Press.

Newton, R.G. & C. Renfrew 1970, British faience beads reconsidered, *Antiquity*, 44(175), 199–206.

Oakley, K.P. 1967, *Man the Toolmaker*, London: British Museum.

O'Brien, M.J. (ed.) 1996, *Evolutionary Archaeology: Theory and Application*, Salt Lake City: University of Utah Press.

O'Brien, M.J. & R.L. Lyman (eds.) 2003, *Style, Function, Transmission*, Salt Lake City: The University of Utah Press.

Odling-Smee, F.J., K.N. Laland, & M.W. Feldman 2003, *Niche Construction: The Neglected Process in Evolution*, Princeton: Princeton University Press.

Olalde, I., S. Brace, M.E. Allentoft, I. Armit, K. Kristiansen, N. Rohland, S. Mallick, T. Booth, A. Szécsényi-Nagy, A. Mittnik, E. Altena, M. Lipson, I. Lazaridis, N. Patterson, N. Broomandkhoshbacht, Y. Diekmann, Z. Faltyskova, D. Fernandes, M. Ferry, E.

Harney, P. de Knijff, M. Michel, J. Oppenheimer, K. Stewardson, A. Barclay, K.W. Alt, A.A. Fernández, E. Bánffy, M. Bernabò-Brea, D. Billoin, C. Blasco, C. Bonsall, L. Bonsall, T. Allen, L. Büster, S. Carver, L.C. Navarro, O.E. Craig, G.T. Cook, B. Cunliffe, A. Denaire, K.E. Dinwiddy, N. Dodwell, M. Ernée, C. Evans, M. Kuchařík, J.F. Farré, H. Fokkens, C. Fowler, M. Gazenbeek, R.G. Pena, M. Haber-Uriarte, E. Haduch, G. Hey, N. Jowett, T. Knowles, K. Massy, S. Pfrengle, P. Lefranc, O. Lemercier, A. Lefebvre, J.L. Maurandi, T. Majó, J.I. McKinley, K. McSweeney, M.B.G.A. Modi, G. Kulcsár, V. Kiss, A. Czene, R. Patay, A. Endrődi, K. Köhler, T. Hajdu, J.L. Cardoso, C. Liesau, M.P. Pearson, P. Włodarczak, T.D. Price, P. Prieto, P-J. Rey, P. Ríos, R. Risch, M.A.R. Guerra, A. Schmitt, J. Serralongue, A.M. Silva, V. Smrčka, L. Vergnaud, J. Zilhão, D. Caramelli, T. Higham, V. Heyd, A. Sheridan, K-G. Sjögren, M.G. Thomas, P.W. Stockhammer, R. Pinhasi, J. Krause, W. Haak, I. Barnes, C. Lalueza-Fox, & D. Reich 2018, The Beaker phenomenon and the genomic transformation of northwest Europe, *Nature*, 555, 190–196.

Olsen, B. 2003, Material culture after text: re-membering things, *Norwegian Archaeological Review*, 36(2), 87–104, DOI: 10.1080/00293650310000650.

Olsen, B. 2010, *In Defense of Things: Archaeology and the Ontology of Objects*, Lanham: Altamira Press.

Olsen, B. 2012, After interpretation: remembering archaeology, *Current Swedish Archaeology*, 20, 11–34.

Olsen, B. 2013, Reclaiming things: an archaeology of matter, in P.L. Carlile, D. Nicolini, A. Langley, & H. Tsoukas (eds.) *How Matter Matters: Objects, Artifacts and Materiality in Organization Studies*, Oxford: Oxford University Press, 171–196.

Olsen, B., M. Shanks, T. Webmoor, & C. Witmore 2012, *Archaeology: The Discipline of Things*, Berkeley: University of California Press.

Olsen, B. & C. Witmore 2015, Archaeology, symmetry and the ontology of things: a response to Critics, *Archaeological Dialogues*, 22(2), 187–197, DOI:10.1017/S1380203815000240.

Outram A.K. & A. Bogaard 2019, *Subsistence and Society in Prehistory: New Directions in Economic Archaeology*, Cambridge: Cambridge University Press.

Oyama, S. 2000, *The Ontogeny of Information: Development Systems and Evolution*, Durham NC: Duke University Press.

Oyama, S., P.E. Griffiths, & R.D. Gray (eds.) 2001, *Cycles of Contingency: Developmental Systems and Evolution*, Cambridge MA: The MIT Press.

Parker Pearson, M. & Ramilisonina 1998, Stonehenge for the ancestors: the stones pass on the message, *Antiquity*, 72(278), 308–326.

Pascoe, B. 2014, *Dark Emu: Aboriginal Australia and the Birth of Agriculture*, Broome Western Australia: Magabala Books.

Pauketat, T.R. 2007, *Chiefdoms and Other Archaeological Delusions*, Lanham: Altimera Press.

Patrik, L. 1985, Is there an archaeological record? *Advances in Archaeological Method and Theory*, 8, 27–62.

Pettitt, P. 2011, *The Palaeolithic Origins of Human Burial*, London: Routledge.

Pettitt, P. & J.R. Anderson 2020, Primate thanatology and hominoid mortuary archeology, *Primates* 61(1), 9–19.

Pétursdóttir, Þ. 2017, Climate change? Archaeology and Anthropocene, *Archaeological Dialogues* 24(2), 175–205.

Piel, A.K. & F.A. Stewart 2016, Non-human animal responses towards the dead and death: a comparative approach to understanding the evolution of human mortuary practices, in C. Renfrew, M.J. Boyd, & I. Morley (eds.) *Death Rituals, Social Order and the Archaeology of Immortality in the Ancient World: 'Death Shall Have No Dominion'*, Cambridge: Cambridge University Press, 15–26.

Pigliucci, M. 2010, Genotype-phenotype mapping and the end of the 'genes as blueprint' metaphor, *Philosophical Transactions of the Royal Society: Biological Sciences*, 365(1540), 557–566.

Plog, F.T. 1974, *The Study of Prehistoric Change*, New York: Academic Press.

Plog, F.T. 1977, Explaining change, in J.N. Hill (ed.) *The Explanation of Prehistoric Change*, Albuquerque: University of New Mexico Press, 17–57.

Powell, T.G.E., J.X.W.P. Corcoran, F. Lynch, & J.G. Scott 1969, *Megalithic Enquiries in the West of Britain: A Liverpool Symposium*, Liverpool: Liverpool University Press.

Pross, A. 2012, *What is Life? How Chemistry Becomes Biology*, Oxford: Oxford University Press.

Rascovan, N., K-G. Sjögren, K. Kristiansen, R. Nielsen, E. Willerslev, C. Desnues, & S. Rasmussen 2019, Emergence and spread of basal lineages of *Yersinia pestis* during the Neolithic Decline, *Cell*, 176, 1–11. https://doi.org/10.1016/j.cell.2018.11.005 Accessed April 2020.

Ratnagar, S. 2001, The Bronze Age: unique instance of a pre-industrial world system? *Current Anthropology*, 42(3), 351–379.

Redman, C.L., E. Curtin, N. Versaggi, & J. Wasner 1978, Social Archaeology: the future of the past, in C.L. Redman, M.J. Berman, E.V. Curtin, W.T. Langhorne Jr., N.M. Versaggi, & J.C. Wanser (eds.) *Social Archaeology: Beyond Subsistence and Dating*, New York: Academic Press, 1–17.

Reich, D. 2018, *Who We Are and How We Got Here: Ancient DNA and the New Science of the Human Past*, Oxford: Oxford University Press.

Renfrew, C. 1969a, The autonomy of the south-east European Copper Age, *Proceedings of the Prehistoric Society*, 35, 12–47.

Renfrew, C. 1969b, Trade and culture process in European prehistory, *Current Anthropology*, 10, 151–169.

Renfrew, C. 1972, *The Emergence of Civilisation: The Cyclades and the Aegean in the Third Millennium BC*, London: Methuen.

Renfrew, C. 1973a, Review of *Explanation in Archaeology: An Explicitly Scientific Approach* by P.J. Watson et al., *American Anthropologist*, 75(6), 1928–1930.

Renfrew, C. (ed.) 1973b, *The Explanation of Culture Change: Models in Prehistory*, London: Duckworth.

Renfrew, C. 1973c, *Before Civilisation: The Radiocarbon Revolution and Prehistoric Europe*, London: Jonathan Cape.

Renfrew, C. 1973d, *Social Archaeology: An Inaugural Lecture*, Southampton: University of Southampton.

Renfrew, C. 1975, Trade as action at a distance: questions of integration and communication, in J.A. Sabloff & C.C.L. Karlofsky (eds.) *Ancient Civilisations and Trade*, Albuquerque: University of New Mexico Press, 3–59.

Renfrew, C. 1976, Megaliths, territories and populations, in S.J. De Laet (ed.) *Acculturation and Continuity in Atlantic Europe Mainly During the Neolithic Period and the Bronze Age*, Bruges: De Temple, 198–220.

Renfrew, C. 1977, Space, time and polity, in J. Friedman & M.J. Rowlands (eds.) *The Evolution of Social Systems*, London: Duckworth, 89–112.

Renfrew, C. 1979, Systems collapse as social transformation: catastrophe and anastrophe in early state societies, in C. Renfrew & K.L. Cooke (eds.) *Transformations: Mathematical Approaches to Culture Change*, London: Academic Press, 481–506.

Renfrew, C. 1980, The Great Tradition versus the Great Divide: archaeology as anthropology? *American Journal of Archaeology*, 84(3), 287–298.

Renfrew, C. 1982, Explanation revisited, in C. Renfrew, M.J. Rowlands, & B.A. Segraves (eds.) *Theory and Explanation in Archaeology: The Southampton Conference*, London: Academic Press, 5–23.

Renfrew, C. 1983, Introduction: the megalith builders of western Europe, in C. Renfrew (ed.) *The Megalithic Monuments of Western Europe: The Latest Evidence Presented by Nine Leading Authorities*, London: Thames and Hudson, 8–17.

Renfrew, C. 1984, *Approaches to Social Archaeology*, Edinburgh: Edinburgh University Press.

Renfrew, C. 1996, The sapient behaviour paradox: how to test for potential? In P.A. Mellars & K. Gibson (eds.) *Modelling the Early Human Mind*, Cambridge: the McDonald Institute for Archaeological Research, 11–14.

Renfrew, C. 2001, Symbol before concept: material engagement and the early development of society, in I. Hodder (ed.) *Archaeological Theory Today* (1st edition), Cambridge: Polity Press, 122–140.

Renfrew, C. 2003, *Figuring It Out: What Are We? Where Do We Come From? The Parallel Visions of Artists and Archaeologists*, London: Thames and Hudson.

Renfrew, C. 2004, Rethinking The Emergence, in J.C. Barrett & P. Halstead (eds.) *The Emergence of Civilisation Revisited*, Oxford: Oxbow Books, 257–274.

Renfrew, C. 2005, Systems thinking, in C. Renfrew & P. Bahn (eds.) *Archaeology: The Key Concepts*, London: Routledge, 259–264.

Renfrew, C. & P. Bahn 2004, *Archaeology: Theories, Methods and Practice* (4th edition), London: Thames and Hudson.

Renfrew, C., M.J. Boyd, & I. Morley (eds.) 2016, *Death Rituals, Social Oder and the Archaeology of Immortality in the Ancient World: 'Death Shall Have No Dominion'*, Cambridge: Cambridge University Press.

Renfrew, C. & J. Cherry (eds.) 1986, *Peer Polity Interaction and Socio-Political Change*, Cambridge: Cambridge University Press.

Renfrew, C. & E. Zubrow (eds.) 1994, *The Ancient Mind: Elements of Cognitive Archaeology*, Cambridge: Cambridge University Press.

Ribeiro, A. 2018a, Ontologies, in C. Smith (ed.) *Encyclopaedia of Global Archaeology*, Cham: Springer. DOI: https://doi.org/10.1007/978-3-319-51726-1_2706-1 Accessed December 2019.

Ribeiro, A. 2018b, *Archaeology and the Historical Understanding*, Bonn: Habelt.

Richerson P.J. & R. Boyd 2005, *Not By Genes Alone: How Culture Transformed Human Evolution*, Chicago: University of Chicago Press.

Rindos, D. 1980, Symbiosis, instability, and the origins and spread of agriculture: a new model (with comments and reply), *Current Anthropology*, 21(6), 751–772.

Rindos, D. 1984, *The Origins of Agriculture: An Evolutionary Perspective*, London: Academic Press.

Robb, J. 2013, Material culture, landscapes of action, and emergent causation: a new model for the origins of the European Neolithic (with comments and reply), *Current Anthropology*, 54(6), 657–683.

Roberts, B.W. & M. Vander Linden (eds.) 2011a, *Investigating Archaeological Cultures: Material Culture, Variability and Transmission*, New York: Springer.

Roberts, B.W. & M. Vander Linden 2011b, Investigating archaeological cultures: material culture, variability and transmission, in B.W. Roberts & M. Vander Linden (eds.) *Investigating Archaeological Cultures: Material Culture, Variability and Transmission*, New York: Springer, 1–21.

Roll-Hansen, N. 2009, Sources of Wilhelm Johannsen's genotype theory, *Journal of the History of Biology*, 42, 457–493.

Rosen, R. 1991, *Life Itself: A Comprehensive Inquiry into the Nature, Origin, and Fabrication of Life*, New York: Columbia University Press.

Roskams, S. 2001, *Excavation*, Cambridge: Cambridge University Press.

Rowlands, M. 2010, Concluding thoughts, in P. van Dommelem & A.B. Knapp (eds.) *Material Connections in the Ancient Mediterranean: Mobility, Materiality and Mediterranean Identities*, London: Routledge, 233–247.

Rowlands, M. & J. Ling 2013, Boundaries, flows and connectivities: mobility and stasis in the Bronze Age, in S. Bergerbrant & S. Sabatini (eds.) *Counterpoint: Essays in Archaeology and Heritage Studies in Honour of Professor Kristian Kristiansen*, Oxford: Archaeopress, 517–529.

Rowley-Conwy, P. 1984, The laziness of the long-distance hunter: the origins of agriculture in western Denmark, *Journal of Anthropological Archaeology*, 13(4), 300–324.

Rowley-Conwy, P. 2004, How the west was lost, *Current Anthropology*, 45(4) (Supplement), 83–113.

Rowley-Conwy, P. 2007, *From Genesis to Prehistory: The Archaeological Three Age System and Its Contested Reception in Denmark, Britain and Ireland*, Oxford: Oxford University Press.

Rowley-Conwy, P. 2011, Westward Ho!: the spread of agriculture from central Europe to the Atlantic, *Current Anthropology*, 52(4) (Supplement), 431–451.

Rück, O. 2009, New aspects and models for Bandkeramik settlement research, in D. Hofmann & P. Bickle (eds.) *Creating Communities: New Advances in Central European Neolithic Research*, Oxford: Oxbow Books, 159–185.

Ruiz-Mirazo, K. & A. Moreno 2004, Basic autonomy as a fundamental step in the synthesis of life, *Artificial Life*, 10(3), 235–259.

Sackett, J.R. 1977, The meaning of style in archaeology: a general model, *American Antiquity*, 42(3), 369–380.

Sackett, J.R. 1982, Approaches to style in lithic archaeology, *Journal of Anthropological Archaeology*, 1, 59–112.

Sahlins, M. 1977, *The Use and Abuse of Biology: An Anthropological Critique of Sociobiology*, London: Tavistock.

Sahlins, M.D. & E.R. Service (eds.) 1960, *Evolution and Culture*, Ann Arbor: University of Michigan Press.

Salmon, M. 1978, What can systems theory do for archaeology? *American Antiquity*, 43(2), 174–183.

Salmon, W. 1982, Causality in archaeology, in C. Renfrew, M.J. Rowlands, & B.A. Segraves (eds.) *Theory and Explanation in Archaeology: The Southampton Conference*, London: Academic Press, 45–55.

Salmon, W. 1993, Probabilistic causality, in E. Sosa & M. Tooley (eds.) *Causation*, Oxford: Oxford University Press, 137–153.

Saussure, F. de 1974, *Course in General Linguistics* (translated by W. Baskin), London: Fontana.

Saxe, A.A., 1970, *Social Dimensions of Mortuary Practices*, Ph.D. thesis, University of Michigan, (Published by University Microfilms, Ann Arbor, 1973).

Scarre, C. 2002, Contexts of monumentalism: regional diversity at the Neolithic transition in north-west France, *Oxford Journal of Archaeology*, 21(1), 21–63.

Schiffer, M.B. 1976, *Behavioral Archaeology*, London: Academic Press.

Schiffer, M.B. 1985, Is there a 'Pompeii premise' in archaeology? *Journal of Anthropological Research*, 41(1), 18–41.

Schloss, J. & M.J. Murray (eds.) 2009, *The Believing Primate: Scientific, Philosophical and Theological Reflections on the Origins of Religion*, Oxford: Oxford University Press.

Schneider, E.D. & D. Sagan 2005, *Into the Cool: Energy Flow, Thermodynamics, and Life*, Chicago: University of Chicago Press.

Schneider, J. 1977, Was there a pre-capitalist world-system? *Peasant Studies*, 6(1), 20–29.

Schrödinger, E. 1944, *What Is Life? The Physical Aspects of the Living Cell*, Cambridge: Cambridge University Press.

Schulting, R.J. & L. Fibiger 2014, Violence in Neolithic north-west Europe: a population perspective, in A. Whittle & P. Bickle (eds.) *Early Farmers: The View from Archaeology and Science*, Oxford: Oxford University Press, 281–306.

Schulz Paulsson, B. 2017, *Time and Stone: The Emergence and Development of Megaliths and Megalithic Societies in Europe*, Oxford: Archaeopress.

Schulz Paulsson, B. 2019, Radiocarbon dates and Bayesian modeling [sic] support maritime diffusion model for megaliths in Europe, *Proceedings of the National Academy of Sciences of the United States of America*, 116(9), 3460–3465.

Searle, J.R. 1983, *Intentionality: An Essay in the Philosophy of Mind*, Cambridge: Cambridge University Press.

Service, E.R. 1962, *Primitive Social Organization: An Evolutionary Perspective*, New York: Random House.

Shanks, M. & R. McGuire 1996, The craft of archaeology, *American Antiquity*, 61(1), 75–88.

Shanks, M. & C. Tilley 1982, Ideology, symbolic power and ritual communication: a reinterpretation of Neolithic mortuary practices, in I. Hodder (ed.) *Symbolic and Structural Archaeology*, Cambridge: Cambridge University Press, 129–154.

Shanks, M. & C. Tilley 1987a, *Re-Constructing Archaeology: Theory and Practice*, Cambridge: Cambridge University Press.

Shanks, M. & C. Tilley 1987b, *Social Theory and Archaeology*, Cambridge: Polity Press.

Shennan, S. 2000, Population, culture history, and the dynamics of culture change, *Current Anthropology*, 41(5), 811–835.

Shennan, S. 2002, *Genes, Memes and Human History*, London: Thames and Hudson.

Shennan, S. 2018, *The First Farmers of Europe: An Evolutionary Perspective*, Cambridge: Cambridge University Press.

Sherratt, A. 1976, Resources, technology and trade: an essay in early European metallurgy, in G. de G. Sieveking, I.H. Longworth, & K.E. Wilson (eds.) *Problems in Economic and Social Archaeology*, London: Duckworth, 557–581.

Sherratt, A. 1990, The genesis of megaliths: monumentality, ethnicity and social complexity in Neolithic north-west Europe, *World Archaeology*, 22(2), 147–167.

Short, T.L. 2004, The development of Peirce's theory of signs, in C. Misak (ed.) *The Cambridge Companion to Peirce*, Cambridge: Cambridge University Press, 214–240.

Shreeve, J. 2015, Mystery man, *National Geographic*, 288(4), 30–57.

Skippington, E. & M.A. Ragan 2011, Lateral genetic transfer and the construction of genetic exchange communities, *Micro Biological Review*, 35, 707–735.

Smith, B.D. 2007, Niche construction and the behavioral context of plant and animal domestication, *Evolutionary Anthropology*, 16, 188–199.

Smith, E.A., K. Hill, F.W. Marlowe, D. Nolin, P. Wiessner, M. Gurven, S. Bowles, M.B. Mulder, T. Hertz, & A. Bell 2010, Wealth transmission and inequality among hunter-gatherers, *Current Anthropology*, 51(1), 19–34.

Smith, J. 2005, Civilizational sociology and perspectives on the Atlantic, *Atlantic Studies*, 2(2), 199–217.

Smith, M.A. 1955, The limitations of inference in archaeology, *The Archaeological Newsletter*, 6, 3–7.

Smith, M.E. (ed.) 2012, *The Comparative Archaeology of Complex Societies*, Cambridge: Cambridge University Press.

Smyth, J. 2014, *Settlement in the Irish Neolithic: New Discoveries on the Edge of Europe* (Prehistoric Society Research Paper 6), Oxford: Oxbow Books.

Steward, J.H. 1949, Cultural causality and law: a trial of the development of early civilisations, *American Anthropologist*, 51, 1–25.

Strein, H-C. 2011, Chronological and social interpretation of the artefactual assemblage, in A. Bogaard, *Plant Use and Crop Husbandry in an Early Neolithic Village: Vaihingen an der Enz, Baden-Württemberg*, Bonn: Habelt, 19–23.

Szécsényi-Nagi, A., V. Keerl, J. Jakus, G. Brandt, E. Banffy, & K.W. Alt. 2014, Ancient DNA evidence for a homogeneous maternal gene pool in sixth millennium cal BC Hungary and the central European LBK, in A. Whittle & P. Bickle (eds.) *Early Farmers: The View from Archaeology and Science* (Proceedings of the British Academy 198), Oxford: Oxford University Press, 71–93.

Tallis, R. 2011, *Aping Mankind: Neuromania, Darwinitis and the Misrepresentation of Humanity*, Durham: Acumen.

Tallis, R. 2020, *Seeing Ourselves: Reclaiming Humanity from God and Science*, Newcastle-upon-Tyne: Agenda.

Taylor, T. 2010, *The Artificial Ape: How Technology Changed the Course of Human Evolution*, New York: Palgrave Macmillan.

Thomas, J. 2013, *The Birth of Neolithic Britain: An Interpretive Account*, Oxford: Oxford University Press.

Thompson, E. 2007, *Mind in Life: Biology, Phenomenology, and the Sciences of Mind*, Cambridge MA: The Belknap Press.

Tilley, C. 1989, Interpreting material culture, in I. Hodder (ed.) *The Meanings of Things*, London: Harper Collins, 185–194.

Tilley, C. 1991, *Material Culture and Text: The Art of Ambiguity*, London: Routledge.

Tilley, C. 1993, *Interpretive Archaeology*, Oxford: Berg.

Tilley, C. 1996, *An Ethnography of the Neolithic: Early Prehistoric Societies in Southern Scandinavia*, Cambridge: Cambridge University Press.

Tilley, C. 1999, *Metaphor and Material Culture*, Oxford: Blackwell.

Tirard, S., M. Morange, & A. Lazcano 2010, The definition of life: a brief history of an elusive scientific endeavour, *Astrobiology*, 10(10), 1003–1009.

Tomasello, M. 2016, *A Natural History of Human Morality*, Cambridge MA: Harvard University Press.

Tringham, R.E. 1991, Households with faces: the challenge of gender in prehistoric architectural remains, in J.M. Gero & M.W. Conkey (eds.) *Engendering Archaeology: Women and Prehistory*, Oxford, Blackwell, 93–131.

Trivers, R.L. 1971, The evolution of reciprocal altruism, *The Quarterly Review of Biology*, 46(1), 35–57.

Tuggle, H.D., A.H. Townsend, & T.J. Riley 1972, Laws, systems, and research designs: a discussion of explanation in archaeology, *American Antiquity*, 37(1), 3–12.

Vander Linden, M. 2011, To tame a land: archaeological cultures and the spread of the Neolithic in western Europe, in B.W. Roberts & M. Vander Linden (eds.) *Investigating Archaeological Cultures: Material Culture, Variability and Transmission*, New York: Springer, 289–319.

Varela, F.G., H.R. Maturana, & R. Uribe, 1974, Autopoiesis: the organization of living systems, its characterization and a model, *BioSystems*, 5, 187–196.

Venkatesan, S. (ed.) 2010, Ontology is just another word for culture: motion tabled at the 2008 meeting of the Group for Debates in Anthropological Theory, University of Manchester, *Critique of Anthropology*, 30(2), 152–200. DOI:10.1177/0308275X09364070.

Viveiros de Castro, E. 1998, Cosmological deixis and Amerindian perspectivism, *Journal of the Royal Anthropological Institute*, 4(3), 469–488.

Viveiros de Castro, E. 2004, Exchanging perspectives: the transformation of objects into subjects in Amerindian ontologies, *Common Knowledge*, 10(3), 463–484.

Viveiros de Castro, E. 2017 [2009], *Cannibal Metaphysics* (translated by P. Skafish), Minneapolis: University of Minnesota Press.

von Wright, G.H. 1971, *Explanation and Understanding*, Ithaca NY: Cornell University Press.

Wallerstein, I. 1974, *The Modern World System: Capitalist Agriculture and the Origins of the European World-Economy in the Sixteenth Century*, London: Academic Press.

Ward, P. 2018, *Lamarck's Revenge: How Epigenetics Is Revolutionizing Our Understanding of Evolution's Past and Present*, New York: Bloomsbury Publishing.

Waterbolk, H.T. & P.J.R. Modderman 1958/59, Die Großbauten der Bandkeramik. *Palaeohistoria*, 6/7, 163–171.

Watkins, T. 2010, New light on Neolithic revolution in south-west Asia, *Antiquity*, 84(325), 621–634.

Watson, P.J., S.A. LeBlanc, & C.L. Redman 1971, *Explanation in Archaeology: An Explicitly Scientific Approach*, New York: Columbia University Press.

Webmoor, T. 2007, What about 'one more turn after the social' in archaeological reasoning? Taking things seriously, *World Archaeology*, 39(4), 563–578.

Webmoor, T. & C.L. Witmore 2008, Things are us! A commentary on human/things relations under the banner of a 'social' archaeology, *Norwegian Archaeological Review*, 41(1), 53–70, DOI:10.1080/00293650701698423.

Wheeler, M. 1956 [1954], *Archaeology from the Earth*, London: Penguin Books.

White, L.A. 2007 [1959], *The Evolution of Culture: The Development of Civilisation to the Fall of Rome*, Walnut Creek CA: Left Coast Press.

Whitley, J. 2002, Too many ancestors, *Antiquity*, 76(291), 119–126.

Whittle, A. 2003, *The Archaeology of People: Dimensions of Neolithic Life*, London: Routledge.

Whittle, A & V. Cummings (eds.) 2007, *Going Over: The Mesolithic–Neolithic Transition in North-west Europe* (Proceedings of the British Academy 144), Oxford: Oxford University Press.

Whittle, A., F. Healy, & A. Baylis 2011, *Gathering Time: Dating the Early Neolithic Enclosures of Southern Britain and Ireland* (2 volumes), Oxford: Oxbow Books.

Willey, G.R. & P. Phillips 1958, *Method and Theory in American Archaeology*, Chicago: University of Chicago Press.

Wilson, E.O. 1975, *Sociobiology: The New Synthesis*, Cambridge MA: The Belknap Press.

Wilson E.O. 1999, *Consilience: The Unity of Knowledge*, New York: Vintage Books.

Wilson, E.O. 2012, *The Social Conquest of Earth*, New York: Liveright Publishing.

Wilson, P. 1988, *The Domestication of the Human Species*, New Haven: Yale University Press.

Winch, P. 2008 [1958], *The Idea of a Social Science and Its Relation to Philosophy*, London: Routledge.

Witmore, C.L. 2007, Symmetrical archaeology: excerpts of a manifesto, *World Archaeology*, 39(4), 546–562, DOI: 10.1080/00438240701679411.

Wittgenstein, L. 1968 [1953], *Philosophical Investigations* (translated by G.E.M. Anscombe), Oxford: Blackwell.

Woolley, L. 1960 [1930], *Digging up the Past*, London: Penguin Books.

Wylie, A. 1989, Archaeological cables and tacking: the implications of practice for Bernstein's 'Options Beyond Objectivism and Relativism', *Philosophy of the Social Sciences*, 19, 1–18.

Wylie, A. 2002, *Thinking from Things: Essays in the Philosophy of Archaeology*, Berkeley: The University of California Press.

Yoffee, N. 1993, Too many chiefs? (or, Safe texts for the '90s), in N. Yoffee & A. Sherratt (eds.) *Archaeological Theory: Who Sets the Agenda?* Cambridge: Cambridge University Press, 60–78.

Zeder, M.A. 2008, Domestication and early agriculture in the Mediterranean Basin: origins, diffusion, and impact, *Proceedings of the National Academy of Sciences of the United States of America*, 105(33), 11597–11604.

Zeder, M.A. 2011, The origins of agriculture in the Near East, *Current Anthropology*, 52(S4), S221–S235.

Zeder, M.A. 2015, Domestication as a model system for niche construction theory, *Evolutionary Ecology*, 30, 325–348.

Žižek. S. 1994, Introduction: the spectre of ideology, in S. Žižek (ed.) *Mapping Ideology*, London: Verso, 1–33.

Zvelebil, M. 1986, Mesolithic prelude and Neolithic revolution, in M. Zvelebil (ed.) *Hunters in Transition: Mesolithic Societies of Temperate Eurasia and Their Transition to Farming*, Cambridge: Cambridge University Press, 5–15.

Zvelebil, M. & P. Dulokhanov 1991, The transition to farming in eastern and northern Europe, *Journal of World Prehistory*, 5(3), 233–278.

Zvelebil, M., & M. Lillie 2000, Transition to agriculture in eastern Europe, in T.D. Price (ed.) *Europe's First Farmers*, Cambridge: Cambridge University Press, 57–92.

Zvelebil, M. & P. Rowley-Conwy 1984, The transition to farming in northern Europe: a hunter-gatherer perspective, *Norwegian Archaeological Review*, 17(2), 104–127.

INDEX

Agean *see* Greece *and* Renfrew, C.: Aegean Bronze Age (study)

agency: external 92; DNA 93; human 36, 66, 84–85, 95, 99, 101, 106, 125; of 'things' 3, 80

agriculture/agriculturalists: agroecology 113; DNA analysis 116–119; failure 134; land management/control 12–18, 45, 115, 129–133; Neolithic Europe 11–18, 43–45, 71–73, 104, 111–120, 129–137; non-European 79, 104, 111–113, 117, 119; productivity 69, 114; storage 63; transition from hunter-gathering 43, 54–56, 71, 111–119; *see also* plants

ancestors *see* inheritance *and* burial practice

animal: activity (taphonomic) 31; bison 82; behaviour 26, 30, 34, 53, 81, 98, 103, 113; bone/remains 21–22, 50, 79, 86, 129, 133; butchery 24, 31, 34, 51, 132; cattle/goats/sheep 114, 133; domestication/management 54–56, 104, 110–119, 126, 129, 132; elk/reindeer 83; horse 82; humans as 93; mouse 33, 89–90, 103; pig 133

anthropology 5, 8, 123–124; and archaeology 10, 20, 47, 56–57, 66–74, 77–79, 83, 90, 122–124, 131; and biology 34; and historians 47; case studies 31–32, 44, 61, 64, 66, 68, 131

architecture 11, 109, 118; domestic 114, 130–132, 137; earthworks *61*, 64, 114, 133, 135–137; henge *61*, 64; monumental/megalithic 11–18, 45, 71–73, 117–119, 135–137; mudbrick

114; naval 62; tells 131, 137; wood/ timber 72, 130, 135, 137

Archaeology and Society 53

Archaeology as Anthropology 10

art 40, *41,* 82–83, 128

Asia: 43, 46, 54, 60, 79, 104, 110–118, 129

australopithecine 31

authority *see* social organisation: hierarchy

'availability model' 116

Bahn, P. 2, 19, 40

Barad, K. 109

barrow *see* architecture: earthworks

beaker/s *see* pottery

Belgium 134

beliefs *see* religion/beliefs

Bhaskar, R. 20, 88

Binford, L.R.: hunter-gatherer studies 40–43, 53–55, 78; methodology 30–37; Mississippi River Valley study 78; systems theory 10, 28–30, 42, 49–56, 122–124

biocultural mechanisms 1, 5, 91, 94–102, 109–112, 117, 125, 129–137

biology: human 5–6, 25–26, 34–36, 57, 91–112, 117–119, 129, 131; theory 34, 49

Bloor, D. 85–86

Bogaard, A. 113–116, 129–137

bone *see* animal *and* human

Botterill, G. 17

Bradley, R. 46, 48, 64

Brain, C.K. 31

bread *see* food